...More Murphy's Laws

Any sufficiently advanced technology is indistinguishable from magic.

(Chapter 5 shows you where the magician hides the rabbit.)

The floppy will be the wrong size.

(How to make sure you have the right size is in Chapter 9.)

Survive first, then do long-term planning.

(See Chapter 22 for how to stay afloat in nine popular programs.)

Important letters that contain no errors will develop errors on the way to the printer.

(See Chapter 10 for ways to take control of the printer genie.)

Regardless of the size of the program, you won't have enough hard disk space to install it.

(Get more space. Read Chapter 13.)

You'll never have enough time, money, or memory.

(See Chapter 6 for help with the memory part.)

Whatever hits the fan will not be evenly distributed.

(Murphy's Laws of DOS tell you how to duck.)

Smart Advice with a Smile
The Murphy's Laws Computer Book Series

Let's face it. Most computer books just don't feature the "can't put it down" excitement of an Ian Fleming spy novel or the heart-palpitating romance of Danielle Steele. But they don't have to put you to sleep, either. **The Murphy's Laws Computer Book Series** gives you the answers you need and keeps you entertained at the same time.

Written with wit and filled with useful information, **The Murphy's Laws Computer Book Series** *helps everyone*, even the most reluctant computer users, get the best of their computer and computing. In the series, there are books on word processing, spreadsheets, PCs, and operating systems—and even more books are planned. Every book in the series promises to give you the information you need on the software you use without boring you into oblivion.

Always smart, never stuffy. Every computer user will want to use **The Murphy's Laws Computer Book Series** whenever there are questions about the computer.

Look for **The Murphy's Laws Computer Book Series** at your favorite bookstore.

For a complete catalog of our publications:

SYBEX Inc.
2021 Challenger Drive, Alameda, CA 94501
Tel: (510) 523-8233/(800) 227-2346 Telex: 336311
Fax: (510) 523-2373

Murphy's Laws of DOS

Murphy's Laws of

DOS®

Charlie Russel

SYBEX ®   San Francisco   Paris   Düsseldorf   Soest

Acquisitions Editor: Dianne King
Series Editor: Sharon Crawford
Editor: Brendan Fletcher
Technical Editor: Sheila Dienes
Book Designer: Claudia Smelser
Screen Graphics: John Corrigan
Technical Art: Cuong Le
Typesetter: Dina F Quan
Production Coordinator/Proofreader: Catherine Mahoney
Indexer: Ted Laux
Cover Illustration: Robert Kopecky
Cartoonist: Robert Kopecky
Special icon font created by Len Gilbert.
Screen reproductions produced with Collage Plus.

Library of Congress Card Number: 93-83691
ISBN: 0-7821-1280-3

Manufactured in the United States of America
10 9 8 7 6 5 4 3 2 1

Acknowledgments

I'VE HAD SUCH fun writing this book that I really want to express a lot of gratitude to everyone involved:

Sharon Crawford, series editor, who came up with the Murphy's idea and without whom the book might have been possible, but not nearly so funny;

Brendan Fletcher, editor extraordinaire, a pleasure to work with;

Sheila Dienes, the ideal technical editor, excruciatingly correct yet tactful;

Claudia Smelser, a wonderful, persevering artist who kept her head while all those about her were losing theirs;

Armando Ablaza and Greg Clark, whose patience and understanding gave me the time I needed to get the job done;

Mac Dunn, who supplied the dBASE expertise;

and all the usual suspects at SYBEX, who did everything they were supposed to except better and faster: production coordinator Catherine Mahoney, technical artists John Corrigan and Cuong Le, typesetter Dina Quan, and indexer Ted Laux.

Others who supplied inspiration, support, and succor in time of need include, but are not limited to, Dianne King, David Clark, Jan Aragon-Denno, Kenyon Brown, Kathleen Lattinville, Richard Mills, Drew Benjamin, Dr. Rudolph Langer, Dianne Robbins, Margaret Rowlands, Savitha Varadan, Veronica Eddy, Janna Hecker-Clark, Dean Denno, Ed Holbrook, Michael Gross, Jamie Wright, Linda Gaus, Perla Martin, Gene Weisskopf, Harold Turner, Gerald Jones, Sonja Banford, Christian Crumlish, and the Moon-Light Indian Restaurant.

Thank you one and all.

Contents at a Glance

Table of Contents

Part 4

I'm FLUGGED!
How to Get UnFLUGGED

Part 5 Murphy Was an Optimist
How to Stay Afloat

Introduction

Murphy's Law: Anything that can go wrong,
will go wrong.

MURPHY WAS ABSOLUTELY right. The natural tendency in the universe is to go from bad to worse. And in today's universe the source of a lot of things that can go wrong is the computer! Everywhere the cry is "The computer's down!" or "It won't print!" or "I HATE computers!"

But help is on the way. Computers are only machines and all they have to get themselves going in the morning is DOS. We humans have large brains, opposable thumbs, and a variety of caffeinated beverages. And now there's *Murphy's Laws of DOS*, the book that can make things in your DOS universe go right for a change.

This book was written to provide all the answers about DOS a real human would need. In English. Quickly. You can use a computer without having to have a degree in computer science or (worse) having to read a lot of pious platitudes about how The Computer Is Your Friend.

Who Are You?

All this book assumes is that you have a PC and it appears to be "alive" when you turn it on. You want to use this computer to actually *do* something. (Or perhaps it's your boss who has expressed this wish.) You have no interest in becoming a computer expert. Rest assured it's not necessary. Just as you don't need to know a lot about the internal combustion engine in order to drive, you don't need to have to have a lot of technical knowledge to get results from a computer.

Inside This Book

This book is set up so that it can be used as an easy reference. You can jump in, find the answer to your questions, and quickly escape. You will not be burdened with boring explanations you don't need to know, because all that techie stuff is set aside in clearly marked boxes. If you are interested you can read some (it *is* allowed), but you don't have to.

There are five parts, thus:

Part 1: The Bare Minimum (Skinny-Dipping into DOS)

Here's where you'll find all the basic stuff: how to turn on the computer, what you'll see when you do. Easy ways to move around inside the system (sort of like *Fantastic Voyage* but without Raquel Welch), do stuff with files, and generally get going. You'll find chapters on the cool DOS Shell and the uncool DOS prompt.

Part 2: PC Hardware—Just Enough to Dazzle the Crowd without Baffling You

In this section are chapters on all the things that make up a computer: the screen thing, printers, keyboards, mice, and more. This is all in normal non-nerd talk so you can get real answers that don't leave you more confused than when you started.

Part 3: A Gentle Guide to Software

Here's where you can get help with the software that runs on your computer. How to use DOS to protect and serve instead of letting it beat you over the head. There's a special section on how to buy software without buyer's remorse.

Part 4: I'm FLUGGED!—How to Get UnFLUGGED

Sooner or later you will be stricken with that combination of **F**ear, **L**oathing, **U**ncertainty, and **G**rief that signifies you are FLUGGED and something has gone seriously awry. The chapters cover things you can fix and things you need an expert for and how to tell the difference.

Part 5: Murphy Was an Optimist (How to Stay Afloat)

Here are chapters with all the DOS commands you'll ever need to know with definitions and descriptions for normal people. Also here are suggestions for helpful programs that can make your life easier as well as cautions against mistakes that can make your life a lot harder.

What Those Things in the Margin Mean

This guy is to alert you to really cool tips and shortcuts nearby. Here's also where you'll find cross-references to related stuff.

This is to let you know that we're dealing with scary material. Read this because there's a possible risk to your files or your hardware or both. (The computer will not, however, blow up or catch on fire.)

This icon is in a couple of places because it represents an opportunity to do something heroically stupid. Read the warning and resist the temptation.

This is to let you know that this is technical or background information that you certainly don't *have* to read. Mostly it is pretty interesting stuff, but if you skip it your life will go on without a hitch.

How to Use This Book

The intent is for this book to be used as a reference. Look for the topic you want in the index or table of contents and you should be able to go right to the answer.

Where it's necessary to show you things to type in, you'll see them as

```
things to type in
```

on the page. You should always press the Enter key after typing something in.

Because DOS is so literal-minded, take care to type things in exactly as they're shown—including characters like \ or : and blank spaces.

Sometimes you need to substitute something specific from your computer like a real name instead of *filename*. But that's made clear when it does come up.

You should be able to find everything you need to know about DOS in this book. If you have an unwholesome interest in becoming an expert, there are a few recommendations scattered around for some books that you'll find helpful. Also there are about a zillion other books available about every aspect of computers. They won't be any more helpful than the *Murphy's* books, just more boring.

If you think there's something missing or something I could have done better, write to me:

Charlie Russel
c/o SYBEX Computer Books
2021 Challenger Drive
Alameda, CA 94501

Don't expect me to answer your letters because I *hate* being corrected. But after I sulk for a while, I will fix what's wrong for the next edition.

So jump right in and have a good time.

Here's all the basic stuff you need to get going. How to turn on the computer and what you'll see when you do. There's advice on how to move around and handle files with aplomb. This section also covers how to make the most of the cool DOS Shell and the not-so-cool DOS prompt.

THE BARE MINIMUM
Skinny-Dipping into DOS

Chapter 1

BASIC TRAINING
(No Marching Required)

Edison's Rule: It works better if you plug it in.

Anza's Paradox: You $_{\text{almost}}$ work better if you don't.

LET'S FACE IT, computers are appalling machines from hell. They can do lots of cute tricks, but just as often they drive you nuts. The key to surviving your life with a computer is to remember that it is only a machine, and therefore not as smart or as good-looking as you are. With a little bit of effort (and this book), you can control your own computer destiny.

First, let's say a few words about your computer. Just what is it? Is it The Box With Buttons and Switches That Hums and Gurgles When Turned On? Or is it The Entire Package Including Screen, Keyboard, Mouse and All That Stuff?

Yes.

So to keep the bewilderment quotient down, let's say that when we're talking about The Box That Hums, etc. specifically, we'll say "the computer box." Otherwise, we'll just say "computer" when the talk is of computers-in-general.

Turning It On

Most of the time computers are put together out of separate pieces (sort of like stereo components), so you have to turn on the computer box with one switch, the monitor with another, and maybe the printer with still another. Start by flipping the switch on the computer box. If the computer doesn't immediately start making noises, plug it in. Then flip the switch on the monitor, and within a few seconds, it will come on. If it doesn't, plug it in and turn it on. If you don't get any action from one or both, see "It's Just DEAD" in Chapter 17. Once the computer and monitor are humming along, you can turn on your printer.

Highly Important Stuff You Really Ought to Read

Electricity is scary stuff, especially when it threatens your expensive computer. Here are two important things you can do to protect your investment:

☞ Get a surge protector so that variations in electrical current (and they happen everywhere) won't fry your circuits.
Don't buy one that costs less than $30. The real cheapies offer so little protection, you might as well go bare.

☞ Plug your computer into grounded outlets only (the kind with three holes for the three-pronged plug). If you have doubts about the grounding or if you don't have three-holed outlets, call someone who knows something about electricity and have them ground your system for you.

☞ *One way to avoid having to flip all those switches every morning is to set up your computer with a power strip or other central control device. Then you can turn everything on with a single switch.*

Where Am I?

When the computer is on, you should see something that looks like one of the following:

```
C>
C:\>
```

This is the DOS prompt. More information on how to relate to the DOS prompt is in Chapter 2.

If you see a letter followed by a colon and a backslash (C:\) and maybe some other stuff too (like the > sign) you're in luck. DOS is set up to show you where you are. But if you have only a letter followed by the greater-than sign (C>), you'll need to type the character **C** followed by the character **D** and press the Enter key to find out your location. The Enter key sometimes has the word *Return* printed on it, and sometimes only a ↵. Whatever it is called on your computer, it will be on the right edge of the main part of the keyboard.

When you type in **CD** it will show on the screen as you type it, and when you press the Enter key, the cursor (that little flashing line) moves down a line and the screen will show something like

```
C:\SPORTS
```

This means you are at drive C—the hard disk—and in the directory named SPORTS. If a directory (such as SPORTS) already shows at the prompt, typing in **CD** will only show that yes, you are in the SPORTS directory.

You can always type this command, CD, to locate your current directory.

☞ *If you type CD alone, it stands for Current Directory. If you include a directory name, you can remember it as standing for Change Directory.*

☞ *Until you press the Enter key or ↵, nothing will happen. Press Backspace to erase your typing, letter by letter. You can continue to type in as many versions as you want because the computer pays no attention until you press that Enter key.*

☞ *To change that C> prompt into something useful, see "What Does the DOS Prompt Really Mean?" in Chapter 2.*

Changing Directories

DOS can divide up individual disks into areas called *directories*. You certainly don't *need* directories on floppy disks, but on a hard disk they're indispensable.

The programs you install usually have their own directories. For example, a directory called PDOX will have files for Paradox. WordPerfect 5.1 makes a directory called WP51. You can also organize stuff into directories based on function, such as a directory called GAMES for all your fun stuff.

The main directory on a disk is called the *root directory* and is symbolized by the backslash character (\). So if you see a prompt like

    C:\

you know you're in the root directory. All the other directories on that disk are under the root directory.

Directories can have *subdirectories* of their own. So if you find yourself at a prompt like

    C:\WP51\FISH

then you are in the FISH directory (presumably full of fish stories), which is a subdirectory of your WordPerfect 5.1 (WP51) directory. The WP51 directory is in the root directory of drive C.

To change to another directory, type the CD command followed by the name of the directory, as in

    CD \WP51\DAWGS

and press Enter. This will take you to the DAWGS subdirectory (where you keep all your canine files) under the WP51 directory.

☞ *A subdirectory is no lesser a being than a directory. The term subdirectory is used to indicate that it is a directory under another directory, not that it is smaller or functions differently.*

☞ *You can always get to the root directory of a disk by typing in*

CD \

and pressing Enter.

☞ *For enough information on directory structure to make you barf, see "Directory Assistance" in Chapter 13.*

Changing Drives

The computer can only work with one disk (or drive) at a time. If you're working with drive C (the hard disk), you are said to be *logged to* drive C. To change to, or log to, drive A, just type

A:

Make sure you include the colon and press Enter. To change back, type in

C:

and press Enter.

☞ *Sometimes when you change drives, you will find yourself at a strange directory, \WP51\FELINES for example, instead of at the root directory like you expected. This is because the last time you left the drive, that's the directory you were in. DOS always "remembers" where you were the last time you visited that drive and plops you down there again. To get to the root, just type in*

CD \

and press Enter.

☞ *Don't change to a floppy drive unless a disk is in that drive.*

☞ *Your first floppy drive is drive A; the second floppy drive is drive B. Your first hard drive is always drive C. Additional drives you may have will start with letter D and go on through the alphabet.*

Scouting Your Location—The DIR Command

Once you know what directory you are in, you probably want to know what else is around. Type in

    DIR

and press the Enter key.

All the files in your current directory will show up on your screen. If there's a lot of stuff, it will go scrolling by faster than you can read. To solve this problem, try one of the following:

    DIR /W

The *W* stands for "wide." This will give you the files in five columns across the screen as in Figure 1.1. This is useful if you're looking for a particular name, but it leaves off all the other information about the files.

FIGURE 1.1:
What you get with
DIR /W

```
C:\MEMOS>DIR /W

    Volume in drive C is BigDOS5Disk
    Volume Serial Number is 0000-14CA
    Directory of C:\MEMOS

    [.]              [..]           ALFIE.TXT      GUSANO.TXT     HAROLD.TXT
    MEEP.TXT         PRISCLLA.TXT   STANLEY.TXT    INDEX.TXT      BASEBALL.TXT
    BIRDS.TXT        APPNOTE.TXT
            12 file(s)         30065 bytes
                            20688896 bytes free

C:\MEMOS>
```

Or you can use

    DIR /P

which gives you a screen's worth of files at a time as in Figure 1.2. Think of the *P* as standing for "page-at-a-time." Press Enter to get another screen's worth, until you've seen everything.

FIGURE 1.2:

What you get with DIR /P

```
Volume in drive C is BigDOS5Disk
Volume Serial Number is 0000-14CA
Directory of C:\DOS

.              <DIR>      11-03-91    8:55p
..             <DIR>      11-03-91    8:55p
HIMEM    000      11552   04-09-91    5:00a
GORILLA  BAS      29434   04-09-91    5:00a
MONEY    BAS      46225   04-09-91    5:00a
EXRC                160   01-11-92    9:17a
PROTOCOL 001         24   08-23-92    3:11p
DOSHELP  BAK       8205   01-12-92   10:53a
ASSIGN   COM       6399   04-09-91    5:00a
COMMAND  COM      47845   03-29-92   12:39p
DISKCOMP COM      10652   04-09-91    5:00a
DISKCOPY COM      11793   04-09-91    5:00a
DOSKEY   COM       5883   04-09-91    5:00a
DOSSHELL COM       4623   04-09-91    5:00a
FORMAT!  COM      32911   04-09-91    5:00a
GRAFTABL COM      11205   04-09-91    5:00a
GRAPHICS COM      19694   04-09-91    5:00a
KEYB     COM      14986   04-09-91    5:00a
LOADFIX  COM       1131   04-09-91    5:00a
Press any key to continue . . .
```

COOL TIP

☞ *If you just want to see the names of the files and not all this other stuff, type*

DIR /B

The B gives you just the "bare" names. This works fine for smallish directories. If you have a bigger directory, use

DIR /B/P

to get a screen's worth of files at a time.

☞ *See "Directory Assistance" in Chapter 13 for lots more on bending the DIR command to your will.*

What You're Seeing When You Type DIR

When you see a list of files after typing DIR, the information is in five columns. First is the file's name followed by the three-character extension. The extension is part of the file's name, though some files may not have an extension. See Chapter 15, "Whither Files?" for the lowdown on file names and extensions.

Next is the file's size, in *bytes* (or characters), followed by the date and time the file was created, or if the file's been changed, the date and time of the most recent change.

If the directory you're in has subdirectories, you'll see those too. Unless you use /W, the directories will have <DIR> next to them in the listing, so you can easily tell them from the files. See "Directory Assistance" in Chapter 13 for help in organizing directories.

Insert Disk 1 in Drive A

Most computer boxes have two slots for floppy disks. These days you usually see one for 5¼-inch disks and one for 3½-inch disks. Each one of these slots is a disk drive—one is drive A and the other is drive B. The one on the top is drive A unless some smartass has switched things around.

Inserting a 5¼-inch disk

If there's a latch or door in the way, open it. Remove any disk already in the drive. Hold the disk by the label and slide it in the drive with the label side up. Close the latch or the door.

Removing a 5¼-inch disk

Open the latch or door. Pinch the center of the edge that's toward you and pull it out.

When the disk is not on the drive it should be in its protective paper sleeve. You should never touch the shiny, exposed surface of the disk, anyway, and if it's in the sleeve you *can't* touch it.

Inserting a 3½-inch disk

Hold the disk by the label and slide it into the slot, label side up. When the disk is all the way in, you will hear a nice, satisfying click. The button under the slot will pop out (if it isn't out already).

Removing a 3½-inch disk

Push the button under the disk drive. The disk will pop out about an inch so you can pull the disk out.

☞ *Don't put the disk in the little space between the two drives. Unless you have the computer box right in front of you and are very careful, eventually you will do this and feel foolish beyond imagining. Especially since you will have to bribe some snickering nerd to dismantle your computer box and retrieve the disk. Save yourself this embarrassment and put a piece of tape over part of that space, so the disk won't go in.*

☞ *In line with that, don't force the disk into the slot. If it doesn't go in easily, either there is already a disk in the drive, you are putting the disk in upside down or backwards, or you have already embarrassed yourself as described in the item above.*

☞ *You can get 5¼-inch disks to slide in easily—even if they are upside-down and backwards. They won't work that way (you'll get a "Drive not ready" error message) and it won't do your drive mechanism any good, either.*

☞ *For more information on disks, go to Chapter 9, "Floppy Disks."*

Wait for the drive light to go off before removing a disk from the drive. The light means that something is happening and if you remove the disk, you will interrupt that something. Just like people, computers hate to be interrupted and will show their displeasure by fouling up whatever was being written to that disk. Don't risk it! Wait for the light to go off.

Looking at Files

If you want to look at a file using DOS, you need to know the file's name. If you're not sure of the name, look for it using the DIR command as described in "Scouting Your Location—The DIR Command" earlier in this chapter.

Once you know the name, type in the following at the DOS prompt

```
TYPE FILENAME.EXT
```

In other words, if the file is called BUSINESS.DOC, the prompt line will look like

```
C:\>TYPE BUSINESS.DOC
```

Press the Enter key, and the contents of the file will show up on the screen. Unfortunately, you may see some weird stuff. Not all files are in normal-looking ASCII code (see "How to Sound Cool," below).

> ### How to Sound Cool
>
> Files that can be read by mortal eye are called *ASCII files* (pronounced *AS-key*). These files can be easily seen by using the TYPE command.
>
> Programs (files with the .EXE or .COM extension) are in a type of code that looks extremely peculiar on the screen. Even nerds can't read it because it has been through a translator that makes it the private property of the computer's processor.

Don't try to look at files with the extensions .EXE, .COM, .BIN, or .OVL. There is nothing there to see and you may lock up your computer and have to reboot.

Help and How to Get It

Gross's Law: When trying to resolve a problem, it always helps to know the solution.

Frankly, your best source of help is in your hands right now—this book.

If you don't panic, you can extract some useful information from the DOS 5 Help system. If you do tend to panic, you'd better upgrade to DOS 6. And if you're really nervous, stick with me, kid. No double-talk here.

DOS 5 Help—when all you need is a little help

When you know what the command is, but can't remember exactly how it works, just add a space and a /? to the command. Asking for help on the COPY command, then, would look like this:

```
COPY /?
```

DOS will respond by giving you a short list of the different ways the command can be used. One command I use about once a month, but can never remember exactly, is REPLACE. I use this when I need to update a set of files at work, after working on them at home. So, when I get back to work, I put the floppy in my A drive and type

        REPLACE /?

The result is shown in Figure 1.3. Since I already know what the command means, and just need a quick reminder about how it works, this is perfect.

FIGURE 1.3:
A quick brushup on the REPLACE command. If the sight of this makes your blood run cold, try the Help system in DOS 6.

```
C:\>REPLACE /?
Replaces files.

REPLACE [drive1:][path1]filename [drive2:][path2] [/A] [/P] [/R] [/W]
REPLACE [drive1:][path1]filename [drive2:][path2] [/P] [/R] [/S] [/W] [/U]

  [drive1:][path1]filename Specifies the source file or files.
  [drive2:][path2]         Specifies the directory where files are to be
                           replaced.
  /A                       Adds new files to destination directory. Cannot
                           use with /S or /U switches.
  /P                       Prompts for confirmation before replacing a file or
                           adding a source file.
  /R                       Replaces read-only files as well as unprotected
                           files.
  /S                       Replaces files in all subdirectories of the
                           destination directory. Cannot use with the /A
                           switch.
  /W                       Waits for you to insert a disk before beginning.
  /U                       Replaces (updates) only files that are older than
                           source files. Cannot use with the /A switch.

C:\>
```

DOS 6 Help—when you need more help

With DOS 6, you can still use the /? to get a quick summary, but if you can't remember the command at all, this isn't going to be much good. So, just type

        HELP

and DOS will give you a list of commands to choose from like that in Figure 1.4. You can use your mouse or the cursor keys to move around through the list. When you find a command you think might be it, either click on it with your mouse or highlight it with the cursor keys

FIGURE 1.4:
Whole lotta help topics

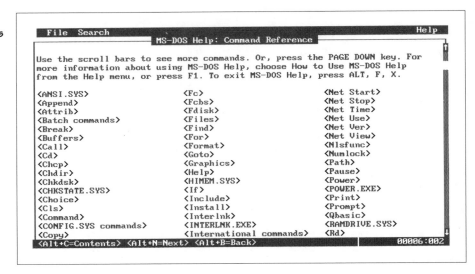

and hit Enter. You'll see a detailed explanation of the command. Select Syntax or Notes or Examples (depending on where you are in the Help system) at the top of the page for more explanations. Figure 1.5 shows part of the Examples page for the DIR command.

When you're ready to return to the DOS prompt, click on File in the menu bar. Then click on Exit.

FIGURE 1.5:
Big-time help for the DIR commands. If this is way more help than you had in mind, forget DOS Help.

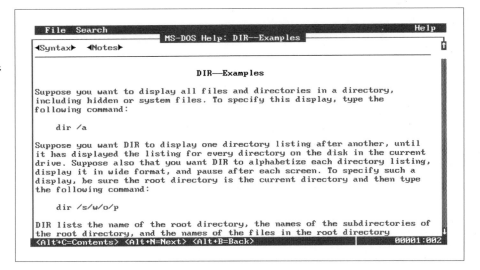

If you have a pretty good idea which command you want help on, but know you need more than the limited help you get with a /?, type **HELP** and then the command. For example, to get detailed help on copying, enter

```
HELP COPY
```

If all this gives you a big pain, don't bother with it. Look up what you need in the index of this book. If what you want isn't there, go find someone who knows the answer.

Getting with the Program

The reason you have a computer, of course, is to get some work done. Even if that work is nothing more serious than playing Flight Simulator. In order to do that, you must *run* a program.

Mildly technical drivel about file types

There are three kinds of files that you can run on your computer. These programs are called "executable" files. Any file that ends in .COM (short for *command* file), .EXE (short for *executable* file), or .BAT (short for *batch* file) can be run. .COM and .EXE files are ones that programmers created. .BAT files are files that more-or-less ordinary humans create to simplify their lives. Batch files run a series of commands automatically, just as if they had been typed in by hand. For more on batch files, see "Batch Files" in Chapter 11.

Running programs

In order to run a program, you simply type in the name of its main executable file and press Enter. The hard part may be figuring out what that name is. Usually the best place to look for the main program file name is the (shudder) manual. Almost all programs use letters that are related to their names. The main executable file for WordPerfect, for example, is WP.EXE. For Quattro Pro, it is Q.EXE. And to make life easier, you only need to type the part *before* the period. DOS is smart enough to figure out the rest. Table 1.1 lists the names of some of the major DOS programs. Type the name at the DOS prompt to start the program.

Program	Name to Type In
dBASE	DBASE
Harvard Graphics	HG
Lotus 1-2-3	123
Norton Commander	NC
Norton Desktop for DOS	ND
Paradox	PARADOX
Prodigy	PRODIGY
Quattro Pro	Q
Quicken	Q
Windows	WIN
WordPerfect	WP
Word for DOS	WORD
WordStar	WS

A Small Point of Interest to Very Few

Sometimes you will hear the term *application* used interchangeably with *program*. An application is really a collection of files that may include several programs. Lotus 1-2-3 is an application, and 123.EXE is the program that starts the thing working. Mostly this is a distinction without a difference.

Let Me Out!

Manzi's Axiom: The easier it is to get into a program, the harder it will be to get out.

So you went ahead and started a program. You've puttered around for a while and now you can't figure out how to get out.

There is, needless to say, no *standard* way to exit all programs. However, most programs respond to at least one of the following. I list them here in order of their likelihood of working, so try them in order:

1. Try pressing the Esc key energetically several times. This may not work, but you'll feel better.

2. Tap the Alt key. Frequently this will turn on the menus at the top of the screen. If it does, and there is a choice called Exit or Quit, try selecting that. If there isn't a choice like that, then try one called File. This should drop down a list of choices, one of which is often Exit.

3. Press the F10 key. Again, this sometimes activates a menu.

4. Try the F7 key. For reasons known only to the original WordPerfect programmers, this is the Exit key in WordPerfect and those few programs that use similar keystrokes.

5. Tap the / key. In Lotus, and all sorts of other spreadsheet programs, this activates the menus. See step 2 above for what to do once you get a menu.

6. You can always try Ctrl-C or Ctrl-Break. These key combinations work on a few old programs.

If none of these works, you are the victim of a truly ingenious programmer. See the next section, "Reset, Reboot, and the Fine Art of Ctrl-Alt-Del."

Reset, Reboot, and the Fine Art of Ctrl-Alt-Del

Computers are reliable, friendly, and dependable assistants. And if you believe that, I have some oceanfront property to sell you in Arizona. So what happens when something really goes wrong and you can't make it do what you want (or sometimes, anything at all)? First, try the steps in the previous section to get out of the program you are running.

Go through as many as necessary to get out of the program if at all possible. But if none of these things work, your last resort is to reboot.

There are three ways to reboot the computer—a warm boot, a cold boot, and a power-off boot. The first is the quickest. Give it a "three-finger salute" by pressing and holding down the Ctrl, Alt, and Del keys all at the same time. This usually takes two hands, just so you don't do it by accident. Most of the time, this will cause your computer to reboot, but if nothing happens, more serious measures are called for.

If there is a reset button on the front of your computer box, try pressing it. This will force the computer to reboot, and run all its initial tests.

Finally, if all else fails, turn the power off, wait ten seconds, and turn it back on.

Don't turn the power off and immediately back on. Because of the nature of computer power supplies, this can cause additional electrical stress leading to premature component failure. In other words, you can fry a small and expensive little part.

Be patient. Wait about ten seconds after you initially turn the power off before turning it back on. You can use this time to contemplate homicide, suicide, or computercide.

Why Is a Boot Called a Boot?

This is a reference to "pulling oneself up by one's bootstraps." (A noble, if peculiar, sentiment.)

When you boot your computer, it pulls itself up by its bootstraps. It first loads a tiny little "bootstrap" program that is part of the BIOS (Basic Input Output System). This bootstrap program is just (barely) smart enough to load the first of the system files on your boot disk (usually the hard disk, but sometimes a floppy), which then loads the second of these hidden files, which then sets your configuration and loads the shell you actually see as DOS.

A cold boot first runs a series of tests on your hardware to make sure that all is well. These tests are called the *Power On Self Test*, or POST. The POST checks how much memory you have, and if it is OK, tests to see what devices are attached and if any have failed, etc. After the POST is over, the bootstrap program is loaded and run.

A warm boot (the Ctrl-Alt-Del kind) assumes that all is well with your hardware, and proceeds directly to the bootstrap program.

To Turn It Off or Leave It On, That Is the Question

Probably the oldest debate about PCs is whether you should turn them off when you're finished or leave them on all the time.

If you turn the computer off, you save a little bit of energy and maybe a bit of wear and tear on the hard drive motor. This meant something years ago, but current hard drives are rated to run 100,000 hours or more without a failure.

Besides, leaving it on reduces stress on the hard drive motor caused by the initial surge of electricity when you flip the switch. There's also the problem of stress on the chips and connections caused by repeated heating up and cooling down.

So, I vote for leaving the computer on with the monitor turned off, but if it's too noisy for you or your dreams are haunted by Reddy Kilowatt, feel free to turn it off.

If you want to leave the computer on all the time:

☞ *Turn the monitor off, or better yet, get a really cool screen saver program.*

☞ *Make sure the room where you keep the computer is kept reasonably cool. Computer innards generate a lot of heat, and if the room is too hot for you to work in, it's too hot for your computer to work in.*

☞ *Don't put a dust cover on any component that is on. The net effect is that of a sauna, and it is not healthy for the machinery.*

Chapter 2

THE DOS PROMPT

Denno's Law: To err is human, but it takes a computer to really screw things up.

Aragon's Commentary on Denno's Law: At the source of every error blamed on the computer, you will find at least two errors, including the error of blaming it on the computer.

DOS HAS TO have a way of communicating with you, so it can spit out obscure messages designed to "help" you. Its method of communication is known as the *DOS prompt*. In this chapter you'll learn how to talk to DOS nicely, so it won't respond (too) rudely.

What Does the DOS Prompt Really Mean?

The DOS prompt is DOS telling you that it's ready and waiting for you. In its simplest form it is

```
C>
```

or some other letter. This is, of course, unhelpful in the extreme. Yes, it does tell you which drive you are on, but nothing else. At the very least you can set it up so that the prompt shows where on the drive you are.

To make DOS do this, type

```
PROMPT $P$G
```

After you do this, the prompt will show what directory you are in as well as the drive name. To make this prompt permanent, you will need

TECHNO NOTE

Useless Nerd Stuff You Can Ignore Completely

You can do a lot more with your prompt if you want. For example, any text that you include will display exactly as you would expect. So, if you want an impertinent prompt, try this one:

```
PROMPT $P$G So, speak to me:
```

And if you want a totally subservient one, try

```
PROMPT $P$G Your wish is my command, master:
```

But you can use the prompt command to do far more. For example, if you have a color monitor, you can clear the screen, change the screen colors to bright white on blue, then display the current time and date, the drive, and the path with the following:

```
PROMPT $e[0;1;37;44m$e[2J$d$_$t$_$p$g
```

Hard to believe anyone with still-functioning brain synapses would do such a thing, isn't it?

The possibilities for nerding up one's screen are nearly endless, so if you have lots of free time and no productive way to spend it, see "Playing with Prompts" in Chapter 11.

to include it in your AUTOEXEC.BAT, the little batch program that runs every time you start your computer. For help on doing this, see Chapter 11, "Your System Defined."

The Literal Truth
(Or, Computers Are Stupider Than Cats)

Computers do exactly what you tell them, and not one thing more. They don't read your mind, they don't do what you meant to tell them, etc. And the responses you get back are about as enlightening as those you get from a cat.

But unlike a cat, a computer doesn't sit in your lap and purr, or catch mice, or keep your feet warm at night.

As you type at the prompt, the cursor (the blinking underline) moves forward and marks the spot where the next typed-in character will appear.

The information you type in at the prompt is called the *command line*. This command line is the cause of 99^{44}/100% of the curse words directed at computers.

The good news is that though it's easy to type in a wrong command and have nothing happen, it's not all that easy to make something really horrible happen. Just remember if you type in something and you get a choice to answer Yes or No (Y/N?) and *you don't understand the question*, the answer is **NO**. (Generally a good rule when you're not at the computer, too.)

DOS Grammar

There are only a few rules for what you can type at the prompt, but those that exist aren't flexible (see "Stupider than Cats" above).

Fortunately, DOS is NOT case-sensitive. It doesn't care whether you type DIR, Dir, or dir. The bad news is that it doesn't have a spell checker. If you misspell *format* as *fromat*, it can't guess what you mean; it simply says "Bad command or file name."

Spaces

The easiest mistake you can make when typing in a command at the DOS prompt is to add a space where it shouldn't be, or leave one out that should be there. Here are the rules:

☞ After the command, leave a space (but only one space).

☞ Between separate items, leave a space.

☞ Within file names, don't include a space.

Commas, periods, and semicolons

Commas, semicolons, colons, and other miscellaneous punctuation marks have no business in a file name or command. Some you can get away with, but there is nothing to gain, and everything to lose, so listen up for Murphy's Rules for Punctuation at the DOS Prompt:

☞ You can use a period before the last three characters of the file name.

☞ You can use a colon after the drive letter.

That's it, no more.

Slashing—not as grim as it sounds

The keyboard has two different slash keys. For more about keyboards and which slash key is which, see "What Do Those Weird Keys Do" in Chapter 7. But here's how DOS sees them:

☞ The \ key is used to separate parts of the path. And ONLY to separate parts of the path. See "Finding Your True Path" in Chapter 13 for more information on paths.

☞ The / key is used to tell DOS that the next series of letters is an instruction to modify the command that came before.

Command Line Syntax

When you look up a DOS command in the DOS manual or in the DOS Help system, you will see all sorts of weird stuff after the name of the actual command. This is known as the command line *syntax* or *format*, and it is actually there to *help* you, not confuse you. With friends like this, who needs enemies?

The command syntax may have four parts:

☞ The command name itself

☞ The required part (required parameter)

☞ The optional part (optional parameter)

☞ Switches

Take a look at each of these parts.

The command name

An example of a command name is the command to find out the current version of DOS. You enter in

```
VER
```

Here, only the command is needed because there are no required parts nor any options or switches.

The required part

For a command like the one to prepare a floppy disk for use by DOS, you have the following:

```
FORMAT drive
```

FORMAT is the command name itself, and the *drive* in italics is the required part. For safety, FORMAT insists that you specify which drive is to be formatted.

The optional part

The command to find out the name of a disk (its *volume label*) can also take a drive letter as a parameter, but here it is optional. So it is usually shown like this:

```
VOL [drive]
```

The square brackets indicate that the drive letter is optional. If you don't include the drive letter, DOS assumes you mean the current drive.

A command can also have toggles, which are special optional parameters. These are shown with both options enclosed in square brackets and separated by a vertical bar called the pipe symbol (¦), which is on the keyboard above the backslash. An example of such a command is ECHO, which controls whether DOS displays commands in a batch file while the file is executing. You probably have ECHO as the first command in your AUTOEXEC.BAT file:

```
ECHO [ON¦OFF]
```

Typing in the command name by itself will tell you whether the command is ON or OFF. You type either **ECHO ON** or **ECHO OFF** to set it on or off.

Switches

Finally, a command can have *switches*, which are always optional. Switches modify how the rest of the command is carried out.

Put them all together, they spell "syntax"

Here is the FORMAT command, but in a much fuller syntax:

```
FORMAT drive [/V[:label]][/F:size][/S]
```

First in the line is the command itself, FORMAT. The required parameter is *drive*, so you must type in a drive letter (like **A:**, to direct the command to your first floppy drive).

Next in line is a switch, [/V[:*label*]], which includes an optional parameter to that switch. Notice that this switch has two sets of square brackets: one to indicate that the switch itself is optional, and another to indicate that *label* is optional. If you choose to use the switch (the /V switch adds a volume label to the disk) you can specify the label here or wait to be prompted. The [/F:*size*] switch, if you use it, includes a required parameter, so there's only one set of square brackets here. The /F switch, which specifies size, has to include a specific size and will look like /F:360. The last item in the line is a switch that requires no additional parameters, [/S]. Add this switch to copy system files to the disk and make it bootable. (For more information on bootable disks, see "How to Make a Boot Floppy and What to Do with It" in Chapter 16.)

All the switches are themselves optional, since they are shown in brackets.

Whew! That was pretty intense there, especially at the end.

So if you want to format the 360K floppy in your A drive, put on the volume label CUTEDISK, and you want it to be bootable as well, you would enter

```
FORMAT A: /V:CUTEDISK /F:360 /S
```

Remember that this way of showing the command syntax is pretty consistent in most books, and in DOS versions 5 and above when you get command line help by including the /? switch to the command. So, if you see a command with all those brackets and slashes after it in a manual or other book, just remember that everything in brackets is optional and things with slashes (but not backslashes) are called switches.

Canceling an Order at the DOS Prompt

If you haven't pressed the Enter key, you can cancel a command by pressing the Esc key. The cursor drops to the next line and you can type in the correct command.

If you *have* pressed the Enter key and DOS has started something you must stop **NOW**, hold down the Ctrl key and type a C. This is the all-purpose cancel key. A stronger version of this is Ctrl-Break. Use this key to cancel the current command. Sometimes it even works!

Most programs have their own cancel key, so try that first if you're running a program. This is usually Esc. (Except in WordPerfect, which always has to be different. There it's F1.)

Try Ctrl-C next. You don't want to reboot or turn your computer off in order to extract yourself from a bad spot if you can avoid it.

To Err Is Human

Everyone makes misteaks, and most of us make a LOT. One of the perturbing things about typing at the DOS prompt is that DOS makes it difficult to fix those little typos. There are ways to edit the command you just entered, but only two are worth learning.

The extremely cool F3 key

The first is the F3 key, which will repeat the entire last command you entered.

For example, say you are copying the contents of a series of disks from your drive A to your hard drive, using the command

```
COPY A:*.* C:\LETTERS
```

When that's finished, you remove the disk and put a new one in the drive. Press F3 and the command is displayed again.

F3 can help with typing errors too. If you were attempting to do a DISKCOPY and instead typed in

```
DISHCOPY
```

DOS would respond with "Bad command or file name." Rather than type the whole thing over, press the right arrow key once. You should see a *D* appear on the command line. With each press of the arrow key, DOS fills in with the key from the previous command. Press the arrow key two more times and then type **K** to replace the mistyped *H*. Now, press the F3 key. Voila! DOS fills in the rest of the line.

The moderately terrific F2 key

The other trick is using the F2 key. If you press this key, followed by a character, DOS will fill in the previous command right up to (but not including) that character. So, if you typed, for example,

```
CHK DSK C:
```

and accidentally inserted a space in the middle of the command, press the F2 key, then the Spacebar. DOS fills in the *chk* and leaves the cursor where the space was. Press the Del key once to delete the space, then press the F3 key to fill in the rest of the line. Now the command should work.

Do Function Keys Leave You Feeling Nonfunctional?

You can forget all the dumb stuff above if you have DOS 5 or DOS 6, because you have a handy little program called DOSKEY. DOSKEY does all the stuff F3 and F2 can do and more. See the section "DOSKEY—Is It for Me?" below.

DOS Versions

Most books, including this one, make reference to what works with what version of DOS. DOS comes in a variety of flavors (though they're all basically vanilla). To see what you have, enter

```
VER
```

DOS will respond with the version and type of DOS running on your computer.

The two basic flavors are MS-DOS and IBM Personal Computer DOS. Both were written primarily by Microsoft, and they are virtually identical. You only really care about which is which if you are going to upgrade. If you currently have IBM's version of DOS 5 and you want to upgrade to DOS 6, for example, you will need the IBM upgrade. If you have MS-DOS, you must get the Microsoft upgrade.

DOS versions started at 1.0, but realistically the lowest version that is usable on modern personal computers is 2.11. If you have anything lower than version 5, you should upgrade. DOS is cheap and the upgrade will save aggravation. Besides, you will then have the DOS Shell and can skip all this stuff about using the DOS prompt.

Some hardware manufacturers put their own name on DOS, calling it Everex DOS, Wombat DOS, or something like that. It's all the same at heart. Sometimes they add stuff specific to their own machines, but the core commands will not change.

Program Versions—What Do All Those Numbers Mean?

Software is usually spoken of in terms of version numbers. You will see references to Version X or Version X.xx of various programs. What do the different numbers mean? The same rules apply to all programs:

☞ Whole numbers refer to major changes in the program. For example, if you have version 4.0 of a program, the release of version 5.0 is a major deal. With DOS, the change from DOS 4 to DOS 5 meant real improvements. So if you use the program a lot, you probably want to pay to get the new version.

☞ Changes of a $1/10$, such as from DOS 3.2 to DOS 3.3, usually provide an incremental improvement. Maybe only one significant feature is added. In the example of DOS 3.2 to DOS 3.3, support was added for high-density $3^1/2$-inch drives, as well as for large hard disks. Actually, a pretty worthwhile update at the time. So whether or not to upgrade depends on how valuable the new feature is to you and how much they want you to pay.

☞ Changes of $1/100$, such as from DOS 4.00 to DOS 4.01, generally provide no new features of significance, they just make the ones that *are* there work. Usually, this kind of a version change is a bug fix. Maybe a minor improvement is made, but usually not enough that you would want to pay for it.

But the bug fixes can make a difference to you. If they are in areas you use, you should get the upgrade. And you shouldn't have to pay for it. If they tell you there is a charge, suggest that in your case this should be waived, since the only reason you are getting the new version is to fix bugs they made you pay for in the old version. If that doesn't work, ask for a supervisor. Persist! This is a campaign for justice!

McDonnal's Rule: The squeaky wheel gets the grease.

Annoying Error Messages and How to Defeat Them

DOS has many ways to annoy you, but at the prompt there are only a few error messages that will pop up repeatedly.

Here are the five most common with accompanying translations.

Bad command or file name

Translation: You mistyped something. Maybe you spelled it wrong, maybe you typed in a file or program that isn't in your path. Try Chapter 15, "Whither Files?" for help in finding lost and strayed files. See "Finding Your True Path" in Chapter 13 for information on paths.

File not found

Translation: The file isn't in that directory, bozo. This means you tried to copy or delete a file that doesn't exist, at least not where you thought it did. Again, the simplest answer is that you mistyped the file name. If you want to check to see if the file is there, type

```
DIR X*
```

where *X* is the first letter of the file name. This will give you a list of all the files in the current directory that start with the same first letter.

Invalid directory

Translation: The directory doesn't exist. You either mistyped it, or mis-remembered it. The usual reason for this message is that you forgot to include the correct path to the directory you want to go to. If you are in the WordPerfect directory (\WP51) and try to change to the DOS directory (\DOS) by typing

```
CD DOS
```

you will get this error message because DOS will think you are trying to go to a subdirectory of WordPerfect. The correct command is

```
CD \DOS
```

For more nonsense about paths, directories, and how to move around in them, see Chapter 13, "Care and Feeding of Your Hard Disk."

Path not found

Translation: The directory doesn't exist. You either mistyped it, or misremembered it. Check your typing, and check to make sure you haven't inadvertently left out a leading \.

Not ready reading drive A:

Translation: Put the floppy in first, please. Usually it means that you forgot to put a floppy disk into the drive, or didn't turn the little handle (the scientific term is *latch*) on a 5¼-inch drive. Or if you are at someone else's computer, the drive on top might be B, not A.

This one is simple if it refers to a floppy drive, but may be very bad news if the drive letter is that of your hard disk. If it *does* refer to your hard disk, see "The Case of the Disappearing Hard Drive" in Chapter 17.

Chapter 18 provides a more detailed list of error messages and what to do about them other than sob uncontrollably.

DOSKEY—Is It for Me?

If you are running DOS 5 or greater, then the answer is a resounding Yes. Even if you spend all your time in the DOS Shell or Windows and only occasionally use the command line, this little gem makes your life easier.

Finally, you can make changes in the command line without remembering exactly how to use F2, F3, and all that stuff.

What is DOSKEY?

DOSKEY is a little program that comes with DOS 5 and DOS 6. Type in

    DOSKEY

at the command line, and instead of only being able to recall your last command using F2 or F3, you can cycle through the last several commands.

Just press the ↑ key. Press it once, get the last command, press it twice, get the command you used time before last, and so forth.

You can move around in the command line using the → and ← keys. With DOSKEY you can use the Del key to delete characters and the Ins key to insert characters.

If you want to use DOSKEY every time you turn on your computer, you need to add it to your AUTOEXEC.BAT file. See "Using DOS EDIT to Change Your Files" in Chapter 11 for E-Z instructions.

Chapter 3

FILES AND THE THINGS YOU DO WITH THEM

Clark's Law: Once you open a can of worms, the only way to recan them is to use a larger can.

MOST OF WHAT you do on a computer has to do with files: moving, copying, deleting, (OOPS!) undeleting, renaming, and so forth. That's what this chapter is about. For making up new files and finding ones that are lost or strayed, see Chapter 15, "Whither Files?"

Making a Duplicate

To make a duplicate of a file, you need to know the name of the file and the new name you want to give to the copy. For example, if you have a file called GRIPE.TXT and you want to make a copy called PROTEST.TXT, you would type in

```
COPY GRIPE.TXT PROTEST.TXT
```

When you do this, you get the message "1 file(s) copied." You then have two files that are identical in content but have different names.

☞ *If you get the message "File not found," you probably made a mistake typing in the name of the original file. Just try again.*

☞ *If you get a message like "Invalid switch" or "File creation error," you are trying to give the new file a name that DOS doesn't allow. For more information on file names, see "Legal Names for Files" in Chapter 15. In general, file names can be up to eight letters and/or numbers long. If you want, you can add a period and three more characters.*

☞ *You can't have two files in the same directory with the same name.*

☞ *You can have copies of files with the same name in different directories. But a real can of worms is opened when you have files with the same name and different contents. Don't do it.*

Be sure that a file with the new name doesn't already exist. For example, if you already have a file called PROTEST.TXT, the COPY command shown above will write GRIPE.TXT on top of it, replacing the old file with the new. If that's what you want to do, fine. Just don't do it by accident.

Copying a File from Where You Are to Somewhere Else

To copy a file from the directory you're in to another directory, use the COPY command:

```
COPY GRIPE.TXT \LETTERS
```

This will copy the file GRIPE.TXT to the LETTERS directory on the same disk. Be careful here. If there isn't a directory called LETTERS, you will end up with a file called LETTERS in the root directory (COPY looks for the directory LETTERS, and if it's not there, assumes you want to make a file called LETTERS). Probably not what you had in mind.

To copy the same file to a disk on drive A, type in

```
COPY GRIPE.TXT A:
```

This will put a copy of GRIPE.TXT on the floppy in your drive A.

If you want to copy this file to a directory on another drive, you have to specify the full path:

```
COPY GRIPE.TXT A:\COMPLAIN
```

This will copy the GRIPE.TXT file to the COMPLAIN directory on drive A.

☞ *Don't forget to put a colon after the drive letter. If you don't you will end up with a file called A on your hard disk. I can't tell you how many times I have done this.*

Copying a File from Somewhere Else to Where You Are

Copying a file from some other directory to where you are can be done using the short form of the COPY command. Suppose the file MAMBO.DOC is on drive B and you want to copy it to where you are on drive C. Type in

```
COPY B:MAMBO.DOC
```

If the MAMBO.DOC happens to be in a directory called \DANCE\LATIN, you would type in

```
COPY B:\DANCE\LATIN\MAMBO.DOC
```

In both the examples above, a copy of the file MAMBO.DOC will end up in your current drive.

☞ *This short form of COPY only works when the file you want to get is not in the same directory you are.*

☞ *For more information on directories, see "Directory Assistance" in Chapter 13.*

Copying Multiple Files

You can use the COPY command to duplicate several files at once. This requires the * wildcard. The * wildcard can stand for a group of characters in a file name. So if you want to copy all the files in your current directory to the floppy in drive A, you type

```
COPY *.* A:
```

The first * stands for all characters before the dot, no matter what they are; the second * stands for all characters after the dot.

If you only want to copy the files with a .WK1 extension to drive A, type in

```
COPY *.WK1 A:
```

You can do lots of other weird and obscure things with wildcards. For more info, see "What's a Wildcard?" in Chapter 15.

Including Subdirectories (The XCOPY Command)

There is another form of the COPY command, called XCOPY (short for extended copy), which allows you to copy not only the files in the current directory, but also files in any subdirectories of the current directory. I use this a lot when I have to take work home on the weekends. I have a directory called \REPORT with three subdirectories under it, HOURLY, NONEXEMPT, and EXEMPT. These are used to generate a monthly report on overtime in the department. To copy the entire structure to a floppy disk, I simply type

```
XCOPY \REPORT A: /S
```

The /S tells the XCOPY command to include any subdirectories, and keeps the structure intact.

For more on directories and how they're put together, see "Directory Assistance" in Chapter 13.

Moving Files—A Reason to Get DOS 6

Often you don't really want to copy a file to somewhere else—you actually want to move it.

In older versions of DOS you have to copy the file to the new location and then delete the old copy. See "Moving Files If You Don't Have DOS 6," below.

But if you *do* have DOS 6, this process is very easy. To move a file called KITCHEN.WQ1 that has all the costs of the kitchen remodeling you did from the \PLANNING directory to the \COSTBASE subdirectory, type

```
MOVE \PLANNING\KITCHEN.WQ1 \COSTBASE
```

DOS will respond with

```
c:\planning\kitchen.wq1 => c:\costbase\kitchen.wq1 [ok]
```

telling you that the file was successfully moved.

If you move a file to a directory containing a file with the same name, DOS will quietly, and without warning, overwrite the old file. This is fine, if that is what you had in mind. If that is not your intent, get a directory listing of the destination directory before you do the move.

Moving Files If You Don't Have DOS 6

If you don't have DOS 6, you can still move a file—it just takes a two-step operation. First you copy the file to the destination directory, and then you delete it from its current location. See the sections in this chapter on copying and deleting files.

Deleting a File

To get rid of extraneous junk on your computer such as multiple copies of the same file or old versions of a file, you will use the DEL command (short for *Delete*). When you use the DEL command there is no chance to change your mind, so use it with care.

Type in **DEL** followed by the name of the file. For example, if you have an old version of a document called OLDVER.DOC, type in this:

```
DEL OLDVER.DOC
```

If the file you want to delete isn't in the current directory, you'll have to specify the path. So if OLDVER.DOC is in a directory called 123, type

```
DEL \123\OLDVER.DOC
```

☞ *For more information on directories and paths, see Chapter 13, "Care and Feeding of Your Hard Disk."*

☞ *You can also use a command called ERASE to do the same thing as DEL.*

Deleting Multiple Files

You can use the DEL command to wipe out several files at once. This requires the * wildcard. The * wildcard can stand for a group of characters in a file name. If you want to delete all the files in your current directory with a .WK1 extension (the file extension for Lotus 1-2-3 worksheets), type in

```
DEL *.WK1
```

All of your Lotus worksheets will vanish silently and without warning.

If you accidentally delete a file, or worse, a whole group of files, you should immediately undelete them. Don't wait! If you do this right away, your chances of complete recovery are very good. If you wait, they will go down drastically, because DOS will start to overwrite the old files with new stuff. See the section "Undeleting a File" in this chapter for instructions.

If you want to delete all the files on the floppy drive A, type

```
DEL A:*.*
```

Here, at last, you will get a warning. DOS will put the following message on your screen:

```
All files in directory will be deleted!
Are you sure (Y/N)?
```

If you have any doubts, press N and think it over. Otherwise, press Y and the files all disappear.

Do NOT delete a file called COMMAND.COM or you will be in serious trouble.

Bad Guests—Files That Refuse to Leave

Someday you will try to delete a file and get the message "Access denied." Have you suddenly been transported into an old spy movie? Well, maybe. But a more likely explanation is that the file is being protected by DOS.

Special features called attributes are assigned to some files to protect them from the itchy-trigger-finger crowd. One of these attributes is the R attribute, short for *read-only*. When a file is marked read-only, you can look at it, print it, copy it, and so forth, but you can't change it in any way. And deleting a file is just about the most serious way you could change it!

But if you are sure you want to delete the file, then you can remove this protection by using the ATTRIB command. You type in

```
ATTRIB FILENAME.EXT -R
```

You can now delete this file using DEL as shown above. You can use the * wildcard to remove the R attribute from a group of files.

Don't use the ATTRIB command unless you are absolutely sure you know what you're doing. If you delete a file your computer needs to run, you will be in serious trouble.

Dangerous Info about Attributes That Mustn't Be Allowed to Fall into the Wrong Hands

DOS allows files to have up to four attributes. These attributes help to determine how a file behaves, and how it can be treated. The four attributes are A, R, H and S. These letters stand for the following:

- ☞ A is for *archive*. When this attribute is "on" or set, the file has not been backed up since it was last changed. This attribute is used by backup programs to determine if the file should be backed up. See Chapter 14, "An Ounce of Prevention," for more on backing up files.

- ☞ R is for *read-only*. This is the "Look but don't touch" attribute. You can copy, print, and view the file, but you can't change it in any way.

- ☞ H is for *hidden*. With this attribute on, the file is hidden from normal view. This is only limited protection, though, because there are lots of ways to see what files have been hidden.

- ☞ S is for *system*. This attribute means the file is a special file used by DOS. Like hidden files, system files are not visible if you just get a simple directory listing.

Don't fool around with the attributes of files, especially those marked *system* or *hidden*. It is easy to do something you really didn't mean to do and that you will regret.

Undeleting a File

Martin's Law: As soon as you delete a worthless file, you'll need it.

Sooner or later (and probably sooner) you will delete a file you shouldn't have. As soon as you realize this, your impulse will be to panic. You can do that if you want, but it's much easier on your nerves to use the UNDELETE command.

For example, to rescue the deleted file DIARY.WP5, type in

```
UNDELETE DIARY.WP5
```

DOS will display the file's name and whether or not it can be undeleted. Press Y if you want to undelete it. You'll also have to provide
the first letter of the file name. If you can't remember, supply any old
letter. Once you have the file back, you can rename it if you need to.
(See "Renaming Files," below.)

If you're not sure of the file name, type in

```
UNDELETE /LIST
```

You'll get a list of all the deleted files that can be recovered.

Use UNDELETE as the not-so-evil twin of DEL. If you killed files with
DEL, you can type in the same command, substituting UNDELETE, and
raise the file(s) from the dead.

☞ *For UNDELETE to be successful, you must use it quickly. In other words,
don't do anything else first. If you do any other file copying, moving,
etc., you stand a very good chance of writing over the deleted file.*

☞ *A file that has been written over cannot be undeleted. If you copy a file
on top of another file, the one underneath cannot be undeleted.*

☞ *UNDELETE is available only in DOS versions 5 and 6. If you use an earlier version of DOS, there are a number of programs you can buy that
will recover deleted files in ingenious ways. See Chapter 21, "Seven
Programs That Can Save Your Cookies," for serious help in case of
serious need.*

Additional Protection If You Have DOS 6

The newest version of UNDELETE allows for a fail-safe version of delete
protection. This is called Delete Sentry. You don't have to use Delete
Sentry, but if you frequently find yourself slapping your forehead and
crying "Oh NO! My file's gone!" it makes sense.

Delete Sentry works by making a hidden directory called SENTRY on
your hard drive. All deleted files are escorted to this directory and held
in protective custody in case you want one or more of them back.

To install Delete Sentry, you need to add the following line to your
AUTOEXEC.BAT file:

```
UNDELETE /SC
```

The /SC stands for Sentry, drive C. If you have a drive D, add a space and /SD. When you want a file back, use UNDELETE as described in the previous section.

☞ The SENTRY directory will be assigned up to seven percent of your hard drive. In other words, if you have a 50-megabyte hard drive, the SENTRY directory will take up to 3.5 megabytes for itself (assuming you have that much space available). When it gets full, the oldest files are permanently jettisoned. But unless you are deleting files willy-nilly, there should be enough room to hold deleted files for at least a week.

☞ See "Using DOS EDIT to Change Your Files" in Chapter 11 for information on how to edit your AUTOEXEC.BAT file.

Renaming Files

Changing the name of a file in DOS is amazingly simple. You just use the command REN (short for RENAME, which also works). For example, to change the name of the file HAROLD.TXT to HARRIET.TXT, type

```
REN HAROLD.TXT HARRIET.TXT
```

To rename all the files with the extension .BAK to .SAV, use the following:

```
REN *.BAK *.SAV
```

If the file you want to rename isn't in the current directory, you need to specify the path:

```
REN \BOOKS\SEPT SEPT93
```

This way, the file called SEPT in the BOOKS directory has been renamed SEPT93. As you can see, when renaming a file that's not in the current directory, you need to provide the path for the old name but not the new one.

☞ *REN and RENAME are one and the same. Use the shorter version and save wear and tear on your fingers.*

☞ *If you have more than one file to rename in another directory, change to that directory first. It is faster, takes less typing, and is subject to fewer mistakes.*

☞ *For help on file names, see Chapter 15, "Whither Files?"*

☞ *Help with paths and directories can be found in Chapter 13, "Care and Feeding of Your Hard Disk."*

Putting It on Paper

Most programs provide an easy method for printing files that is specific to that program, and you should always do your printing from within the program where possible. But two kinds of files can be printed directly from DOS:

☞ Simple text files such as those created with DOS's EDIT program

☞ Printer image files, which are created by programs such as Microsoft Word or Quattro Pro when you select the Print to File option from the Print menu

To print a simple text file like PHONES.TXT from DOS, you can COPY it to the printer. Yes, it's your old pal, the COPY command. Just type in

```
COPY PHONES.TXT PRN
```

If the file you want to print is a printer image file, you do almost the same thing, except you have to tell DOS that the file is a *binary* file that may have some special characters in it. To print BUDGET.OUT, therefore:

```
COPY BUDGET.OUT PRN /B
```

My Last Page Didn't Print!

Ever printed something on your laser printer only to have the last page stuck in the printer with the lights on? Here's a simple little trick to eject that page from your printer. From the DOS prompt, enter

```
ECHO ^L > PRN
```

Remember that ^L means Ctrl-L, and you get that by holding down the Ctrl key while pressing the L key. The command may look like gibberish to you, but your printer will recognize it and spit out that last page.

File Basics

The /B tells DOS that the file is binary.

Finally, if your file is a large file, you might want to get something else done while it is printing. DOS provides a special program to print files while letting you do something else. The program is called (ingeniously enough) PRINT. To print the file README.TXT using the PRINT program, type

```
PRINT README.TXT
```

Chapter 4

THE DOS SHELL
(Or, Why Didn't You Say This in the First Place?)

Muysenberg's Law: There's an easier way to do anything.

THE DOS SHELL lets you copy, move, and delete files, plus it lets you see your directory structure and even start programs, without ever having to deal with the dread command line. The command for the DOS Shell is DOSSHELL, so you will see it referred to both ways. But when you want to talk to the computer about the DOS Shell, you have to call it DOSSHELL.

Why do we call DOSSHELL a shell? Like the shell on a turtle, it provides a nice, safe place to hide from the ugly details of the operating system. You can stick your head out every once in a while and do things from

> ### Loathsome Background Information You Can Skip
>
> DOS 4 made the first attempt at providing a graphical tool from within DOS for those of us who find the bare DOS command line intimidating. It was awful.
>
> With DOS 5 came DOSSHELL, a program that actually worked. DOS 6 has the same program, and if you really, truly hate the command line (like all good Americans) you will spend most of your time using the Shell.

the command line, but whenever you find the command line too threatening, just duck back into the DOS Shell. Actually, the DOS prompt itself is really a shell, too, but not exactly a comfortable one.

Starting It

To start the DOS Shell from the DOS prompt, type in

    DOSSHELL

The Shell will soon appear on your screen. If you want to do all your work from within the DOS Shell, you can add this command as the last item in your AUTOEXEC.BAT file, so that every time you start your computer you will get the Shell. (See Chapter 11, "Your System Defined," for how to edit your AUTOEXEC.BAT file.)

If you get the message, "Bad command or file name," then DOSSHELL was probably not included when DOS was installed. This can be remedied, but you may need the assistance of someone with DOS smarts.

Keep in mind that all the info about DOSSHELL in this chapter applies only to DOS 5 and DOS 6.

Do I Really Need a Mouse?

Well, it is possible to do everything from the keyboard, but why would you want to? Let's face it, the world is rapidly being overrun with the little rodents, and there is almost no way to avoid them. Sooner or later you're going to have to buy one anyway, so go do it now. I'll wait here.

Changing Drives

At the top of the screen you'll see a series of cute little buttons, each one of which corresponds to a drive on your machine. To change to another drive, click on that button with your mouse.

Switching Directories

To move to a different directory, you need to make the Directory Tree panel active. Move the mouse pointer somewhere inside that panel and click once.

You select a directory like you select a file, by clicking on it once with the mouse. The contents of that directory will then appear in the File panel to the right.

If there's a plus sign next to the directory name, it means there are sub-directories under it. Click on the plus sign and the subdirectories will be listed.

Moving around in the Shell

The DOS Shell can have anywhere from one to four different panes (as in "window panes"). To change the look, click on the View menu, then select one of the options. The choices are as follows:

☞ *Single File List:* As shown in Figure 4.1, this gives you two panes or panels, with directories shown on the left and the files in the current directory shown on the right (the current directory is whichever one is highlighted in the left panel).

☞ *Dual File Lists:* This gives you two completely separate directory and file lists, for a total of four panes. This view is especially useful for doing stuff between different drives or directories. Figure 4.2 shows how this option looks.

☞ *All Files:* This gives you a single pane on the right side of the screen with all the files on the current drive shown. The left side shows statistics for that drive. This view is useful for finding lost files. See "How to Find a Lost File" below.

FIGURE 4.1:

Select Single File List from the View menu and you'll get something that looks like this.

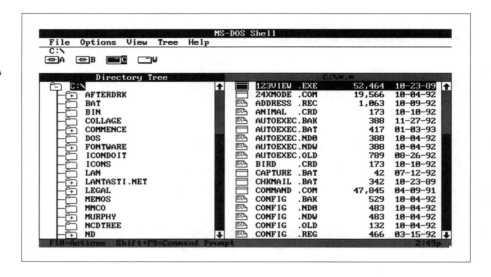

FIGURE 4.2:

If you select Dual File Lists you get two sets of files and directories.

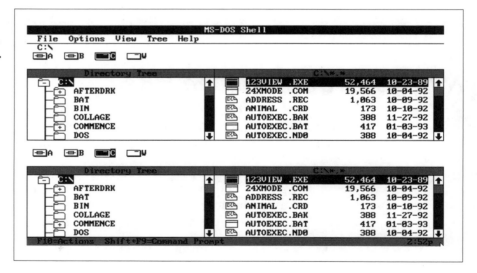

☞ *Program/File Lists:* As shown in Figure 4.3, this view has three panes (four if you have Task Swapper turned on, which you shouldn't) with the directory and file panes on top and a list of available program options on the bottom.

FIGURE 4.3:
The Program/File Lists
option

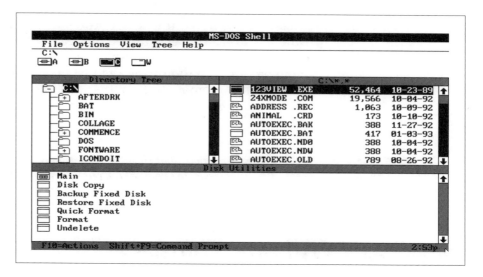

Task Swapper—What It Is and Why You Shouldn't Use It

Task Swapper allows those with plenty of free memory to have several programs open at once and switch between them. This is not "multitasking" because each program is doing something only while it is the open program. But it does allow switching between programs without closing one and opening another. That's the good part.

The bad part is that computers are the ultimate believers in Murphy's Universal Law—"If it can go wrong, it will." If something goes wrong while you are working in one program, the worst that can happen is that you will lose the work you did in that one program. If you are switching back and forth between several programs, you may well lose far more work. If you really need to move back and forth between several programs, use Windows or even DESQview. Both provide enough isolation between tasks that if something goes wrong in one task, you have at least a fair chance of only losing the work in that single task. Of the two, Windows is far friendlier and infinitely cuter. DESQview is more powerful but is really only for the hopelessly nerdy.

DOS Shell

☞ *Program List:* Shows either one or two panes, depending on whether Task Swapper is turned on (see "Task Swapper" above). This view can provide you with an elaborate menu system for running programs. It's fairly messy to set up yourself, but if you want to run all your programs from the Shell and have them organized into customized groups, see the "Bribe-a-Nerd" section later in this chapter.

☞ *If you're wondering what view you're looking at, click on the View menu. In the list of views, the name of the one currently on the screen will be in a lighter shade.*

File Stuff (All the Things You Did the Hard Way Before)

The DOS Shell provides an easy way to copy, move, rename, and delete files. But in order to do anything with a file or files, you must first select them. A selected file is, by definition, highlighted on the screen.

Selecting files

To select a file or files, click inside a file pane with your mouse.

☞ To select a single file, position the pointer above the file name and click. The file should be highlighted.

☞ To select multiple files, click on the first file, then hold down the Ctrl key while you click on the other files.

☞ To select a group of adjacent files, click on the first, then hold down the Shift key and click on the last one in the group.

Copying files

Once you have selected the files you want to copy, there are three ways to copy them.

☞ Press the left mouse button and hold it down while pressing down the Ctrl key. Move the mouse cursor till the drive or directory where you want to copy the files to is highlighted, then release the left mouse button. (The scientific term for using the mouse to move stuff is *drag-and-drop*.)

☞ Press F8 and type in where you want the copy to go.

☞ Select Copy from the File menu and type in where the files are to go.

Make sure you press the Ctrl key first. If you don't you will be *moving* the file, not copying it.

Moving files

Once you have selected the files you want to move, there are three ways to get the job done.

☞ Press the left mouse button and drag-and-drop the files into the drive or directory where you want to move them.

☞ Press the F7 key and then type in where you want the files moved to.

☞ Select Move from the File menu and type in where the files are to go.

Renaming files (and even directories!)

The DOS Shell allows you to rename files easily. You can even rename directories, something you can't do from the DOS prompt.

To rename a file, highlight it and click on Rename in the File menu. A box will appear on the screen with the file's old name and a place in which to type the new name.

To rename a directory, highlight the directory name and click on Rename as described above.

☞ For help on naming files, see "Legal Names for Files" in Chapter 15.

☞ The rules for naming files also apply to naming directories.

DOS Shell

Rodentophobia? Here's How to Do It with the Keyboard

While you are waiting for your mouse to arrive (you *did* order one like I told you, right?), here is how to move around and do things within the DOS Shell using only a keyboard. It can be done, but it is a bit awkward.

☞ Press the Tab key to move from pane to pane and to the drive buttons on top.

☞ Use the ↑ and ↓ keys to move to a different file in the file pane or to a different directory in the tree pane.

☞ To change drives, use the ← and → keys to move the drive button you want, and press the Enter key when the new drive is selected. Or press Ctrl plus the letter of the drive you want to move to.

☞ To select an individual file, use the arrow keys to move the cursor to it. To select a group of adjacent files, hold down the Shift key and move the cursor from the first to the last file in the group.

☞ To select multiple files, press Shift-F8 and use the Spacebar to select/deselect individual files.

☞ To activate the menus, press F10 key or the Alt key, then press the key for the first letter of the menu you want to drop down.

☞ To copy files, select them and press the F8 key. Type in where the files are to go.

☞ To move files, select them and press the F7 key. Type in where the files are to go.

☞ To start a program, highlight its .EXE or .COM file in the file pane and press Enter.

Deleting files

Once you have selected the files you want to delete, there are two ways to get the job done.

☞ Press the Del key. You'll get a message asking you to confirm that you want to do this dire deed. Select Yes if you want to go ahead. Press the Esc key if you've had second thoughts. Depending on how the options are set on your computer, you may also be asked to confirm each individual file deletion.

☞ Select Delete from the File menu. The same confirmation rules will apply.

How to Find a Lost File

One of the things DOSSHELL does best is finding a lost file. Click on Search from the File menu. A window will open that lets you type in as much about the name as you remember. If the file was an annual report and called 93REPORT or 93RESULTS or something like that, type in **93*.*** in the Search For box, then click on the OK button. DOS Shell will find all the files which begin with 93 on the current drive. If your file isn't there, it means the file is probably on a different drive or disk. Press the Esc key to close the Search For box, change to that drive, and try again.

☞ See "What's a Wildcard?" in Chapter 15 for more information on using the * wildcard.

Running Programs from the Shell

The DOS Shell lets you run other programs without ever leaving the Shell. There are three basic ways to do this, and two of them are even for mere mortals.

Using one of the views that includes a file pane, find the .COM, .EXE, or .BAT file that starts the program. Highlight it with the mouse or the cursor, then either double-click with the mouse or press the Enter key.

Bribe-a-Nerd, the Easiest Way

Another way to run programs from within DOS Shell requires that they be set up on the Program menu. While this is handy, I suggest you con one of your nerdy friends to set up your favorite programs. Offer her or him some nice, high-calorie, low-nutrition treat and you can probably get it done for no more than the cost of the treat and having to listen to her/him explain far more than you wanted to know about how to do it. Be patient, or better yet, get some good cheap ear plugs.

DOS Shell

For example, to run your spreadsheet program, Quattro Pro, you would highlight the file Q.EXE in the QPRO subdirectory, and either double-click on it or press Enter.

The second way is to select Run from the File menu. This will open up a dialog box, where you can enter in the command for the program you want to run. So, for example, you can type in WP and start Word-Perfect. With this method you can also open a particular file at the same time. So if you want to start WordPerfect and have it immediately open your letter to Mom, you can type in

```
WP MOM.WP5
```

(This assumes that good old MOM.WP5 is hanging out in your Word-Perfect document directory. Otherwise, you'll have to provide a path.)

Enough, Let Me Out!

Once you are in DOS Shell, you may think you never need to get out, but just in case, here are three ways to escape:

☞ Press the F3 key.

☞ Press Alt-F4. (This is the default way to get out of things in Windows, too.)

☞ Press Alt-F to drop down the File menu (or click on File with your mouse), and then press X or click on Exit with the mouse.

When Not to Use the Shell and Why

There aren't a whole lot of times you don't want to use the Shell to get your DOS work done, unless you have a better shell. (And there are several better shell programs out there, though most are not free. One of the best is Norton Desktop for DOS. See Chapter 21, "Murphy's Eleven Favorite Pain-Relieving Programs.")

There is only really one time when you don't want to use the Shell: when you're starting a memory-resident program. These programs, which are designed to hang around and be always available, are also called TSRs (short for Terminate and Stay Resident). They must be started before you start DOS Shell.

So, for example, if you are going to run DOS's PRINT program, you need to start it before you start DOS Shell. If you have already started DOS Shell and suddenly remember you need to load PRINT, exit the Shell completely by pressing Alt-F4, and type

```
PRINT
```

Press Enter. Press Enter again to make PRN the device you're printing to, then type in

```
DOSSHELL
```

and as soon as you press the Enter key you'll be safely back in the Shell.

DOS Shell

2

This section covers hardware, but not in a scary way. Here are chapters about all the things in a computer and the things attached to a computer and how to keep all of them under control. Plus a chapter with the best description of memory ever written.

PC HARDWARE

Just Enough to Dazzle the Crowd without Baffling You

Chapter 5

E-Z HARDWARE

Ablaza's Observation: Every machine will eventually fall apart.

THE ARE FEW things more boring than listening to a bunch of people talk shop—when it's not *your* shop. Even if their work is interesting, they use a lot of technical terms and inside jokes and leave outsiders feeling very much like outsiders.

Computer people do that too. Some of them do it on purpose. So, just in the interest of making it easier for you to nod knowledgeably the next time a nerd tries to baffle you with bull, take a look at the translation list in Table 5.1.

TABLE 5.1:
Scientific Terms
Explained

Primary Name	Alternate Nerdy Names	Translation
Monitor	Video display, CRT, VDT, video display terminal	The thing that looks like a TV
Keyboard	Manual input device, 101 enhanced	The part you type on
Computer box	System unit, tower case, desktop case	The main box that everything else plugs into
Mouse	Ergonomic graphical input device, rodent, pointing device	Mouse
Trackball	Ergonomic graphical input device, Trackman	Upside-down mouse
Floppy drive	5¼-inch, 3½-inch, removable storage drive, floppy	The slot(s) in the front of the computer box you put floppy disks into
Hard drive	Hard disk, Winchester, mass storage device, IDE, MFM, RLL, ESDI, SCSI	C drive
Memory	RAM, DRAM, extended, expanded, HMA	Where programs actually run
Floppy disk	1.44, HD, 1.2, 360, 720, 3½-inch, 5¼-inch	What programs come on, and where you back up to
Printer	Laser, dot-matrix, ink-jet, PostScript, PCL	Printer
Board	Card, PC board	Something you buy to increase the capabilities of your computer and that is installed inside the computer box
Motherboard	Motherboard	The main board inside the computer box that everything plugs into
CPU	Central Processing Unit, chip, 8088, 80286, 286, 80386, 386, 80486, 486, Pentium, 586	The brain of the computer

Processors (What Is All This SX, DX, DX2 Stuff, Anyway?)

Two things determine how much basic horsepower your computer has: the type of microprocessor and the speed of the microprocessor.

The entire computer will sometimes be described in terms of the processor. For example, it may be described as a "386SX-20" or a "486-33." The first part refers to the processor itself and the second part to the speed of the processor. The processor, also known as the *CPU* (Central Processing Unit), is the brains of the outfit. The entire range of PC processors can be summed up in the following numbers: 8088/8086, 80286, 80386, 80486. (See "Tedious Facts about the Processor Family Tree" below.)

Generally speaking, the bigger the number, the more powerful the computer. And the more you'll have to pay for it. If you are buying a computer, don't buy anything less than an 80386-based computer. And if you're buying a new computer, go for a 486.

Most of the time it won't matter what chip is in your computer until you buy a piece of software that won't run on the processor you have. If you already have a computer and you aren't sure what chip it has, ask a nerd.

What about all those letters after the numbers? The letters are less important than the numbers, but they designate gradations within chips of the same basic number. The rules are

☞ SX is less (powerful and expensive) than DX.

How to Sound Cool

The 8088 and 8086 are always referred to by their full numbers. But everyone refers to the last three processors as the 286, 386, and 486 (two-eighty-six, three-eighty-six, and four-eighty-six).

☞ DX2 is less (powerful and expensive) than DX at the same speed.

☞ SL is mostly for portable computers and uses less power than an equivalent DX.

Software that needs a 386 to run will run on any 386. It generally won't run as fast on a 386SX as on a 386DX, but it will run.

Software that runs on a 386 will run on any 486. The real break is between the 286 and the 386. Some software that runs on the 386 and 486 balks at having anything to do with the lowly 286.

Another topic directly related to the performance of your computer is memory. There are two types of additional memory that may be in your PC, *expanded memory* and *extended memory*. Chapter 6, "Memory (What You Need and What You Don't)," is where you'll find all you need to know about both types.

Tedious Facts about the Processor Family Tree

The first IBM Personal Computer (where "PC" got its start, in 1981) was based on the 8088 microprocessor made by the Intel Corporation. Since then, we've have had the 80286, the 80386, and the 80486. The first computers based on a chip called the Pentium are now appearing, but the Pentium is really just an 80586 with a new name so Intel can trademark it.

Chip Speed and Other Astronomical Numbers

The internal speed of processors is measured in megahertz—that's how many million operations per second. So a chip described as a 386-25 allegedly performs 25 million operations every single second! Don't think about this for too long or your brain will implode.

This seems like useful information. After all, a 386-33 should be able to do 8 million more somethings every second than a 386-25. But there are too many other factors involved to take the chip speed over seriously. Buy a fast one but don't take out a second mortgage.

Math Coprocessors— What Are They and Do I Need One?

While computers are really good at doing lots of simple calculations very fast, they tend to have problems with complex calculations. The math coprocessor was developed to get around this problem. It is a special chip whose only task is to handle these complex calculations that the conventional microprocessor doesn't handle well.

Do you need one? Maybe. If your software is written to take advantage of it, and if you are actually doing the things it does well, it can make a significant improvement in the speed of your computer.

Generally, if you are doing heavy-duty graphics work, or working with complicated spreadsheets, a math coprocessor can speed things up. Here are some simple rules:

☞ If all you are doing is simple addition and subtraction, save your money. You will see no gain.

☞ The speed of the math coprocessor should be the same as the speed of the main processor. The math coprocessor should match the number of your main microprocessor, except have a 7 at the end instead of a 6. So, if you have an 80386SX microprocessor, you get an 80387SX math coprocessor; if you have an 80386DX, you get an 80387DX.

E-Z Hardware

☞ Don't try to install one yourself. Bribe a friend or pay the store where you buy it to do the job.

☞ If you have an 80486DX chip or higher, you already have a math coprocessor. Don't let someone convince you to spend big bucks on another one. If you have that much money, give me a call. I'll help you spend it.

Any Port in a Storm

The back of your PC has lots of interesting places to plug stuff into. If you can bear to look, you'll see that your printer and monitor are hooked up there. Maybe your keyboard and mouse are connected there too. Instead of being called plugs or something obvious, these places are called *ports*.

There are two types of general purpose ports: serial ports and parallel ports.

Computer mice are plugged into serial ports sometimes, but some computers have their own mouse ports.

Serial ports—dangerously techie stuff

The serial ports (also called COM ports and RS-232 ports by very tiresome types) are used for certain mice, modems, plotters, and other devices.

Most computers have one or two serial ports, but they can have up to four. If you have more than two serial ports, you'll probably need some help to use all of them. But if you only have one or two, you can probably handle it yourself.

To use a serial port for a printer or plotter, you must configure the port so that it uses the same protocol that the printer or plotter is using. *Protocol* is a fifty-cent word for a set of rules that control how data flows.

Configuring the port is done with the DOS command called MODE, and with tiny little switches on the printer or plotter called DIP switches. The documentation that came with the printer will show you where these switches are, and which ones do what. But first, some definitions:

☞ *Baud* is the speed at which data is transmitted. This is actually bits per second (BPS), and to be totally correct, the two terms are not exactly the same, though the terms are used interchangeably all the time. (People who make a big deal about the difference need to get a tiny little life. However, you do have my permission to laugh derisively at anyone who says "baud per second.") Valid speeds are 110, 150, 300, 600, 1200, 2400, 4800, 9600, and 19200. Only the first two digits of each speed are used for the MODE command.

☞ *Data bits* are the pieces (bits) of information communicated in each block of transmitted data. The default setting is 7, and the most common numbers are 7 and 8. (See "Whose Default Is It, Anyway?" below.)

☞ *Parity* is the method of error checking used. The most common settings are Even (the default) and None.

☞ *Stop bits* are the bits of dead space between blocks of data. Valid values are 1, 1.5, and 2.

So, if your plotter is set for 9600 baud, 8 data bits, no parity, and 1 stop bit (a pretty typical setting), then the MODE command to connect it to the first serial port would be

```
MODE COM1 BAUD=96 DATA=8 PARITY=N STOP=1
```

Substitute COM2 for COM1 if you are using your second serial port.

Whose Default Is It, Anyway?

Default is one of those annoying terms that are thrown around all the time without explanation. Basically, default means the way things are set when they come from the factory. Both software and hardware come with default settings, and most of the time that's the way you'll use them.

E-Z Hardware

Parallel ports

Parallel ports are generally only used for printers, and they are frequently referred to as printer ports. The nice thing is that printer cables have connectors on each end that keep you from hooking them up wrong.

☞ Most PCs have only a single parallel port, though you might have two.

☞ If you have a choice between a serial port version of a printer or plotter and a parallel port version, take the parallel port version. Parallel ports are faster and don't require you to know anything about speed, stop bits, or any of that wretched stuff that serial printers make you struggle with. If you don't have a choice, read "Serial ports—dangerously techie stuff" above for details.

With the advent of laptop computers, there are now all sorts of specialized devices that can attach to parallel ports. While these were designed for portable computers, they work just fine on regular computers as well. They include network adapters, floppy drives, hard drives, and SCSI adapters.

Woody's Rule of Computer Repair: If it jams, force it. If it breaks, it needed to be replaced anyway.

Marginally Sexist Information about Serial and Parallel Ports and How to Tell Them Apart

Serial ports on the back of your computer come in two different sizes. One has 25 little pins and the other has 9 little pins. In both cases these are called "male" pins for reasons that should be fairly obvious.

Parallel ports (*aka* printer ports) have 25 "receiving" pins and are therefore called "female" plugs.

Look, these names weren't *my* idea! Write your congressperson or something!

Read This Before You Decide to Buy Scuzzy

A SCSI (pronounced *scuzzy*) port is a high-speed way to hook a chain of devices up to your computer all at once. You can attach printers, hard drives, tape drives, CD-ROM drives, and all sorts of other stuff to a single port. The problem is that manufacturers have spent the last several years fighting about how to do this, with the result that they haven't really settled on any one, single way. You can't just buy a new SCSI CD-ROM drive and stick it into your SCSI port and expect everything to work. Here are a few reasons why:

☞ There are three kinds of SCSI ports: SCSI-1, SCSI-2, and FAST SCSI.

☞ Each SCSI device has to have a different address from any other SCSI device.

☞ The device on each end of the chain has to have a terminator.

So, my advice is to buy SCSI devices only if you have extremely good relations with your local computer store (or have a live-in expert). And get a guarantee from the store that they will either make it work or give you your money back.

Modems, or Phun with Phones

Modem is short for *modulator/demodulator*. There, that helped, didn't it? Actually, a modem is just a way to attach your computer to the outside world by way of your phone line. Modems let you send and receive information to and from other computer users (friends even), use online services like CompuServe and Prodigy, and generally waste loads of time and money (like Nintendo but better because you can pretend to be working!).

Modems can be internal or external. If the modem is internal, you need to plug it into one of the slots on the main board of your computer. This requires opening up the case of your computer. Get your System Administrator or a knowledgeable friend to do this. It isn't hard, and once you have watched someone do it, you can probably take it on yourself the next time; but the first time, let someone else do it.

If the modem is external (that is, outside the computer box), it plugs into one of the serial ports on the back of the computer, plus it will need a separate outlet to plug into for electrical power.

☞ *Modems are rated by the speed at which they communicate. This speed is measured in bits per second (BPS), but this speed is frequently misstated as baud. They aren't really the same, but you will hear them used interchangeably. You can ignore the difference.*

☞ *The most common modem speed choices are 1200, 2400, 9600, or 14400 BPS. Don't buy anything less than 2400 baud, because 1200 is painfully slow. If you intend to use the modem very much, spend the extra money for 9600 or 14400 BPS. The prices on modems are dropping hourly as new and faster ones are introduced.*

☞ *You can't use a modem without special software to control it. Many modems come with their own communications software, but you will probably want better (read "more expensive") software if you use the modem very much. If you intend to use the modem to connect to a commercial service, such as CompuServe or Prodigy, see if they have specialized software that makes that connection easier. Most do. Otherwise, you can start out with what came with the modem until you know more about what you want and need.*

☞ *You can buy a combination fax modem for no more than the cost of the modem alone. (See "Just the Fax, Ma'am" below.)*

☞ *For the ultimate in portability, you can buy a very cool pocket modem (some have fax capability). These little guys are no bigger than a deck of cards and are fun to show off to your friends.*

Just the Fax, Ma'am

Ten years ago, fax machines were very specialized equipment used by very few people. Now it seems like everyone has one. They are even becoming a common addition to the personal computer, in the form of a specialized kind of modem called a fax modem. Like regular modems, they come in both internal and external versions, and can handle both fax chores and regular modem communications.

If you need a fax machine, especially for *sending* faxes, then you should seriously consider a fax modem. The advantage is that you can send the document directly from your word processor or spreadsheet program, without having to print it. The disadvantage is that you can only send stuff you created on the computer unless you also have a scanner.

Evaluate your needs carefully before deciding that a fax modem is a reasonable substitute for a fax machine. If you do get a fax modem, get one that operates at 14400 BPS so it can do both jobs efficiently.

Chapter 6

MEMORY
(What You Need and What You Don't)

Kofsky's Law: You can never be too rich, too thin, or have too much memory.

COMPUTER MEMORY CAN be a very confusing subject, because there's more than one kind of memory and there are at least three different names for every kind. Even the most hardened technodweebs can find their brains softening sometimes.

Let's start at the top and you can lie down and put a compress on your forehead anytime you feel faint.

Memory is where things happen in your computer. The processor does the work, but it can only hold so much information inside itself (not much).

The hard disk stores your programs and files, but it doesn't *do* anything. When you start up a program, the program and any files you need to work with are retrieved from the hard disk and loaded into memory. Once this stuff is in memory, the processor can do things with it.

Memory is also volatile (though not flammable). Whatever you have in memory vanishes the instant power is turned off to your computer. This isn't a problem if you've saved your work to the hard disk, but if you haven't, you've lost it. This is why all the books and all the computer yentas make such a fuss about saving your work in the programs you use. One blip in the power supply (or the baby pulls the plug out of the wall) and all the work you've done since your last save is gone with the wind.

How Much Memory Is Enough?

See Kofsky's Law above.

How much memory you need depends on what you need to do. Most programs will run better with lots of memory, and many programs require a substantial amount. The trend these days is toward programs that are bigger and bigger memory-hogs. This is because memory has gotten cheaper and cheaper in recent years. Get as much as you can afford, because the trend is not going to reverse any time soon.

When you buy software, the box will have on it somewhere the shameless amount of memory needed to run the program. Usually it will be stated in terms of the amount of conventional memory, extended memory, and hard disk space the thing requires.

☞ *If a program says it requires 2 megabytes (2MB) of memory but 4 megabytes are "recommended," this means that it will sort-of run at 2 but needs 4 to be functional. (And it will be truly happy with 8.)*

> ☞ *Confusingly enough, sometimes the box will say that the program needs 512K to run or 475K to run. This kind of number (in K's instead of MB's) always refers to the amount of conventional, or DOS, memory the program needs to even get started.*

> ☞ *See the sections below on conventional, expanded, and extended memory for information on those terms.*

What We Talk about When We Talk about RAM

The first way RAM is talked about is in terms of RAM that you put into your computer on a chip. The RAM in your computer is on a physical device that may be called

- ☞ *DIP (Dual Inline Package):* A single RAM chip. DIPs are either plugged into the main board of the computer or are mounted on SIMMs or SIPPs.

- ☞ *SIMM (Single Inline Memory Module):* A small circuit board with up to nine DIPs on it. Plugs into a slot on the mother board.

- ☞ *SIPP (Single Inline Pin Package):* Similar to a SIMM but not interchangeable (naturally).

- ☞ *DRAM (Dynamic Random Access Memory):* The kind of memory contained on a DIP. Dynamic just means that when you pull the plug, the memory's gone.

- ☞ *SRAM (Static Random Access Memory):* Another kind of memory found on a DIP, though more rarely. Static RAM is faster and lots more expensive than DRAM.

This RAM, in whatever physical form it takes, functions in your computer as conventional memory, extended memory, expanded memory, and a couple of other designations that you needn't trouble yourself with. See Chapter 5, "E-Z Hardware," for more on the innards of your computer.

How Memory Is Measured

Memory is measured in bytes. A thousand bytes is a kilobyte (abbreviated K or KB), a million bytes is a megabyte (abbreviated M, MB, or meg), and a billion bytes is called a gigabyte (abbreviated G, GB, or gig). Other kinds of storage, such as hard disks and floppy disks, also use these terms.

The numbers used to describe RAM are somewhat approximate since computers count in multiples of two instead of multiples of ten. A nibble is 2^2, or 4, bits; a byte is 2^3, or 8, bits; and a word is 2^4, or 16, bits. Thus one kilobyte, which common sense would tell you is 1000 bytes, is actually 1024 bytes; and one megabyte (common-sense figure: one million bytes) is actually 1024 kilobytes, or 1,048,576 bytes; and 1 gigabyte (no such thing as a common-sense figure) is 1024 megabytes, or 1,048,576 kilobytes, or 1,073,741,824 bytes. And one terabyte is 1024 gigabytes, or a number too big to even contemplate without getting a headache.

Hall's Rule of Explanations: Any simple idea will be worded in the most complicated way.

Conventional Memory

Conventional memory is the first 640K of RAM in your computer. This is sometimes called DOS memory because DOS can run programs only in this part of memory. This is a limitation of DOS, because your microprocessor could use any memory and in considerably larger qualities.

To get the most out of conventional memory:

☞ *Upgrade to DOS 6. This will allow you to reduce the amount of this memory that DOS uses for itself.*

☞ *If you have a 386SX or better processor (See Chapter 5, "E-Z Hardware," for details), use DOS 6's MEMMAKER program.*

☞ *If you are still getting "out of memory" messages when loading DOS programs, consider getting a copy of QEMM and using its memory-optimizing program. (See Chapter 20, "Murphy's Eleven Favorite Pain-Relieving Programs.")*

Background Information of Dubious Value

When the original version of DOS was written in 1982, the typical personal computer had only 16 to 64 kilobytes of memory. So when the designers of DOS placed a limit of 640 kilobytes into DOS, they thought they had left *plenty* of room.

As a miscalculation this ranks right up there with the Edsel and New Coke.

Programmers have come up with some very ingenious tricks to get the most out of that 640K, but it is still the most important and precious memory on your computer.

Getting More Conventional Memory Using DOS 6

DOS 6 comes with a very cool program called MEMMAKER.

If you have a computer with a 80386 or 80486 processor and extended memory, you can use MEMMAKER to free up some conventional memory by loading device drivers and memory-resident programs into high DOS memory.

To run MEMMAKER, go to the DOS prompt and type in

```
MEMMAKER
```

Follow the prompts. Choose Express Setup. Answer No to any questions you don't know the answer to. If you need help at any point, press the F1 key for help.

After you answer the questions, MEMMAKER tells you to press Enter to restart your computer. Cooperate and press Enter. Then after some period of mysterious activity you'll be asked to press Enter again. Go ahead.

When the computer has restarted (again), MEMMAKER displays a screen asking if your system appears to be working properly. If you haven't seen any error messages and everything seems to be OK, press Enter. If something too strange for words has happened, press the Spacebar to select No and then Exit.

After you press Enter, MEMMAKER displays a memory before-and-after screen. You should at least act impressed.

Press Enter again to quit MEMMAKER.

☞ MEMMAKER will change your AUTOEXEC.BAT and CONFIG.SYS by adding new stuff or editing existing commands.

☞ Quit any programs that are running before starting MEMMAKER. Don't try to run it from inside Windows or while you're in the DOS Shell.

How Do I Tell How Much Memory I Have?

Type **MEM** at the DOS prompt. You'll see a summary of your computer's memory that will look like Figure 6.1 if you have DOS 6 or Figure 6.2 if you have DOS 4 or DOS 5. Even though the looks are a good bit different, the words you are looking for regardless of version are "largest executable program size." This is the amount of DOS memory you have available.

FIGURE 6.1:

What you get with MEM if you have DOS 6

```
C:\>MEM

Memory Type          Total =   Used  +   Free
--------------       ------    ------    ------
Conventional          640K      204K      436K
Upper                 131K       65K       66K
Adapter RAM/ROM       253K      253K        0K
Extended (XMS)       3072K     1396K     1676K
--------------       ------    ------    ------
Total memory         4096K     1918K     2178K

Total under 1 MB      771K      269K      502K

Largest executable program size     436K   (446128 bytes)
Largest free upper memory block      66K   (67216 bytes)
MS-DOS is resident in the high memory area.

C:\>
```

FIGURE 6.2:
What you get with
MEM if you have DOS 5

```
C:\>MEM

    655360 bytes total conventional memory
    655360 bytes available to MS-DOS
    492096 largest executable program size

   7684096 bytes total EMS memory
   6766592 bytes free EMS memory

   7340032 bytes total contiguous extended memory
         0 bytes available contiguous extended memory
   6766592 bytes available XMS memory
           MS-DOS resident in High Memory Area

C:\>
```

With earlier versions of DOS, use the CHKDSK command. A whole lot of numbers will appear (most having to do with your hard disk), but at the bottom of the list will be numbers that show the amount of conventional memory on your machine and how much is available.

Expanded Memory

When software designers started figuring out that 640K of memory might not be enough, a group of them got together and came up with a standard way to get around this limit called *EMS* (Expanded Memory Specification). This created a special kind of "paged" memory and is really smoke and mirrors, since this memory doesn't actually have an address. It is a lot like an old party phone line, where several houses share the same phone number, except here it is memory sharing the same address.

This kind of memory can be used by most DOS programs and PCs of all levels. On an 8088 or an 80286, you'll need to install a special memory board and driver to get this memory. If you already have an expanded memory board, great. If you have an older computer and are thinking getting such a board, save your money. You'll be better off getting a new computer, since most of the new programs will not run acceptably on your older machine, anyway.

☞ *If you insist on buying an expanded memory board, make sure it meets the LIM 4.0 (Lotus-Intel-Microsoft) standard.*

☞ *You will need to put an expanded memory manager driver in your CONFIG.SYS file to make the board work. The driver will be supplied on a disk that comes with the memory board. See "Using DOS EDIT to Change Your Files" in Chapter 11 for help on adding to your CONFIG.SYS file.*

☞ *If you have a 386 system or better, your computer's extended memory can be converted into expanded memory so that DOS programs can use it. To do this you can use either a third-party memory manager like QEMM (see Chapter 20, "Murphy's Eleven Favorite Pain-Relieving Programs"), or you can use two programs that come with DOS: HIMEM.SYS and EMM386.EXE. Both these guys need to be in your CONFIG.SYS file, so see "Using DOS EDIT to Change Your Files" in Chapter 11 for instructions.*

Useful Memory Terms You Can Probably Ignore

☞ *High DOS memory:* The area between the end of DOS memory (conventional memory) and the start of extended memory. This is the area from 640K to 1MB. MEMMAKER (DOS 6) and other merry memory optimizers play neat tricks in here. The original DOS designers reserved this area of memory for device drivers of various types, so DOS can't normally touch it without the use of MEMMAKER or some other program.

☞ *UMB (Upper Memory Blocks):* Chunks of high DOS memory.

☞ *HMA (High Memory Area):* The area that DOS versions greater than 5 can load themselves into. This is the first 64K of memory after 1MB.

☞ *Address:* The location of a given bit of memory. The numbers are expressed in the numbering system called hexadecimal, which is just as bad as it sounds.

☞ *Page frame:* The area used by expanded memory to do its smoke and mirrors thing.

Extended Memory

Extended memory is memory whose address is higher than DOS memory or even high DOS memory. It is not available on older 8088 or XT computers, and most older programs and some newer programs cannot use this memory.

However, Windows loves this type of memory. Many other popular programs are starting to take advantage of it directly (Paradox, Lotus 1-2-3 Release 3.0) and more are sure to follow.

If you have an 80386SX or higher processor (See Chapter 5, "E-Z Hardware"), then even older programs can use this memory by converting it to expanded memory. You will need HIMEM.SYS and EMM386.EXE from DOS or a memory-managing program such as QEMM.

Memory Show and Tell

Figure 6.3 shows a representation of what the relationship is among all these different types of memory. The memory does not *look* like this

FIGURE 6.3:
What memory would look like if it looked like something

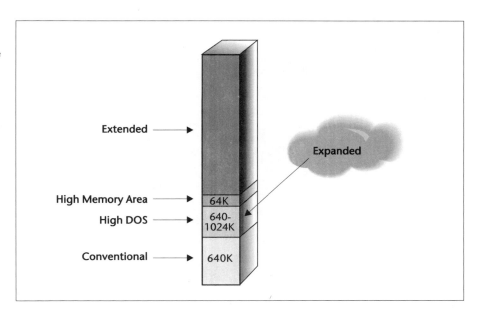

inside your computer, but the addresses of memory locations are laid out like this more or less in order.

Adding Memory

You actually *can* install memory yourself, but it means opening up the computer box and deciding where to snap those little SIMMs in. It also means figuring out how much you have and in what increments it's installed in order to figure out how to get where you want to be.

Just take your little baby to the shop and tell the techie there how much memory you think you'll need. Many stores where you buy memory will install it for you for no extra cost. (Which means they don't give you a discount if you install it yourself, so *let* them do it.)

Chapter 7

THE KEYBOARD, MOUSE, TRACKBALL, ET AL.

Cathy's Postulate: If you hit two keys on the keyboard, the one you don't want will appear on the screen.

IN SCIENCE-FICTION movies people just speak to the computer and it does their bidding. And in *this* world there are articles every year claiming that voice-recognition computers are right around the corner. Maybe. But right now we have to use a keyboard and/or a mouse to boss the computer around.

Why a Good Keyboard Is Important

You can safely order just about any part of a computer by mail without a tryout. But a keyboard is something you have to get personal with before you buy it. One person's delightfully responsive keyboard is another's mushy mess. If you don't like the keyboard on your computer, you will not "get used to it," so get one you like!

Some keyboards make a nice crisp click every time you press a key. However, *you* may hear this click as clattery and chintzy-sounding. If you are a touch typist, the placement of certain keys may drive you crazy, so be sure to try out a keyboard before you buy it.

Keyboard Layout

The computer keyboard has all the normal keys you associate with a typewriter, plus 50 or so more. Figure 7.1 shows a typical, "enhanced" keyboard layout (sometimes called the "101" because it has 101 keys). Figure 7.2 is the older, AT-style keyboard with 84 keys.

Regardless of the type or manufacturer, all keyboards will have four main parts.

FIGURE 7.1:
A typical enhanced keyboard has 101 keys. You can also get one with the function keys on the side instead of at the top.

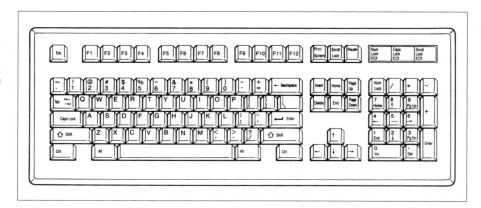

FIGURE 7.2:
A typical PC keyboard,
also called the AT-type

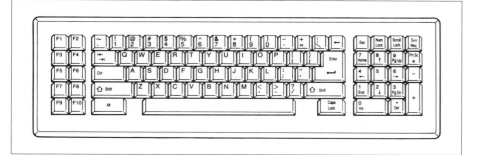

Keyboard & Mouse

Typewriter keys

The typewriter keys are the keys in the middle of the keyboard. The keys are arranged just like those on a typewriter (remember those?), and perform pretty much the same functions. Along the outside edge of these keys are the modifier keys. They are sometimes a darker gray and include Ctrl (Control), Alt (Alternate), CapsLock, and Shift. Each of these keys modifies how the other keys on the keyboard behave.

☞ *The Tab key will move the cursor to the next tab stop. This will be the equivalent of five or eight spaces or whatever the program is set for. From the computer's point of view, this is a single character. When you backspace over a Tab, it disappears in one bite, not one space at a time.*

A Useless Aside You Can Safely Ignore

The layout of the typewriter section of the keyboard is referred to as a QWERTY layout. This comes from the first six characters of the first row of keys below the number keys. This layout was designed in the early days of the mechanical typewriter to overcome the problems of adjacent keys jamming together, but it is really quite inefficient for touch typists.

An alternative layout that was supposed to provide faster touch typing, called the DVORAK layout, was developed, but this has never really caught on. One can, if one wants to be viewed as seriously peculiar, buy a keyboard that can be converted to this DVORAK layout.

Function keys

PC keyboards have 10 or 12 function keys. These keys, which are labeled F1, F2, and so forth, are arranged across the top of the keyboard or in a double row on the left side. Many programs attach special actions to each of these keys (though F11 and F12 are not called upon often). If you are a touch typist, get a keyboard with the function keys on the left.

Cursor control keys

The cursor control keys include the ←, →, ↑, ↓, Home, End, PgUp, and PgDn keys, as well as the Insert and Delete keys. These keys either form a special block of keys to the right of the typewriter keys, or are combined with the numeric keypad on older keyboards.

These keys move the cursor around the screen without changing anything on the screen. The arrow keys work pretty much as you'd suspect. Depending on the program, the Home key will move the cursor to the beginning of the document, the beginning of the page, or the beginning of a line. The End key will move to the end of the document, the end of the page, or the end of a line.

The numeric keypad

One of the enhanced keyboard's major improvements is a separate numeric keypad that doesn't share keys with the cursor control keys. This keypad will help you to enter numbers while moving from cell to cell in your favorite spreadsheet program. Of course, if you use this block of keys primarily to move the cursor around, you may find the change more of a nuisance than an enhancement.

☞ *A computer really and truly cares about the difference between a 0 (zero) and a capital letter O. It can also get very huffy if you use a lowercase l (L) in place of the number one (1). If you mix them up you may get a rude error message (if you're lucky), or worse, something won't work and you won't know why.*

What Do Those Weird Keys Do?

Those strange keys on the keyboard are there because a computer can do so many more things than a typewriter. So, it needs keys to do them with.

The toggle keys

The toggle keys are the CapsLock key, the NumLock key, and the Scroll Lock key. They change the state of certain other keys on the keyboard, and are either ON or OFF.

The CapsLock key affects the characters of the alphabet, converting *a* to *A*, *b* to *B*, and so forth, but it has no effect on any other keys. The Shift key, on the other hand, affects all the keys on your keyboard. If you use the Shift key while the CapsLock key is on, you get lowercase letters.

The NumLock key converts the block of keys on the far right of the keyboard from cursor control keys to a numeric keypad and back. On enhanced keyboards, this is usually toggled to numeric keys by default, whereas the older, AT keyboards had this toggled to cursor control keys by default. In either case, however, tapping the NumLock key switches this, and holding down the Shift key changes it for as long as you hold it down.

The Scroll Lock key toggles how some programs scroll the screen. Other programs completely ignore this key. But if you are working in a spreadsheet, for example, and suddenly your whole screen starts jumping around instead of just the cursor moving, try tapping the Scroll Lock key. That should fix it.

The Ctrl, Alt, and Shift keys

These are the modifier keys that affect every other key on the keyboard. They are frequently combined with other keys, and with each other, to perform special functions within programs.

These keys are never used by themselves. They are used to alter the meaning of a second key. For example, in WordPerfect you press the F7 function key to exit the program, but if you hold down the Alt key

Keyboard & Mouse

while pressing F7, you can create a table. Holding down the Shift key while pressing F7 gets you to the Print menu. Some programs also have three-way combos. For example, you can print an Excel spreadsheet by pressing Ctrl-Shift-F12. This means you hold down all three keys at once.

The slash and backslash keys

These keys look alike, just tilted in opposite directions so it's easy to confuse them. The slash (/) key is combined with the ? key, and is always on the bottom right of the typewriter part of the keyboard. In DOS, the / key is used to add modifiers to a command, as in

```
DIR /P
```

The *P* in this command stands for "pause" and tells DOS to stop the display when it has filled the screen instead of letting it just scroll past.

The backslash (\) key, on the other hand, is liable to be in any of several different places, depending on the keyboard you have. It is usually somewhere along the right edge of the typewriter keys. The \ key is used to designate the root directory or to separate directories in a path. (See Chapter 13 for more on directories and paths.)

Ctrl-S, Ctrl-C, Pause, and Break

The combination of the Ctrl key plus the S key (Ctrl-S or ^S) is used in DOS to stop the scrolling of the screen. If text is scrolling up your screen faster than you can read, press Ctrl-S to stop the scroll. You can also press the Pause key on most keyboards to have the same effect. When you have caught up with reading what's on the screen and are ready to read some more, press any key and the scrolling will continue. (See "The Any Key" below for information on this essential key.)

The Ctrl-C combination (hold down the Ctrl key and press the C key) is the universal cancel key when you are working with DOS. This will almost always cancel your last command, hopefully before it is too late. If you want to be a bit more forceful about it, the Ctrl-Break combination will sometimes work when Ctrl-C won't.

And Now, Let Us Return to the Enter Key

Perhaps the single most important key on your keyboard is the Enter key. Until you press this key, DOS pretty much ignores what you type at the command line. But what happens when you have a keyboard that doesn't have a key on it with a label "Enter?" Glad you asked. The Enter key on some keyboards is called the Return key, and on other keyboards it simply has a ↵ symbol printed on it. All are the same, but sometimes manufacturers just like to make things difficult.

Too Boring to Read

The Enter or Return key is actually two keys in one. When you press the Enter key, you are sending a line feed to move the display up one line and a carriage return to move the cursor back to the beginning of the line.

The Any Key

Probably the most common thing DOS or any other program says to the user besides "Bad command or file name" is "Press any key to continue…" But no matter how hard you look, you won't find a key on your keyboard labeled "Any."

Which key should you press? Well, in theory, it doesn't matter, since the program or DOS is implicitly promising you that all keys are the same. OK, next time you get this message try the Shift key. Didn't work, did it? Actually there are several keys that won't work. These are the Shift, Ctrl, Alt, PrintScreen, Scroll Lock, Pause, CapsLock, and NumLock keys.

Are all the rest the same? The answer is that they *should* be, but I stick to a key that I know won't have any unexpected effect, even if I accidentally press it several times, or the program screws up and doesn't disregard it. My favorite is the Spacebar because it doesn't do anything irreversible in any program.

I have heard that some smart keyboard manufacturer is going to come out with a keyboard that includes an Any key. Sounds good to me.

Keyboard & Mouse

But it had better be a special heavy-duty key, since it will sure get a lot of use.

Rosen's Axiom: The probability of anything going wrong is in inverse proportion to its desirability.

Windows Keys Are for DOS, Too

These days, with Microsoft Windows becoming so common, even programs that run in DOS and don't require Windows at all are starting to adopt Windows keystrokes. Here are some of the more widely used in case you find yourself in an unfamiliar program that is trying to be Windows-like.

Alt this and Alt that

Look at the top of the screen in whatever program you are running. If there is a line that has File Edit and so on all the way over to Help, then you are already most of the way there. Just hold down the Alt key and press the underlined letter, and you will most likely get a *drop-down menu* that will offer you additional choices. Under File you will get a choice of things to do with files. This will usually include such things as Open, Close, Save, Save As, Print, and that all important one—Exit. A common shortcut for Exit, by the way, is Alt-F4.

☞ *Save As is the choice you want if you want to save your work under a new name. This lets you keep multiple versions of a document just in case something horrible happens to the one you are working on.*

☞ *Why is Exit hidden under File? Good question. This is obviously the most important command in the program, and ought to be right out in the open. But that's where it usually is.*

☞ *You can also use your mouse to open a menu in most programs. Instead of pressing Alt-F to open the File menu, click on the word* File *with the left mouse button.*

Windows editing commands

The most common editing commands are Cut, Copy, and Paste. Cut means to remove a portion of the document and save it on a "Clipboard" so you can later paste it back into the document. Copy means to make a copy of the portion of the document and save it on the Clipboard, and Paste means to insert whatever is on the Clipboard into the document in the current location. The Windows keys for this are

☞ *Cut:* Shift-Delete or Ctrl-X

☞ *Copy:* Ctrl-Insert or Ctrl-C

☞ *Paste:* Shift-Insert or Ctrl-V

Of Mice and Trackballs

The computer mouse, an oddity in the PC world only a few years ago, has become ubiquitous (that means they're all over the place). The main culprit is Windows, which really requires a mouse. But now all sorts of DOS programs (including the DOS Shell) are really a pain without a mouse, and only computer-Luddites are grumbling along rodentless.

The only practical alternative to using a mouse is to use a trackball instead. A trackball is kind of like an upside-down mouse, with the ball on the top instead of the bottom. A trackball does have one decided advantage over a mouse—it takes up less real estate on your desk. And with the pile of stuff that always seems to accumulate on desks, this is a big plus. For all intents and purposes, though, a trackball is absolutely interchangeable with a mouse, so if you have a trackball the actions and terms for it are exactly the same as for a mouse.

☞ *Comfort levels for mice and trackballs are just as subjective as they are for keyboards. Try before you buy!*

☞ *If you are working with a CAD (Computer Aided Drafting) program or a drawing program, don't get a trackball. Even the best don't have the fineness of control that a good mouse has—critical for artsy endeavors.*

☞ *Also for CAD, get a mouse with three buttons, not two. Most CAD programs let you program that third button to do something very useful.*

Mouse Terminology

When you have a mouse, there's a certain amount of mouse lingo you need to understand.

☞ *Button:* This is one of the two or three buttons on top of the mouse.

☞ *Left button, right button, center button:* Wait, I only have two buttons! (No sweat, just press both the left and right together. You just created a middle button!)

☞ *Click:* This is the cute little sound made when you press one of the above buttons. Usually you'll be instructed to do something like "Click on OK." This means find the thing on the screen that says OK, move the mouse around until the pointer on the screen is on the thing that says OK, and then press the left mouse button.

☞ *Double-click:* Two quick clicks in a row.

☞ *Select, highlight:* To select something on the screen, you position the mouse pointer on top of it and click on it. The thing will then be highlighted. To unselect it, just move the pointer somewhere else and click again.

☞ *Drag:* Some things can be dragged around the screen by the simple expedient of clicking on them, holding the mouse button down, and moving the mouse to some other spot.

☞ *Drop:* After you drag something, release the mouse button and you drop whatever it was you were dragging.

Not everything on the screen can be selected or highlighted or dragged and dropped. It depends on the program and what it will let you do. Play around and see what happens.

Most programs that use a mouse have some special functions for the right button and sometimes even the middle button. It's up to the individual application what those functions might be.

My Mouse Went Berserk!

Even though mice have been around for years, they are still the source of problems for many programmers, including those who write for the mouse companies. As video standards have been stretched, pushed, and prodded to higher and higher resolutions, the mouse hasn't always been able to keep up. One problem is what are called "mouse droppings." These are little flecks of color that form a trail behind where you have moved the mouse cursor. Sometimes this is the fault of the program you are in, other times it is a weird interaction between the mouse software (called a driver) and some other completely unrelated program you are also running.

If the problem is frequent and annoying, you probably need a new mouse driver. See "Drivers and How to Get Them" in Chapter 16.

Another weird mouse happening is the disappearing cursor. This is most common in programs that switch from displaying text to displaying graphics and back. If you have had your mouse for years, but just got a new copy of Quattro Pro, for example, you might see this. You need an update to your mouse software. In fact, if you buy any new program, and your mouse doesn't work in it, chances are that you need an update to your mouse software. See Chapter 16 for help with getting mouse drivers (no, not little, tiny rodent chauffeurs).

The Care and Feeding of Your Mouse

These things just take Mouse Chow, right? Not quite. The number one cause of jerky mouse movement isn't an outdated mouse driver, but a dirty mouse ball. If you use a mouse pad, this will help, since a nice, shiny desktop is about the worst possible surface for a mouse. But mostly you need to clean the little things periodically. Just take a damp cloth with a little bit of window cleaner on it and wipe the outside, then lay the cloth down and run the mouse around on it for ten seconds or so. Now do the same thing using a clean, dry cloth. Seems to do the trick. But I will probably get swamped with mail from mouse manufacturers telling me all that is wrong with this. So read their instructions, and do what they suggest.

Chapter 8

THE SCREEN, MONITOR, OR WHATEVER YOU WANT TO CALL IT

Benjamin's Law: Any sufficiently advanced technology will be indistinguishable from magic.

THE PART OF your computer that looks like a TV goes by a lot of different names: VDT (video display terminal), screen, display, CRT (cathode ray tube), and monitor. We'll stick with "monitor" in this chapter because it's the most common term. VDT and CRT are really kind of old-timey terms, and "screen" or "display" refer more to what's on the monitor than to the monitor itself.

The keyboard is *your* main communications line with the computer, but the monitor is how the computer communicates with *you*. That's why it's important that the monitor be fast in conveying the news to you and that it look good while doing so (sort of like a TV anchor).

Video 101

Your PC's video system is made up of the monitor and the video display adapter. The monitor is just the box that looks like a TV without the knobs. There'll be an on/off switch of some kind and controls for brightness and contrast that you can fiddle with to make the screen look the way you want. There will probably be other controls either on the back or hidden behind a little door. Leave them alone.

The monitor by itself is not much more than a hollow shell with very few brains of its own (see "TV anchor," above). The other half of the video system is the video display adapter, which is inside your computer box. Usually this is an actual card inside the computer box that can be removed and changed. In lots of new computers the video display adapter is built into the main board of the computer. The video adapter is the brains of the outfit. It processes the information from your computer and then tells the monitor what to display and how.

The important thing to remember is that the monitor and the display adapter are a matched system. You can't just go out and buy a new monitor when you decide you want to upgrade. You probably also need to get a new video adapter as well. But, confusingly enough, you can often get a new video adapter and use it without changing monitors.

Your Monitor as TV

For reasons that escape me, people (read "technoids") have flailed around for years trying to turn their monitors into TVs. Recently, the technology has gotten to be pretty easy, if not cheap. For about $400 you can buy a card, plug it into your motherboard, plug a TV cable connection into the card and (presto!) you have TV on your monitor.

This means that for only slightly more than the cost of a vacation in Mexico, you can add what you've been missing on your computer—commercials!

☞ *The whole system, monitor and adapter, are referred to by the name of the graphics adapter: MDA, VGA, SVGA, and so forth. See "Video Standards—A Life in Letters" below for translations of these and other video acronyms.*

☞ *The video adapter may also be called a video card, video system, or video hardware.*

Color and Why You Don't Want to Live without It

Back in the olden days there were two different video systems, the monochrome display adapter (MDA) and the color graphics adapter (CGA). In those days you had to make a real choice between color with poor quality text, or monochrome and no graphics.

Now you not only *can* have both—you *should* have both. Get a color system. Would you go out and buy a black-and-white TV? Well, you shouldn't buy a monochrome monitor, either. The difference in cost is not all that much when you're already talking bucks, and the satisfaction and enjoyment are well worth it. Besides, your favorite game may not even run on monochrome! (Let's keep our priorities straight here.)

Modes, We Don't Need No Freaking Modes

When talking about video, it is important to understand the differences between text mode and graphics mode. In text mode, the picture on the screen, whatever it looks like, is made up only of text characters. The characters are stored in memory, so changes to the screen happen instantaneously.

In graphics mode, on the other hand, each individual dot on the screen, and the colors that make up those dots, must be drawn and controlled, allowing a far wider range of what can be displayed on the screen, but also slowing down the process. Graphics standards for PCs have become much more demanding since the early days. The end result is the ability to show pictures of virtually photographic quality on some monitors.

Screen & Monitor

Text a la Mode

The normal text-mode screen has 25 lines of text, and each line is 80 characters wide. This is equivalent to about half a page of text. If you have a color display, you can change to a 40-column display by typing

```
MODE 40
```

at the DOS prompt. Don't like the look? Return to the standard 80-column display by typing in

```
MODE 80
```

and pressing Enter.

If you have DOS 5 or DOS 6 and at least a VGA display, you can have more than 25 lines on the page using a smaller size character. To switch to 50-line mode, just type

```
MODE CON LINES=50
```

To change back to the more normal 25-line mode, the command is

```
MODE CON LINES=25
```

The *CON* in these commands refers to the *console*, which is the combination of the keyboard and video system.

☞ *For this to work, you must have a line in your CONFIG.SYS that reads*

```
DEVICE=C:\DOS\ANSI.SYS
```

See "Getting Control of Your Screen with ANSI.SYS" in Chapter 11 for information on how to edit your CONFIG.SYS file.

☞ *If you want to play with the display to achieve all sorts of effects, there are some neat products that can put as many as 132 characters in each line. See Chapter 20, "Murphy's Eleven Favorite Pain-Relieving Programs," for information.*

Video Standards—A Life in Letters

The number of acronyms to describe the various video standards is amazing and seems to be growing hourly. Here is a list of the ones that matter.

☞ *MDA:* Monochrome Display Adapter. The original, text-only standard for PCs.

☞ *CGA:* Color Graphics Adapter. The original (and very limited) color and graphics standard for PCs.

☞ *HGA:* Hercules Graphics Adapter. Provided both text and graphics on monochrome monitors.

☞ *EGA:* Enhanced Graphics Adapter. The first realistically usable combination of color graphics and text modes. Better than CGA but replaced quickly by VGA.

☞ *VGA:* Video Graphics Array. The current minimum standard for a video system. Provides excellent text and acceptable color graphics.

☞ *SVGA:* Super Video Graphics Array. A loose standard that applies to a range of video systems. All provide the exact same text display as VGA, but offer higher resolution displays and cool color possibilities for graphics.

☞ *XGA:* Short for eXtended Graphics Array. This is a standard from IBM that ups the ante in terms of resolution and colors, but it's very expensive and may never catch on.

☞ *8514/A:* Short for 8514/A. Provides the same text as VGA, but even better graphics modes.

A Technodweeb's Guide to Video Advertising

When talking about video, we run into all sorts of language never heard in polite society. Many of the terms below will pop up in computer ads, where they are *never* explained. This is, of course, very annoying, but here's a quick guide that will tell you everything you need to know short of turning into a dweeb yourself.

☞ *Pixel:* The smallest unit of a graphics display. This is a single dot out of thousands or even millions.

☞ *Dot pitch:* The minimum size of each individual pixel on the screen. The smaller the number, the finer grained picture you can get. Don't buy a monitor with a dot pitch larger than .32, because the display will be coarse, vulgar, and tend to spit on the floor.

☞ *Interlaced:* This means that only half the display is updated at a time. Avoid using interlaced displays. They tend to have a barely visible flicker that will eventually drive you insane or to the convenience store for beer, whichever comes first. What you definitely want is non-interlaced.

☞ *Scan Rate/Refresh Rate:* Refers to how often the display is updated. Look for a refresh rate no lower than 72 Hz. That means the screen is rewritten 72 times a second. This should be fast enough for anyone. Higher numbers are even better but not worth what you'll have to pay to get them.

☞ *VESA* (pronounced *VAY-sa*): This is the Video Equipment Standards Association, the folks who set minimum standards for video equipment. Monitors or adapters that don't meet VESA standards may be cheaper but won't be good enough for an illustrious person such as yourself.

A Confession about Pixels

This isn't the only place you'll see pixel defined as a dot, but I cannot tell a lie: a dot it's not. A pixel is equal to a dot only at the highest resolution the monitor is capable of. At lower resolutions, a pixel can be made up of many dots. Does this matter to you? In a word, no.

The Making of a Resolution

Displays are described by their resolution—that's the number of pixels on the screen and the number of colors at the same time. Here are the standard resolutions you'll see:

☞ 640×480: A standard VGA graphics display, this means that the display is 640 pixels wide by 480 pixels high.

☞ 800×600:   A typical SVGA graphics display.

☞ 1024×768: The upper limit of SVGA, and the beginning of 8514/A and XGA graphics displays. A resolution like this has more than twice as many pixels as a standard VGA display. This also means that each pixel is a lot smaller. If you have a monitor smaller than 15 inches, you'll be squinting at this point.

☞ 1280×1024: A resolution like this needs a great big monitor. Otherwise, you can't read a thing unless your nose is pressed up against the screen.

Each of the above numbers could have a third number added. This number gives the maximum number of colors possible on the screen at the same time. The usual choices are

☞ 16 colors, the minimum for business graphics

☞ 256 colors, the minimum for realistic-looking pictures

☞ 32,768 colors, which provides very realistic pictures

☞ 16.7 million colors, sometimes referred to as true color

The trade-off is that as resolution numbers go up, the color numbers have to go down. This is because both high resolution and realistic color require memory, so when you shovel more pixels in, you can have fewer colors. Also, as the resolution increases, the size of the screen necessary generally increases as well, which translates into big differences in cost.

☞ *Buy Super VGA even though it costs more up front.*

☞ *If you plan to use graphics-intense software (drawing programs, desktop publishing), get yourself a video adapter with an accelerator chip and at least one megabyte of video memory.*

Screen & Monitor

Chapter 9

FLOPPY DISKS
(Why Floppy? Why Not Mopsy or Cottontail?)

Ward's Rule of Buying: No matter how long you shop for an item, after you've bought it, it will be on sale cheaper.

FLOPPY DISKS ARE made of thin sheets of plastic and are called floppy to set them apart from *hard disks*, which are inside your computer. Floppies are also called diskettes, flexible disks, and sometimes just disks. They come in two physical sizes:

☞ The 5¼-inch size is (surprise!) 5¼ inches in diameter and looks like an old 45-rpm record inside a paper or plastic sleeve.

☞ The 3½-inch size is 3½ inches in diameter and it's inside a rigid, more or less square plastic case.

Truly Interesting Facts You Never Need to Know

☞ Early personal computers used eight-inch floppy disks that could contain only about ¹/₁₀ as much data as current high-density floppies. Since they were made much like the current 5¼-inch floppy, they could bend easily, hence the name "floppy."

☞ Both floppy and hard disks are made of a substrate—mylar in the case of floppies and aluminum or glass for hard disks—onto which a magnetic oxide has been deposited. The information is stored on this magnetic oxide layer in much the same way that music is recorded on a cassette tape.

What Are Floppies, Anyway?

Floppies are a way to transport information. Your computer contains lots of files and programs, but the only way to get these programs to you or from you is by means of floppies (no fair bringing up networks).

Floppies are not software

When you buy software, it is on floppy disks. You bring the floppies home and put them in your computer. The software is copied from the floppies to the hard disk. Floppies are the medium, software is the message.

What Size Floppies to Buy

Buy the largest capacity your drives will support. There's no way to tell what capacity floppies your computer will accept just by looking. Ask someone. Take a deep breath and look at the papers that came with your computer.

If you bought your computer any time in the past three or four years you probably have *high-density* drives. High-density drives will accept and read low-density disks, but buy high-density floppies anyway.

If you bought your computer more than four years ago or you're working at a company that's been slow to upgrade its equipment, you may have *low-density* drives. Low-density drives will *not* read high-density disks (if you try to use one, you'll get a "General Failure error reading drive A" message), so you'll have to buy low-density (*aka* double-density) disks.

But even if you have a high-density drive, low-density floppy disks will cross your path eventually. So even if you only buy high-density floppies, you need to understand the difference.

What the sizes mean

The 5¼-inch disk comes in two capacities:

☞ *360K:* Called double-density, this size will hold up to 360,000 bytes worth of files.

☞ *1.2MB:* Called high-density, this size will hold up to 1,200,000 bytes worth of files.

The 3½-inch disk comes in two capacities:

☞ *720K:* Called double-density, this size will hold up to 720,000 bytes of info.

☞ *1.4MB:* Called high-density, this size will hold up to 1,440,000 bytes of information.

Boring Facts That You Don't Really Need to Know

The numbers used above are somewhat approximate since computers count in multiples of two instead of multiples of ten. A nibble is 2^2 or 4 bits, a byte is 2^3 or 8 bits, etc. Thus one kilobyte that ought to be 1000 bytes is actually 1024 bytes, and one megabyte (one million bytes) is actually 1024 kilobytes or 1,048,576 bytes. But for most purposes, let's just stick to the simple numbers. A kilobyte is 1000 bytes, and a megabyte is 1,000,000 bytes. Leave the rest for nerds who care.

Mysteries of Floppy Disks, Revealed

Many times floppy disks will not have manufacturer's labels to tell you what capacity they are. But there's an easy way to tell:

☞ Double-density 5¼-inch disks will have a reinforcing hub ring around the hole in the middle of the disk. High-density disks will not have this ring.

☞ Double-density 3½-inch disks will have one hole in the plastic case (to the right of the label as you hold the diskette facing you). High-density 3½-inch disks have an additional hole to the left of the label.

Mildly Interesting, Though Nonessential, Facts

Floppy disks are sometimes marked DS/DD (double-sided/double-density) or DS/HD (double-sided/high-density). Only the density side of the fraction is important. The double-sided reference is to the computer Stone Age when disks were sometimes one-sided.

If you are not careful, you may also hear references to quad density (QD) or the new extended density (ED). Ignore such references; they have nothing to do with real life.

Rules for the Floppy Disk Buyer

☞ Generic vs. Name Brand

1. Always buy generic when possible, or at least the cheapest name brand.

2. Pay for color only if you find it irresistible.

3. Don't whine if you have to throw away a couple of disks out of a hundred.

4. Ignore Rule 3 if you bought a name brand. Whine loud.

5. If you can find them on sale, buy floppies that come in plastic boxes. The boxes are cute and they really are useful.

☞ Formatted vs. Unformatted

1. It takes a minimum of two minutes (more like four or five minutes in real time) to format each and every disk you buy.

2. Formatting floppies is among the most boring chores on the planet.

3. Splurge—buy them already formatted. Even if you have a drudge working for you whose job it is to do the formatting, he/she will think you are such a kind boss, you will gain the few pennies back in increased devotion.

More Extremely Interesting Stuff You Don't Have to Know

The fact that disks are still sold unformatted is a historical relic of the old days when there was no assurance that disks were going to be used on a computer using DOS. You would buy the disks bare and then use your computer to set them up for your particular system. This still applies to the 3½-inch disks. They can be formatted for the Apple Macintosh as well as PCs, so buy formatted disks and let the Apple people buy all those unformatted floppies.

Formatting Metaphor

When building a road, the surface must be graded before the pavement can be put down. In the same way, your floppies have to be formatted before you can put information on them. Even if you buy already formatted disks, you will want to reformat them when recycling them to use again.

How to Format a Floppy

Put the disk in drive A, label side up. The A drive is usually the top slot on your computer box. If it is a wide slot with a lever, pull down the lever to latch the drive closed. If it is a narrow slot, push the disk carefully until you hear a click. Type in

```
FORMAT A:
```

Floppy Disks

and press the Enter key. A message appears on the screen telling you to insert a disk. Since you've already done that, press the Enter key. Wait impatiently. When the formatting is done, you will be asked to enter a volume label. Ignore this and press Enter again. When you're all done, you will get a message on the screen asking if you want to format another diskette. Do what you want, I can't stop you.

You will also get a cryptic message about the number of bytes on your floppy.

To format a floppy in the B drive, just put a floppy in the bottom of the two drives, type in

```
FORMAT B:
```

and press the Enter key.

Important Stuff You Really Do Need to Know

Do not format any drive other than A or B or you will be very unhappy. If you have inadvertently done this, proceed immediately to "Format C:—How to Unformat" in Chapter 16.

Weird Messages While Formatting

☞ If you start formatting and get the screen message "Sector 0 bad," grit your teeth and toss the floppy in the nearest wastebasket. It's history.

☞ If, after formatting, the report on the number of bytes on your disk includes a line saying that some bytes are in bad sectors, proceed as above: toss that disk. You and it have no future together.

☞ If you try to format a floppy in drive A and get the message "Not ready," make sure the drive door is latched (5¼-inch drives) or that the disk is all the way in the drive (3½-inch drives). Still get "Not ready?" Then you have probably guessed wrong about which drive is drive A. Press N for No and try typing in

FORMAT B:

If that doesn't work, try a different disk.

Don't try this at home (or at the office, either)

Because the high- and low-density disks *look* the same, sometimes people are tempted to try to make one size into another by reformatting a disk in a new size. If you take a low-density disk and format it as a high-density disk, it flat doesn't work. If you take a high-density disk and format it as low-density, it may *appear* to work. Don't be fooled! When you actually try to use the floppy, you will sooner or later (and usually much sooner) get one of those "sector not found" error messages, which translates loosely as "You're hosed, pal!"

Recycling Floppies

Over time, you will build up a collection of used disks with all sorts of junk on them. You should recycle these by reformatting them. It not only saves you money, but makes you feel virtuous as well. But don't give them to the drudge to do, or you will spoil all that good will you gained by buying them formatted in the first place. If you are the drudge, proceed as described above in "How to Format a Floppy."

Write-Protecting Floppies

A disk that is write-protected is made read-only. That means you can read whatever's on the disk, you can copy files from it, but you can't change or delete anything on the disk.

Write-protecting a 5¼-inch floppy

Take one of the little black sticky tabs that came with the disk and place it over the notch on the side of the floppy (see the left half of Figure 9.1). When the notch is covered, the disk is write-protected and you

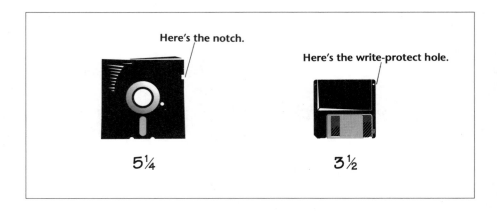

FIGURE 9.1:
Write-protecting
floppies

Here's the notch.

Here's the write-protect hole.

5¼

3½

can't alter the contents in any way. To remove the write protection, peel off the sticky tab. Be careful not to damage the disk with over enthusiastic peeling.

Write-protecting a 3½-inch floppy

Look for the hole on the right side of the label (see the right half of Figure 9.1). This little hole has a sort of window shade in the back that lets you open and close the hole. Slide the cover so the window is open and the disk is write-protected. Slide the cover back so you can't see through the hole, and you can write to the disk, delete files, reformat it, or whatever.

Do Not Fold, Spindle, or Mutilate

Because information is put on disks magnetically, magnets will also take the information off. So in addition to not using a magnet to attach your floppy to the refrigerator, don't put disks on

- ☞ Electric pencil sharpeners
- ☞ Magnetic paper-clip holders
- ☞ The monitor
- ☞ Old-style telephones that have a ring instead of a chirp
- ☞ Any device with a motor, since all motors produce a magnetic field to one degree or another

Be careful how you handle floppies. The 3½-inch size has a protective case that makes it fairly sturdy, but the 5¼-inch size is much more vulnerable. Don't fold, bend, puncture, or touch the actual recording surface. Floppies can handle a certain amount of abuse, but why take risks?

Copy That Floppy

Whenever you get new software, the first thing you should do is make copies of the disks. Then, use the copies to do the installation, so that if you encounter some incredible screwup during installation, you haven't damaged your original floppies.

You will find the above advice in *every* software manual and every book on using computers. Personally, I don't know anyone who actually makes copies before installing a program, but it is good advice if you want to beat Murphy.

Corrigan's Law: All probabilities are 50 percent. Either a thing will happen or it won't.

Holbrook's Commentary on Corrigan's Law: Odds, however, are 90 percent against you.

The other time you may want to make a copy of a floppy disk is when you want to take a file or files home with you, or when the software you just bought came on the wrong size floppy and is fussy about installing only from the A drive. You would think by now that software companies would have got that one figured out, but some of them still seem to have problem with this. So the next couple sections show you how to copy those floppies.

Floppy Disks

> ### Some Legal Notes We All Need to Understand
>
> When you buy a software program, you are legally entitled to make a *single* copy for archival purposes. You are not entitled to make 14 copies to give to everyone in the department. Nor, if you are so fortunate as to have four computers, are you legally allowed to have that same software installed on all four computers. Some software companies allow you to install the software on your computer at home as well as your computer at work, so long as only one of them can possibly be used at once.
>
> Making more than the single archival copy of the software for your own backup is known as software piracy, and it is a federal crime. Admittedly, it's a law broken about as often as the one against jaywalking, but it's still wrong.

Copying a Floppy onto Another Floppy of the Same Type

If there is no copy protection involved, and there usually isn't these days except for a few games, then the process is pretty simple. First, if the floppy is a 5¼-inch floppy, place a write-protect sticker over the notch, or if it is a 3½-inch floppy, open the write-protect window. Next, insert the floppy in the A drive and type

```
DISKCOPY A: A:
```

If you are using the B drive to copy the floppy, substitute *B* for the *A* above. Follow the prompts on the screen, being sure you remember which disk is the source (the original) and which is the destination (the copy).

If the original disk is copy-protected, you will get an error message when you go to install the program using the backup copy. Complain to the store where you got the software and to the manufacturer. Demand an uncopy-protected version of the software. If that doesn't work, and there is a reasonable alternative, demand your money back and buy the alternative. And if there isn't a reasonable alternative, buy

Mostly Boring Background Stuff You Can Ignore

In the early days of PCs, almost all major software companies used copy protection. This copy protection made it difficult to make a copy of the software unless you had a special program to get around the protection, such as COPYIIPC. In fact, this is how Central Point Software got its start. As the copy protection got more sophisticated, so did the software to get around it. Finally, enough users complained loud enough that the major software companies, led by Borland, decided that it wasn't worth the expense to continue this war, and more and more software became available unprotected. Now, only very expensive, specialized software and games are protected. But in order to keep it that way, we all have to do our part. Read "Some Legal Notes" above.

a copy of Central Point Software's COPYIIPC program and make your archival copy with it. And meanwhile, complain long and loud. Most software companies have given up on copy protection, but there are still a few that do it.

Copying a Floppy onto Another Floppy of a Different Type

Sometimes you have a program on 5¼-inch floppy but you need it on 3½-inch, or the other way around. As long as the original isn't on a high-density 3½-inch floppy that is completely full, this is easy. First, write-protect the original floppy. Then, assuming the original floppy fits in your A drive and the copy fits your B drive, type

```
XCOPY A: B: /S
```

If you are going the other way, from B to A, change the order of the drives in the command. Now, if all you wanted to do was copy a disk full of data, you are done. But, if you will be using the new floppies to do a software installation, you may need to do one more step. First, find out the volume label on the original floppy. A DIR of the original will give you this information. It will read something like: "Volume in

Floppy Disks

Drive A is DISK 1." What you want is the part after *is*. This is known as the *volume label*, and many installation programs rely on this label to tell them which disk the user inserted in the drive. To add the label "DISK 1" to the copy you just made, which is in drive B, type

```
LABEL B:DISK 1
```

Be sure to include all spaces and special characters. The copy you made will now have the label it needs to have.

☞ *You can copy a high-density 5¹/₄-inch floppy to a high-density 3¹/₂-inch floppy.*

☞ *You can copy any low-density floppy to any high-density floppy.*

☞ *You cannot copy a full high-density 3¹/₂-inch floppy to any other floppy. This is because a high-density 3¹/₂-inch floppy holds the most data, and copying a full one to any other size floppy is like trying to put ten pounds of potatoes in a five-pound bag.*

☞ *You cannot copy any high-density floppy to any low-density floppy.*

☞ *Not even COPYIIPC will copy a copy-protected program onto a different size disk. Demand that the software company give you an unprotected version. Almost all will do it, but only if you complain strongly. If they won't, demand your money back.*

Chapter 10

PRINTING—GETTING IT ALL ON PAPER

Turner's Observation: The computer only crashes when printing a document you haven't saved.

UNLESS YOU ARE doing a computer graphics slide show from your laptop, the chances are your final product will need to be on paper. It may be a complex report with graphics, a couple of bar charts, and a half dozen or so fonts, or it may be a simple hard copy of your directory. Either way, you need to get it from electronic form inside the computer to a piece of paper.

In this chapter, you will learn about the different kinds of printers and their advantages and disadvantages. You will learn how to hook up your printer to your computer and how to get your computer to talk to it. And, of course, you will learn some tips to make using a printer easier.

Printer Basics

There are more than 1000 different printers on the market. The good news is that they fall into a few basic categories, and within those categories, most work in pretty similar ways. See the "Laser, Dot-Matrix, Color" section below for similarities and differences. But first let's get that printer connected to the computer.

Serial or Parallel—NO! Not Ports Again

The first thing you need to do is figure out which kind of printer you have. If you need a refresher on telling serial ports from parallel ones, see "Any Port in a Storm" in Chapter 5.

Probably better than 98 percent of all printers designed for PCs today are parallel printers, so if you are unsure what you have, chances are in your favor if you guess parallel. About the only serial printers you are likely to run into are printers that were designed primarily for other computer systems, like UNIX or one of those huge computer systems that made IBM rich, a mainframe. The only common serial printer is a plotter, a special kind of printer used in Computer Aided Drafting (CAD) programs. But the easy answer is to look at the printer's manual. If you have a serial printer, see "The Serial Scoop" below.

Connecting the Printer

To connect your printer to the computer, you will need a parallel printer cable (sometimes called Centronics cables after the company that invented them).

One end has 25 pins arranged in two rows inside a metal shell. This is called, if you care, a 25-pin, male, D-shell connector. This end connects to your computer. Your computer should have an equivalent female plug. If it only has one, great. If you happen to have two, you want the one marked LPT1 or Printer 1 or Parallel 1. If they aren't marked, choose either one. You will inevitably pick the wrong one, even though there is a 50/50 chance. (After all, this is a book about Murphy.) It won't hurt anything; just change it when you guess wrong.

The other end of the printer plug has a weird connector that plugs into the back of your printer. With your printer off, plug this cable into the back of your printer. If you have trouble finding where it plugs in, check the printer's manual. It should have a nice picture to make things easier.

☞ *Never plug anything into your computer when either the computer or what you are plugging in is turned on. Remember, Murphy never takes a vacation.*

☞ *Plan your computer work area so that you won't have to use a printer cable longer than 15 feet. You can get longer ones, but for tedious technical reasons, you shouldn't use them.*

Unavoidable Technospeak about Printer Names

DOS's name for your printer is PRN. Which would be fine, except what if you have more than one printer? Then you have to tell DOS which port the printer is connected to. The main port, PRN, is LPT1 (short for Line Printer 1). The second one is LPT2, and you can even have an LPT3. If you have a printer connected to either the second or third parallel port, then when you print, whether from DOS or an application, you will need to let either DOS or the application know. So, for example, if you are using the PRINT command to print a file README.TXT to the printer connected to the second printer port, you would type

```
PRINT /D:LPT2 README.TXT
```

at the DOS prompt. The *D* in the above command stands for "device" and is telling PRINT where to go—in this case, to whatever is connected to LPT2.

If you're using a program and want to print something you made in that program, the commands will vary depending on the application, but they will involve telling the application that the printer you want is connected to either Parallel 2 or LPT2 for the second printer port.

The Serial Scoop

If you have a serial printer or plotter, you will need to configure both your printer and DOS so that they agree about how they are going to talk. First you need to set up your printer. Turn the printer off and pick up the manual. Find the section in the manual where it explains how to set up the tiny switches that control the printer. These are called, by the way, DIP switches. Now, set the switches according to the manual's recommendations. Usually this will be something like

```
9600,8,N,1
```

which, if you reread the section in Chapter 5 like you were supposed to, you will know means that the printer wants a speed (or baud) of 9600, 8 data bits, no parity, and 1 stop bit. Once the switches are set, turn the printer back on. Next, you need to tell DOS how to talk to the printer. Assuming that the printer is connected to the first serial port, type

```
MODE COM1 BAUD=96 DATA=8 PARITY=N STOP=1
```

which will set DOS to the same speed as the printer. Then we only need to redirect the printer to the serial port. This takes one more MODE command:

```
MODE LPT1=COM1
```

I know this is ugly, but once you get it right, simply add these commands to your AUTOEXEC.BAT and you'll never have to deal with it again. For details on how to do this, see "Using DOS EDIT to Change Your Files" in Chapter 11.

☞ *Always change the switches on your printer with the printer off, since the printer only checks these switches when you first turn it on.*

☞ *Unless you have a very good reason not to, always use your printer in the factory default state. This means that all switches and front panel settings are set just as they first were when the printer was unpacked from the box. The printer's manual will tell you what these settings are. (Good to know in case some screwball has messed with them.) Most applications assume that the printer is set this way, and will only work reliably if that is true.*

☞ *Always make sure you are all the way out of any application, including the DOS Shell, when you issue either PRINT or MODE commands from DOS. A quick way to check this is to type*

```
EXIT
```

and press the Enter key. If nothing much happens, then you are all the way out to DOS and it is safe to issue these commands.

Laser, Dot-Matrix, Color

There are four printer types you might run into these days. These are the laser printer, the ink-jet printer (laser wannabe), the color printer (this overlaps all the other categories, but is still pretty much in a category by itself), and finally the lowly but still most popular dot-matrix printer.

Laser printers

Laser printers are what we all wish we had. They are quiet, fast, and produce beautiful output. They are also big, heavy, and expensive. Prices keep coming down, though, and they are now almost down to where real people can afford them.

There are two subclasses of laser printers. The first is HP-compatible. These are printers that use Hewlett Packard's Printer Control Language (PCL) to control what comes out on the paper. If you want one of these, get a real HP. Most of the clones are still only almost compatible. And whether it is an HP or a clone, get one that uses version 5 of PCL (PCL5) or above. This will give you access to scalable fonts, which you will want to have as soon as you know what they are. See the "Horrible Note on Scalable Fonts" below.

The second type of laser printer is the PostScript-compatible. These use Adobe's PostScript language (or a clone of it) to control what comes out on the paper. If you have a lot of graphics, this is definitely the preferred choice. But if most of what you do is straight text, then the PCL printers are a better bet. And you can always stick a PostScript cartridge in your HP printer and make it do PostScript.

Printing

Horrible Note on Scalable Fonts

Scalable fonts are typefaces like balloons. No matter how big you blow them up to be, they retain their nice smooth outline. Other kinds of fonts are called raster fonts and they only look nice at certain sizes. When you blow them up, you really *would* like to blow them up because they're very ragged and clunky-looking.

Another type of font is bit-mapped. Bit-mapped fonts look OK but take up a lot of space on your hard disk. That's because the size you buy is the size you get. It can't be made larger or smaller. So if you want to be able to use several different sizes of the typeface Palatino, for example, you have to have a complete set of each size.

Ink-jet printers

Ink-jet printers are cheaper and smaller than laser printers, but they provide a similar quality of output and are even quieter. They are good for the individual user, but they're slower than what you'd generally need in an office. And though they're not all that expensive to buy, they are pretty expensive to use if you do a lot of printing.

Color printers

This class spans the range from PostScript laser printers to dot-matrix printers. Their advantage is their color, which in the best of them is remarkable, and even in the inexpensive dot-matrix versions provides a interesting extra. However, they are expensive to use, slow, and in many cases do relatively poorly with simple black-and-white text.

Plotters are special color printers that use an actual pen or pens to draw on the paper. For Computer Aided Drafting (CAD) they are indispensable.

Dot-matrix printers

Ah, the lowly dot-matrix printer. Dot-matrix printers used to be slow, noisy, and provide truly horrible output. Not so anymore. The speed has improved, the noise level is down a lot, and the output can be

> ### Don't Read This
>
> If you have a peculiar interest in printers, you should either seek professional help or go buy a copy of *Murphy's Laws of PCs* by Gene Weisskopf (SYBEX, 1993), where you can indulge your fantasies to the fullest.

remarkably good. Some now even provide scalable fonts. These printers are described by the number of pins in the print head, usually 9 or 24. Stick to 24-pin versions from major manufacturers, and you can't go too far wrong. Make sure that the printer is Epson-compatible, since even an application that doesn't directly support your printer will support one or another Epson printer that yours can mimic.

On, Off, and On-Line

A printer can be switched on and still not be ready to print. Many printers will have a button labeled "On-line" or "Select" with a corresponding light. When that light is on, it means the printer is ready to go.

If you have to do something to the printer like move the paper around in a dot-matrix printer or clear a paper jam in a laser printer, make sure you press that button and take the printer off-line first.

If your printer doesn't have a button/light like that, then it is on-line whenever it's turned on. In that case you should turn the whole printer off before probing its innards.

Getting That Last Page to Print

A common problem with a laser printer is getting that last page to print. When that last page won't pop out, press the On-line button (usually the upper left button) so that the light goes out. Then press the Sheet Feed, Form Feed, Page Eject, or similarly named button (usually directly underneath the On-line button). Usually the light is on at this point. Then, when the page starts coming out, press the On-line button again.

Printing

Boring Technical Details about Form Feeds

The reason the laser printer won't give you that last page is because it thinks you aren't done with it yet. Unlike other kinds of printers, it doesn't print a line at a time; instead it prints an entire page. Until you (or your software application) send a form-feed character (Ctrl-L or ^L), or the page is full, it thinks there might be more, so it waits patiently. You can tell the printer you are done by manually sending this form-feed character to the printer. Just type

```
ECHO ^L > PRN
```

Note that you must hold down the Ctrl key while pressing the letter *L* to get the ^*L* in the line above. And don't forget the spaces.

Form Feeds for the Rest of Us

Those of us without laser printers also need to eject a page occasionally. Dot-matrix and ink-jets usually have a button called Form Feed or Page Feed or something similar. First press the On-line button (sometimes called the Select button) to take the printer off-line, then press the Form Feed button. Don't forget to press the On-line or Select button again when you are done to put the printer back on-line.

Nonlaser printers also usually have a Line Feed button as well. This button will push the paper up one line at a time. Again, the printer must be off-line before you can use this, and you must remember to put it back on-line when you get done.

Paper Jams—Dot-Matrix Style

If you have a jammed dot-matrix printer, first turn off the power. Then try slowly backing up the paper, using the large knob on the side of the platen. If this doesn't work, try flipping up the little latches that hold the paper against the pin-feed pins, and gently pull the paper out. And if this still doesn't work, you may have to remove the platen completely. Get help for this, at least the first time. Taking the thing off isn't a problem, but getting it back on may be.

☞ *Don't try to back messed-up sticky labels out of your dot-matrix printer. Move the little lever on the left side of the printer that compensates for the thickness of the paper all the way to its thickest setting. Tear off the labels where they're feeding into the printer and feed the jammed ones slowly forward through the printer until you've gotten all of them out.*

☞ *Watch out for hot parts. The print head on a dot-matrix printer can be hot enough to burn.*

Paper Jams—Laser Printers

If you have a laser printer, you don't have to turn the printer off to unjam it, but be careful. First, take the printer off-line and remove the paper tray. If you see a piece of paper sticking out, gently pull it back out of the printer and put the paper tray back. If you still get the paper-jam signal you will have to open up the printer and peer into its guts. Usually the source of the problem is pretty obvious at this point.

☞ *Never stick anything sharp into your printer. It can only make the problem worse.*

☞ *Never force the paper, and try to avoid tearing it. This generally just makes the problem worse.*

☞ *The inside of a laser printer can get pretty hot. Follow the printer manufacturer's instructions carefully, and be especially careful not to touch or damage the little wires called corona wires.*

Thomas's Troubleshooting Truism: Hot parts look exactly like cold parts.

Fonts Defined in English

In traditional typography, a font is a single size of a single typeface. Type size is measured in points. So 12 point Courier is one font, and 10 point Courier is another. In computer practice, however, font has come to mean typeface alone. So all sizes of Courier are called one font, all

Printing

sizes of Times Roman are another and so on. This is not really correct but hardly anyone cares. So you can use font and typeface pretty much interchangeably unless there's an artist or typesetter you want to impress.

In the computer world, there are different kinds of fonts and it will serve you well to know what they are.

All printers have *internal* fonts. These are fonts built into the printer that any program can use without much in the way of special work on your part. For most dot-matrix printers, you will have perhaps half a dozen fonts available. Older laser printers had two fonts, plain old Courier and Lineprinter. Most newer (PCL5 compatible) laser printers have a dozen or so if you count italic and bold as separate fonts, while PostScript printers come with 35 fonts built in. Internal fonts are the best because they require little intervention on your part and are also the fastest to print.

Next come *cartridge* fonts. These are contained in a little cartridge that you plug into the front or side of the printer. (While the printer is off, please.) These cartridges can contain anywhere from a few to a plethora of fonts. If you have an HP LaserJet, using a cartridge is one of the best and cheapest ways to increase your choice of fonts. For HP LaserJet III and IV printers, an excellent cartridge is the Pacific Data Complete Font Cartridge. It includes a broad range of fully scalable fonts, is available for a reasonable price, and only takes a single cartridge slot.

Cartridge fonts are almost as good as internal fonts. They are fast, and they don't require a whole lot on your part to use them. One thing you *do* need to do, however, is tell your application that you have the cartridge installed. The cartridge manufacturer will include specific directions for how to tell most popular applications how use the fonts. This may include installing a special driver into the program. But once you have done this, you won't have to worry about it again.

The third kind of font is a *soft* (also called downloadable) font. This is a font that has to be sent to the printer every time you want to use it. These fonts are available from Adobe, Agfa, Bitstream, and other font manufacturers.

The problem with soft fonts is that they have to be stored on your hard disk which can take a lot of space, and every time you want to use them, you need to send them to your printer. However, most popular word processing programs can handle sending the fonts once you have installed the necessary drivers. If you use the same fonts all the time, get an expert to set your system up so that the fonts are automatically downloaded to your printer.

What Happened to All Those Neat Fonts I Had?

So, you spent all this time setting up your spreadsheet or document or whatever with all these neat fonts and when you go to print to your laser printer, all you have is plain old ugly Courier? It's enough to make you throw large heavy objects at the printer, the computer, or both.

Usually this means that your application didn't tell the printer to use the fonts. Check to make sure that you didn't accidentally select draft mode printing, and that you have the right type of printer selected. If the fonts you want are on a cartridge, turn the printer off and make sure the cartridge is securely seated. Then turn the printer back on. Turning the printer off and on will also have the desirable effect of reinitializing the printer, so it's a good idea even if you aren't using a cartridge. Finally, if you are using soft fonts that have to be downloaded to the printer, make sure they are downloaded before you start the print job. Turn the printer off and then back on, and redownload the fonts.

Gibberish and How to Stop It

Suddenly your printer starts printing a few characters on each page and then spitting it out. And when you press the On-line button it won't stop. If it's a dot-matrix printer, turn it off and then go tell your application to stop printing. After you have stopped the print job, realign the paper in the printer so that the top of the sheet is where it should be (only experience will tell you where this is) and then turn the printer back on. Now, start the print job from scratch.

If you have a laser printer, it is a bad idea to turn it off in the middle of printing. This will usually leave a piece of paper stuck inside. So

Printing

remove the paper tray. Then when the last sheet of paper has had a chance to get all the way out of the printer, turn off the printer, cancel the print job, and start all over again from scratch.

One cause of gibberish on laser printers is common to those of us who switch back and forth between PostScript and PCL laser printers. If you tell your application to print to a PostScript printer and you forget to put the PostScript cartridge in, what you will get is page after page of PostScript language commands. Cancel the print job, turn the printer off, and insert the PostScript cartridge. Then turn the printer back on and restart the print job from scratch.

Funny Characters in the Upper Left Corner

If you print something and get three or four stray characters in the upper left corner of the first page, it means that you have the wrong printer *driver* selected from whatever application you are printing. A printer driver is the translating layer between the application and the printer. The application knows what you want, since you told it, and the printer driver knows how to speak to your particular printer. The problem comes when you have the wrong driver for your printer. Sometimes this happens because the person who installed the software in the first place made a mistake, and sometimes it happens because some other program has gotten in the way and told your printer to pretend to be a different printer. First, try turning your printer off and then back on, and try the print job again. If the problem doesn't go away, chances are that the wrong driver was installed. If you feel up to trying to solve it yourself, consult the instructions that came with the program you were printing from. Otherwise, call for help.

Printing a Directory

To print out a list of files on your disk, make sure your printer is on-line and type the following at DOS prompt:

```
DIR > PRN
```

If you want a directory of some other disk, like a floppy, type in

```
DIR A: > PRN
```

If you are printing on a laser printer, you may need to issue a form feed to get the page out. See "Getting That Last Page to Print" above.

Printing What's on Your Screen

Sometimes all you need is a copy of what is on your screen. This is pretty easy—just press the PrintScreen key. This may be labeled PrtScrn or Print Screen or something similar. Unfortunately, if what is on your screen has lines and boxes and such, the result will probably be a little weird. This is because many printers don't print these lines and boxes without special commands, and PrintScreen isn't smart enough to send it the right special commands. So what you get may have a lot of *m*'s where you thought there was supposed to be a line.

☞ *If nothing happens, try pressing the PrintScreen key a second time. Some keyboards require that you press the key twice in a row.*

☞ *If everything seems to freeze, but nothing actually prints, check to make sure your printer is on-line. PrintScreen will wait patiently forever until the printer is on-line. And meanwhile, you can't do anything else until it gets done.*

☞ *If you have a laser printer, nothing will print until you send a form feed to the printer. See the section "Getting That Last Page to Print" earlier in this chapter.*

Here are chapters about software: how to buy it and how to use it. Also there's info on how to change the files that make your computer what it is today into what you want it to be tomorrow. This part also explains backups and virus protection for safe computing.

A GENTLE GUIDE
TO SOFTWARE

Chapter 11

YOUR SYSTEM DEFINED

(What Your Computer Knows about Itself)

Robbins's Rule: The person who smiles when bad things happen knows who to blame it on.

YOUR COMPUTER HAS two critical files that control its configuration and many aspects of its behavior. They are CONFIG.SYS and AUTOEXEC.BAT.

You will need to modify AUTOEXEC.BAT and/or CONFIG.SYS if you want certain programs like DOSKEY and DOSSHELL installed and ready for you every time you start the computer or if you want a custom prompt. (See the section called "Playing with Prompts" below.) When you buy new software or hardware you may need to modify one or both of these files.

If you are using a computer at work, get the person in charge of computers to make the changes. That way, you have someone to blame when things go wrong (see Robbins's Rule above).

But if you don't have any help, you still can edit the files yourself. You do have to be a bit careful with both files because they contain most of what the computer needs to know to get itself going in the morning. So make sure *you* know what it is you're adding or changing and be sure to make a copy of the *original* file before you start.

Absolutely Unnecessary Information

When you turn on your computer, the first program run is the little bootstrap program stored in read-only memory (see "Why Is a Boot Called a Boot?" in Chapter 1 for more). That program goes looking for CONFIG.SYS (short for System Configuration file), which runs next. In this file go things like your memory manager, any information needed to make your hard disk work, and all sorts of other low-level stuff like this. When CONFIG.SYS finishes, it tells DOS to load COMMAND.COM (the DOS command processor).

The very first thing COMMAND.COM does is run a little batch file called AUTOEXEC.BAT (short for Automatically Executed Batch file). This file's job is to load all the stuff you don't want to live without that doesn't get loaded by CONFIG.SYS.

How to Find
AUTOEXEC.BAT and CONFIG.SYS

These files are pretty easy to find, since they must be in the same place all the time—the root directory of your primary boot drive. "Primary

Always Make a Boot Disk Before You Start Editing Your Configuration

Your system is working now, right? So, first, before you do *anything* else, make a boot disk just in case. See "How to Make a Boot Floppy and What to Do with It" in Chapter 16 for help on how to make a boot disk for your system.

If you already have a boot disk, before you make a change to either your AUTOEXEC.BAT or CONFIG.SYS file, copy the original file to this boot disk. If you pay attention to no other warning in this book, pay attention to this one. If I followed my own advice, I could save myself many hours and much grief every year.

boot drive" is techspeak for your C drive. If you're not already at a prompt that says C>, type

    C:

and press the Enter key, followed by

    CD \

and Enter again. Now you're in the root directory.

Pinkie's Immutable Law of Configuration:
If you make a copy of your system configuration nine out of ten times, the tenth time is the only time you will need it.

Using DOS EDIT to Change Your Files

If you have DOS 5 or 6, you can use the friendly EDIT program to make changes to AUTOEXEC.BAT, CONFIG.SYS, or any other text file. Otherwise, you must use EDLIN—a horrible but usable editor included with earlier versions of DOS. Skip to the section "Remember Slide Rules? Then You'll Love EDLIN" later in this chapter.

Starting DOS EDIT

To add or change a line in your AUTOEXEC.BAT, type the following at your DOS prompt:

```
EDIT AUTOEXEC.BAT
```

If it's your CONFIG.SYS file you want to edit, then type

```
EDIT CONFIG.SYS
```

instead. Press Enter and the EDIT program will start. The file you specified will be displayed. When you start EDIT without requesting a specific file, that is, you just type in

```
EDIT
```

at the prompt, you will get a display box asking if you want to use the "Survival Guide." Press the Esc key. Then select Open from the File menu to request a specific file or New if you want to create a new file.

Adding a line

To add a line to the end of the file, use the ↓ key to move to the first blank line at the bottom of the screen. Type the line you want to add. For example, if you wanted to add the DOS Shell so that you wouldn't have to look at that miserable C> prompt first thing every morning, you would type

```
DOSSHELL
```

as the very last line in your AUTOEXEC.BAT file. Then whenever you started your computer, the AUTOEXEC.BAT would do its thing, and as its last action before turning the computer over to you, it would start the DOS Shell.

☞ *To add a line in the middle of the file (such as PROMPT PG), use the ↓ key to move to the beginning of the line that is going to be the line after the one you want to add. Press Enter and you've just made a space for the new line. Type it in.*

☞ *Use the Backspace key to back up and erase any typing mistakes.*

☞ *You may need to include a path name for some instructions. See "Finding Your True Path" in Chapter 13 for help on paths.*

Saving your work

After you're sure you've done what you want to do, click on File at the top left of the screen. In the menu that drops down, click on Save. Click on that File menu again and select Exit to leave EDIT.

If you've somehow bollixed things up and just want to escape and try again, don't select Save. Instead, click on Exit from the File menu, and when you're asked if you want to save the file, click on No. Then you can go back to "Starting DOS EDIT" above and start over.

EDIT menus

At the top of the DOS EDIT screen are four menus: File, Edit, Search, and Options. These work more or less like comparable menus in a word processor. If you want to use EDIT a lot, I suggest that the next time you start up EDIT and get a chance to look at the Survival Guide, do it.

Remember Slide Rules?
Then You'll Love EDLIN

Back in the bad old days before DOS 5, DOS didn't include nice, friendly, tail-wagging EDIT. No, it had a snarling, junkyard dog of a program called EDLIN. EDLIN allows you to "edit" only one line at a time and you can't even see what you're doing. But if you must use EDLIN to do something to CONFIG.SYS or AUTOEXEC.BAT, it can be done.

Starting EDLIN

If you need to edit your AUTOEXEC.BAT, go to the DOS prompt and type in

```
EDLIN \AUTOEXEC.BAT
```

which will start EDLIN and load your AUTOEXEC.BAT file. If it's your CONFIG.SYS file you want to edit, substitute CONFIG.SYS for AUTOEXEC.BAT above.

What you will see is

```
End of input file
*
```

☞ *If you don't see this nasty message or you get the "Bad command or file name" error message, check to make sure you typed everything in right. If you did and it still doesn't work, call for help.*

Adding a new line at the end

To add a line at the end of the file, at the * prompt shown above, type in

```
#I
```

That's the pound sign (above the number 3 on the main part of your keyboard) and the letter *I*. You'll get a prompt like the following:

```
15:*
```

The number is the number of the last line in the file and the asterisk is EDLIN's version of a prompt. Type in the line you want. For example, to add DOSSHELL to your AUTOEXEC.BAT file so that you will have the Shell to look at when you start up your computer rather than the C> prompt, you would type in

```
DOSSHELL
```

Check your typing carefully, and when you're sure it's OK, press Enter. You should see

```
16:*
```

That is, the next line number. Press F6 followed by Enter and you'll see that * prompt again. If you're sure you've done everything right, type in the letter **E** and press the Enter key. That will save what you've done and get you the heck out of EDLIN.

Adding a new line in the middle

Follow the steps in "Starting EDLIN" above. After you get the * prompt, type **L** (the letter *L*) and press Enter. EDLIN will **L**ist the first 24 lines of your AUTOEXEC.BAT file, along with the line numbers for each line of it. If you have more than 20 lines, type

    20L

This is short for "**L**ist starting at line 20," which is exactly what you will get: the same sort of line-by-line listing of the file, starting at line 20 instead of line 1. Let's say you want to insert a simple PROMPT command in front of line 15. Type

    15I

That's the number 15 and the letter *I*. Instead of EDLIN's helpful * prompt, you will see:

    15:*

which tells you that you are at line 15, and that the line is blank. Not surprising, since we are adding a new line in front of the old line 15. EDLIN is also saying it is ready to let you add something to the line. So if you want to make your prompt look like C:\>, you type in

    PROMPT PG

followed by the Enter key. This will leave you with

    16:*

because EDLIN thinks you probably want to add even more lines here. But you don't, so press the F6 key, followed by Enter, and you should be back at the * prompt again. To make sure that you didn't make a mistake, do a listing again (**L**, in case you forgot), and then if all looks well, you can exit. Press the letter **E**, followed by the Enter key, and your changes will be saved.

Quitting EDLIN without saving changes

If you make *any* mistake at all, your best bet is to try the whole thing again, from the beginning. So, to **Q**uit EDLIN without keeping any of the changes you made, type

    Q

and EDLIN will respond with

```
*q
Abort edit (Y/N)?
```

to which you can respond with a heartfelt **Y** for yes. Then you can go back to "Starting EDLIN" and try again.

☞ *Don't rush when trying to use something as peculiar as EDLIN. Remember, the computer is infinitely patient. No matter how long you take, it will not start drumming its fingers on the table or making annoyed sounds. So take whatever time you need.*

Rebooting to Make Changes Happen

OK, so you made a change to your AUTOEXEC.BAT. Now what? Nothing happens until you reboot your computer. The computer operates based on the instructions it got when it last booted up. So any changes you make to the AUTOEXEC.BAT or the CONFIG.SYS don't get recognized until you boot up again.

So, exit out of whatever editor you were using to make the changes (EDIT or EDLIN), and don't forget to save the change as you exit. Then, press the Ctrl, Alt, and Del keys all at the same time. When your computer is done rebooting, the changes you made will be in effect.

☞ If you see error messages or other bad news when you reboot, go to Chapter 16 for a chance to use that boot disk you were so smart to make.

☞ For more on booting up and Ctrl-Alt-Del, see "Reset, Reboot, and the Fine Art of Ctrl-Alt-Del" in Chapter 1.

Things That Go in Your CONFIG.SYS

If you want to start making serious changes to your CONFIG.SYS file, you are probably going to need help from your system administrator or favorite nerd. However, as long as you are careful to make a copy of the original file before you start messing with it, there's no reason you can't make modest modifications.

Your CONFIG.SYS is made up primarily of *drivers*. Drivers are little packages of instructions that control things like your printer, your mouse, the monitor, various types of memory, and so forth. Not all the drivers used by your computer are in the CONFIG.SYS file, but many are. CONFIG.SYS can include drivers to let you send commands to your screen (ANSI.SYS) and drivers to control your memory (HIMEM.SYS and EMM386.EXE).

Getting Control of
Your Screen with ANSI.SYS

It's easy enough to add screen control to your computer. DOS supplies a driver called ANSI.SYS that lets you customize your prompt and screen display. First, check to see if ANSI.SYS is already in your CONFIG.SYS file. At the DOS prompt, key in the following line exactly

```
TYPE C:\CONFIG.SYS
```

and press the Enter key. The contents of your CONFIG.SYS file will be displayed on the screen. If ANSI.SYS is there, leave it alone. If not, use DOS EDIT to add the following line to your CONFIG.SYS:

```
DEVICE=C:\DOS\ANSI.SYS
```

Just stick it at the end of the CONFIG.SYS file, since ANSI.SYS isn't fussy about where it goes.

☞ *For information on neat video stuff that ANSI.SYS makes possible, see "Text a la Mode" in Chapter 8.*

☞ *Once ANSI.SYS is in place, you can do all sorts of ridiculous things with your DOS prompt. See the "Playing with Prompts" section later in this chapter.*

Memory Is Made of This

If you have a 80386 or 80486 processor and at least one megabyte of extended memory, you need to have a memory manager installed, or that memory sits there doing nothing. Go to your DOS prompt, type in the following line exactly

```
TYPE C:\CONFIG.SYS
```

and press the Enter key. The contents of your CONFIG.SYS file will be displayed on the screen. Toward the top you should see two lines that say

```
DEVICE=C:\DOS\HIMEM.SYS
DEVICE=C:\DOS\EMM386.EXE
```

There may be some additional numbers and/or letters, but if the above information is there, let it be.

If, however, there's nothing that resembles these lines, you will need to add them. Use EDIT and put the two lines, in the same order shown above, at the beginning of your CONFIG.SYS file.

☞ *If you have special drivers for your hard disk (which you probably don't), make sure they go before any memory drivers.*

☞ *See the section "Using DOS EDIT to Change Your Files" earlier in this chapter for help on adding lines to CONFIG.SYS.*

☞ *If you're queasy about changing your CONFIG.SYS or AUTOEXEC.BAT, go find someone with DOS smarts. You certainly don't have to do any of this.*

Buffers and Files

Two lines that should be in your CONFIG.SYS file are

```
BUFFERS=30
FILES=30
```

If you have these lines but the numbers are bigger, fine. The BUFFERS command helps DOS get stuff to and from your hard disk faster, and the FILES command makes sure that programs that work with more than one or two files at once have enough *handles* to do so.

You can use EDIT to change either or both of these numbers if you get an instruction from your software to do so. Sometimes when you install something new, you'll get a "Too many files are open" error message.

That means increase the FILES= number. But don't get carried away; more than 40 files and 30 buffers just eats up memory without improving performance.

Things That Go in Your AUTOEXEC.BAT

Your AUTOEXEC.BAT is a batch file that contains mostly DOS commands, such as PATH and PROMPT, and all those things that need to be installed before you can do any real work, such as network drivers, DOSKEY, and DOSSHELL.

☞ *Never change more than one thing at a time in either the CONFIG.SYS or AUTOEXEC.BAT file. That way, when it doesn't work, it will be a lot easier to figure out why.*

☞ *For information on PATH and path names, see "Finding Your True Path" in Chapter 13.*

☞ *To customize your prompt, see "Playing with Prompts" later in this chapter.*

Adding DOSKEY to Your AUTOEXEC.BAT

If you haven't been using DOSKEY and you decide you like the idea of having a better behaved command line, here is how to add it. If when you reboot your computer, you end up looking at the DOS prompt (C> or something similar), then you will want to load DOSKEY on the last line of your AUTOEXEC.BAT. If you usually end up either in some sort of menu system or in DOS Shell, then you should load DOSKEY just before the line that starts the menu or the Shell. Using DOS EDIT, add the following line to your AUTOEXEC.BAT file:

```
C:\DOS\DOSKEY
```

Save the change and reboot your computer to make the change happen. See "DOSKEY—Is It for Me?" in Chapter 2 for more information on how this program works.

Batch Files

Batch files are little programs written in text. They always have the extension .BAT, and when you type their names in at the DOS prompt, they run just like any other program. Batch files can be very complicated, but they can also be within the range of normal humans. For example, if you have Quicken and Quattro Pro on your computer, you will soon discover that they both are started with a file called Q.EXE. So if you type in **Q** at the DOS prompt and you always get Quicken because that's the one DOS finds first, you can write an easy batch file to find Quattro Pro for you. Go to the root directory of your hard drive by typing in

```
CD \
```

Then start DOS EDIT and type in the following:

```
C:
CD \QPRO
Q
```

Type it exactly like this, on three lines. When you run the batch file, the first line, C:, will move you to drive C's root directory, CD \QPRO will move you to your Quattro Pro directory, and the letter *Q* will finally start up Quattro Pro. Of course, if your Quattro Pro files are in a directory with another name, substitute that name for QPRO above.

Save the file by selecting Save from the File menu. Give it a name like QPRO.BAT or any other easy name—just be sure to give it the extension .BAT. The file will be saved in the root directory of your hard drive. Then when you type **QPRO** (or whatever you have named it) at the prompt, you will be quickly escorted to Quattro Pro and nowhere else.

☞ *Batch files can be ornamented in lots of ways. If you're interested, you can find a zillion books on the subject.*

☞ *To make it easier to find all your batch files, create a directory called \BAT and put all your batch files there. See "Making a New Directory" in Chapter 13 for help in making a new directory.*

☞ *If you do the same series of steps at the DOS prompt more than once or twice a week, consider writing a simple batch file to do it for you.*

☞ See "The PATH Command" in Chapter 13 for an explanation of how DOS searches for programs.

Using DOSKEY
Macros instead of Batch Files

DOSKEY allows you do many of the same things that a batch file does. The advantage is that you can store all your DOSKEY macros in a single batch file. This way it's easy to find and change them when you need to.

To create a batch file for your DOSKEY macros and put your very first macro in it, a duplicate of the batch file we just created to run Quattro Pro, start DOS EDIT and type in the following line:

```
DOSKEY QPRO=C: $T CD \QPRO $T Q
```

This one line looks intimidating, but it actually means exactly the same thing as the batch file above. First the command DOSKEY tells DOS that this is for DOSKEY to remember, then QPRO= says "Every time I type QPRO, substitute the rest of this line for it." Next, the C: says "If I am not already on my C drive, change to it." The $T is a bit tricky: it says that this is the end of one task, and the start of another. Next, CD \QPRO says to change to the Quattro Pro subdirectory, another $T is there to separate the tasks, and finally the letter Q tells DOS to start Quattro Pro.

OK, now save the file in your DOS directory, calling it MACROS.BAT or some such name. Exit from EDIT and then type

```
MACROS
```

at the DOS prompt and every DOSKEY command in MACROS.BAT is ready to run. When you want to add a new command to DOS, just add the line you want to the MACROS.BAT file.

If you want the contents of this file to be available all the time, add the following line immediately after the line that loads DOSKEY in your AUTOEXEC.BAT file:

```
CALL C:\DOS\MACROS.BAT
```

This tells DOS about the existence of the file.

See the section "Using DOS EDIT to Change Your Files" earlier in this chapter for help on adding lines to AUTOEXEC.BAT.

Pardon Me, Do You Have the Time?

In the bad old days, you had to tell your computer what time it was every time you started it. But these days our computers keep track of the time pretty well, except that they generally don't understand about Daylight Savings Time. But then, who does? You can find out what the computer thinks the current time is by typing

```
TIME
```

DOS will respond

```
Current time is 3:30:17.02p
Enter new time:
```

to which you can either type in a new time, or press Enter to leave it as is. To set the time to 4:30 in the afternoon, type

```
16:30
```

or

```
4:30p
```

and press Enter. Either will work. But if you respond

```
4:30
```

DOS will assume you mean 4:30 in the morning. Though why DOS would think that any rational being would be up at that hour is beyond me.

The DATE command works just like TIME: type **DATE**, type in a new date if you want to change it, and press Enter.

☞ *Some older, XT-class computers require a special program to make the changes permanent. On those machines, the change will only last until you reboot your computer. If this applies to you, ask someone for help in figuring out which program will make the change stick.*

Playing with Prompts—
You Can Ignore This Completely!

The DOS PROMPT command allows you to do some very complicated and sophisticated things to your screen. The possibilities are pretty near endless, but in most cases they are hardly worth the time or energy. If you just type

    PROMPT

you will end up with DOS's most useless prompt:

    C>

This prompt, which is the default, tells you only which drive you are currently on, and doesn't even tell you what the current directory is. The "normal" prompt (the one seen on most computers that looks like C:\>) is the result of typing

    PROMPT PG

This yields a prompt that tells you the current drive and the current directory ($P), followed by a > symbol ($G). However, PROMPT can do a lot more. Officially, PROMPT has all the functions shown in Table 11.1. These include functions to show the current date and time, the DOS version, and other stuff.

TABLE 11.1:
Prompt Options

Parameter	Result
$Q	= (equals sign)
$$	$ (dollar sign)
$T	Current time
$D	Current date
$P	Current drive and path
$V	MS-DOS version number
$N	Current drive
$G	> (greater-than sign)
$L	< (less-than sign)

Parameter	Result
$B	| (pipe)
$H	Backspace (erases previous character)
$E	Escape code (ASCII code 27)
$_	Carriage return and line feed

Additionally, any text may be included.

You can use these to create a prompt that shows the current time, erasing all but the hours and minutes, and then on the next line shows the normal prompt:

```
PROMPT THE TIME$Q$T$H$H$H$H$H$H$_$P$G
```

This command first writes the words *THE TIME* on the screen, followed by = ($Q), followed by the time ($T). Then, since the time is shown in a hopelessly long form, we erase the last six characters of the time we just put on the screen by backspacing six times ($H six times). Then we start another line ($_), and show the usual prompt (PG).

If we have ANSI.SYS loaded in our CONFIG.SYS, we can use the escape character ($E) to send commands to ANSI.SYS. This means you can control the colors, the cursor's position on the screen, and even how many characters show on the screen. If you really care about all this, take a look at your DOS manual under ANSI.SYS to see all the possibilities. But just as an example of what can be done, the following will clear the screen, setting it to bright white on a blue background, and show the regular prompt in green. Note that case matters here. The m must be lowercase, and the J must be uppercase.

```
PROMPT $e[1;37;44m$e[2J$e[32m$P$G$e[37m
```

☞ For a complete description of the possible ANSI.SYS commands you can use, see your DOS manual, or type

```
HELP ANSI.SYS
```

if you have DOS 6.

☞ For help in editing your CONFIG.SYS to include ANSI.SYS to add one of these ridiculous prompts to your AUTOEXEC.BAT, read "Using DOS EDIT to Change Your Files" earlier in this chapter.

☞ See Chapter 2, "The DOS Prompt," for more information on the prompt.

Chapter 12

SOFTWARE BASICS

Schubert's Rule of Installation: The more pounds the package weighs, the harder it will be to find the installation instructions.

THE REASON YOU have a computer is, of course, to get some work done. And you can't get a whole lot done with DOS alone, so you will inevitably need to use some other software. This chapter will help you to figure out which software to buy and what to do with it once you get it. But the hard part is still yours. You will have to make the decision about exactly which software to actually buy.

Buying New Software

There are those for whom a trip to the local software store is fun. Honest. There are even those who cannot be trusted in one without a responsible adult present. They go in, wander around a bit, fondle the boxes, drool and slobber a bit, and inevitably, wander back to the front of the store with one or more boxes clutched under their arm, charge card at the ready. But for most of the world, a trip to the software store is not fun.

So, since you don't want to have to make the trip any more often than absolutely necessary, prepare and plan ahead of time. You will still have to make the trip, but at least you will come out with what you need.

Murphy's Six Commandments of Software Buying

1. First decide *why* you are buying the software. Don't laugh. This is probably the most ignored step on this list. Sit down and write out what you want to accomplish, what things the software needs to be able to do, and what you expect to get out of the whole process.

    ☞ Be honest. If you aren't, you may end up with software that's slick, but doesn't do what you really need.

    ☞ If you need a specific report or output, draw a sketch of what it should look like, if you know. Then when you go to the store, see what it takes to get this kind of report out of the packages you try.

    ☞ Ask others what they use to do similar things.

2. Make a list of your hardware. This list should include what kind of processor you have, how much memory (and what kind) your computer has, how much free space your hard disk has, what kind of video system you have, and what printer you have. Review Part Two on PC hardware if you need to, or better yet, get your computer resource person to give you a hand with this.

3. Armed with your two lists, you are ready to brave the software store. Avoid going at times when they are likely to be really busy. March in, whip out your lists, and ask for help.

4. After the salesperson makes a couple of recommendations, ask him or her to set you up on one of the store computers so you can

try the software out. Most will be happy to do this, if they aren't horribly busy. If they can't right then, ask them to set up a time for you to try the software. If they still won't, find another store.

☞ See how hard it is to create the kind of report or document you described back in Commandment 1.

☞ Try to get a feel for how easy or hard to use the software is overall. Remember, you will have to live with the result.

☞ Check out the help system. Does it actually help? This can make a big difference in usability.

☞ Find out what kind of support the manufacturer provides. Do they have phone support, preferably toll-free? Ask the salesperson what she or he knows about the quality of support the company provides.

☞ Ask what the store's return policy is, and don't be shy about demanding the right to return the software if it doesn't do what you need it to. Also, many software companies now offer guarantees.

5. Trust your instincts. If it feels like the salesperson is trying to snow you, or push you into an overpriced and far more complicated package than you think you really need, go somewhere else. If the salesperson is rude or can't be bothered, go somewhere else. (And tell the store manager *why*.) Don't be afraid to shop around, but be fair. If you find a helpful, knowledgeable salesperson, buy the software from him or her. In fact, cultivate this person. You may need their help on another purchase.

6. Buy the darn thing. Whip out that MasterCard and just do it. But avoid the temptation to buy several things at the same time. Buy the software you need to do the job at hand and no more. If you succumb to the siren call of the Visa, you will end up with a collection of "shelfware" that just gathers dust.

Rucinski's Rule: If the new software you want requires new hardware to run, you don't need the new software.

Installing Your New Software

OK, so you finally escaped from the store with your purchase, and you are back home, ready to rip off the shrink wrap. Most people will now tear open the box and rummage through all the papers, books, etc. until finding the floppies, immediately insert one of the floppies into the computer, and start pounding away on the keyboard. Some time later, when things don't seem to be working quite as expected, this same person will start pawing through the stack of discarded manuals, leaflets, registration cards, and what all, and actually try to *read* some of it to figure out why nothing is working. Everyone does this. So will you. But read on to see how you should be doing it.

What is installation?

In the olden days of personal computers, when software cost less than $100 and came on one or two floppies, all you really had to do was create a directory and copy all the files on the floppies to it.

These days that just won't work. Virtually all software now comes in a compressed form that won't work without being *installed*. This involves uncompressing the files that make up the software, copying them to your hard disk, and configuring the software to work with your hardware.

The good news is that virtually all software you buy today comes with an installation program to walk you through the process.

Read me, please

When you open the software package, there will be one or more books and a raft of other papers. Carefully inspect the loose papers to make sure that none of them says something like "READ ME FIRST!" or "Installation Instructions." If you find one that does, read it carefully and follow the instructions on it. If you don't find such a paper, you will have to find the section of the manual that covers installation. This may be called "Getting Started" or "Installing" or some such, but it is often *not* the first chapter of the manual.

Read the directions carefully, and when you are ready, put the first disk in floppy drive A (or B if that is where it fits, but then adjust these instructions accordingly) and type

    A:

and press Enter. Next, type in the name of the installation program. This should be given in the installation instructions, but you can type

    DIR /P

and look for something like INSTALL.EXE or SETUP.EXE. These days, probably 60–70 percent of the installation programs are called IN-STALL, with the rest called SETUP.

☞ *Whatever it's called, the installation program will probably have the extension .EXE.*

☞ *Microsoft programs all use SETUP, while all Borland programs use INSTALL.*

Assuming it is INSTALL we want, type that in and press Enter. Read the instructions on the screen and follow them. No, really, *read them!* This is the first and most important chance that most software companies have to communicate with you, and they generally spend a fair amount of energy to make sure that what they have to say is useful.

Where, oh where does it go

One of the first things that the installation program will ask you is where to install the software. It will almost always offer you a suggestion. Unless you have a strong and compelling reason not to, accept its suggested location. This has the very real advantage of making it easier to figure out later where the software is. Plus any instructions in the manual will agree with what you actually have.

Configuring your new program

Once you have answered the big question of *where* the software will go, there are two essential steps left. One will copy all the stuff on the floppies to your hard disk, and the other will configure the software to work with your particular hardware. The order here is unimportant.

The copying part is pretty straightforward, just feed it whichever floppy disk it is asking for. But eventually it will ask you some questions about your hardware. This is really fairly stupid, since in most cases it *ought* to be able to figure this out for itself, but humor it. If you are at all unsure, ask someone.

One of the most important questions it may ask you is what kind of printer you have. This allows it to select the necessary printer driver to communicate with your printer. Look through the list for your printer's make and model, and select it. If your printer is not listed, try selecting another one from the same maker that has a similar name. If your printer maker is not listed at all, look in the manual for your printer and see if it can *emulate* one of the choices. This is a fancy way of saying that it can pretend to be the same as another manufacturer's printer. If you don't have the manual or it offers no help, you can try one of three selections:

☞ If you have a dot-matrix printer, select Epson FX or Epson MX. Chances are that this will at least work fairly well.

☞ If you have a laser printer, select HP LaserJet.

☞ If you have a PostScript printer, you can select any of the PostScript printers you see listed, such as Apple LaserWriter.

More README stuff

Finally, when the installation is almost all done, it will frequently offer you a chance to read a special file with last-minute instructions and manual corrections, called READ.ME or README.TXT or something similar. If this option is offered, take it.

Read the text carefully to make sure that none of it applies to you. If you aren't offered this option, you will have to do it the hard way. First, return to your hard disk by typing

```
C:
```

and then change to the directory you told the installation program to install the software in. If this was, say, C:\QPRO for Quattro Pro, then the command would be

```
CD \QPRO
```

Now, you need to find the README file. This can have all sorts of different names, but it will almost always start with *READ*, so to find it, type

```
DIR READ*.*
```

which will give you a list of all the files that start with *READ*. Now, to read it, type in

```
MORE < READ.ME
```

substituting the actual name for READ.ME above. This will display the file a page at a time so you can read it. If there's anything interesting in it, you'll probably want to print it out. To do that, type

```
COPY READ.ME PRN
```

again substituting the real name of the file for READ.ME above. You can always come back and do this later if you discover that you need some information from this file.

What do I do with the little white card?

All software comes with a registration card. This card asks all sorts of impertinent questions and has the main function of building the software company's mailing list. Filling out this card is virtually guaranteed to add 20 pounds to your junk mail collection for the year. So, should you fill it out? Yes, unfortunately. In many cases, software companies get downright snippy about answering questions if you call their support line and they haven't gotten a little card from you.

However, many software stores will let you return a package only if you have everything that came in the box. So don't send in the card until you are sure you want to keep the software or have passed the return deadline.

When the deadline is passed, however, fill the card out and send it in. Sometimes new versions of software are shipped with little problems. These problems have all sorts of euphemisms such as "anomaly" or my personal favorite, "undocumented feature," but the most common name is *bug*. Nothing is said at the time, of course, but occasionally the software company will actually 'fess up that a bug exists and send a fix (also called a *patch*) to its users. If you have sent in your little white card, you will get the fix. Otherwise, you may keep beating your head against the wall trying to make something work that is in fact, buggy.

Besides, if you send in the card, the company will then be able to try to separate you from your hard-earned cash when they upgrade the software in six months. See "Updating Your Software" later in this chapter for information on upgrading.

Using and Learning Your New Software

You'll probably have to reboot the computer to use your new software. This allows any changes the installation program made to your system files to take effect.

Sometimes the program you're installing says "Press Enter to Reboot" or something like that. Go ahead and reboot that way if you get the offer.

If you don't get any friendly help from the program, you'll need to exit the program and go to the DOS prompt before rebooting. Press the Ctrl, Alt, and Delete keys simultaneously, or press the reset button on the front of the computer box.

Once your computer has rebooted, change to the directory where you installed the program and type its name to start it. Check the manual if you are unsure of the name and it isn't on the list of common names in the table in Chapter 1.

The point here is to make sure that the program runs and that you haven't made some silly mistake. So, once you start the program up, type in some lines and try to save them. Then maybe print out what you typed in. If anything doesn't seem to work or doesn't work as expected, check with a knowledgeable friend or give the software company's tech support number a call. This second approach has the added advantage of letting you know early in the game just how helpful they can be. Since you have a limited time to be able to return the software, it's better to find out now rather than later that there is a problem.

☞ For more information on rebooting, see "Reset, Reboot, and the Fine Art of Ctrl-Alt-Del" in Chapter 1.

☞ For a list of common programs and the commands to start them, see Table 1.1 in Chapter 1.

☞ If you do have to call a company's tech support number and you are not happy with the help you are getting, ask to speak to the supervisor. The good companies have outstanding technical support departments, but even the best can have a weak link or a bad day. But if you are patient and persistent, you will get the best results.

Learning how to use your new software

Learning a new software program is a lot like learning a new language. At first you can only do the simplest things, but the more you use it the better you will get with it. So be patient, and don't be afraid to try something new.

Most programs these days come with a tutorial or some sort of workbook to teach you the basic features of the software. Use them. These tutorials are not designed to teach you everything there is to know about the software, but they should cover most of the major features. A little time spent now will save you lots of time later.

As you go through the tutorials, make notes on the features you will need the most. Don't try to remember it all; write it down. Keep a little notebook with solutions to common problems, or stick little flags on the page in the workbook where it shows you how to do something.

Tutorials vary from the useful to the hopelessly boring. If you are stuck with the latter and you find that it is not helping you, give it up. And write a letter to the software company to complain. Believe me, they will take that letter *very* seriously.

If the software is commonly used in your company, chances are that they will have classes on using it. Sign up. If it is a major software package, the local community college may well have classes on it and the store where you bought the software may even teach a class on it. But be a little cautious about signing up for a class that will cost money. Some are worth it and some aren't. Try to find someone who has already taken the class and get their opinion. And think seriously about what level user the class is aimed at to make sure you have a good match.

Software

After you have used the software a bit, play around with it, trying out something you haven't used yet. Stretch yourself. Or ask someone who uses it all the time how to do something. But if you do, make sure you take notes so you don't have to ask the same question again.

☞ *Always take notes, especially on new things. Keep them with the software manuals, or even write the notes right in the manual.*

☞ *Don't be afraid to try reading the manual to figure out how to do something. The quality of software manuals has improved tremendously in the last few years. But don't try to read them cover to cover. Look up what you want in the index, and then try it out.*

☞ *If the software is a company standard, there may be macros or templates that have been developed to make common tasks easier. These can greatly simplify everyday tasks. Ask a coworker or the computer resource person (fancy word for nerd) in your department.*

☞ *The most important manual your software comes with is usually called the* Reference Manual *or something similar. This will have short but complete descriptions of all the program's features and explanations of how to use them. The* User's Guide *tends to have a lot more fluff and a lot less useful information.*

Roger's Rule: Installing a new program will usually screw up at least one old one.

Updating Your Software

There are two reasons to update your software. The first happens when you change something about your computer—you get a new printer, you change video cards, add a mouse, and so forth. This may require you to reconfigure your software so it will work with the new equipment. If you are at all unsure about this, get help for this one. Some programs make it pretty easy to add a new printer driver or whatever, but others can be a pain. Especially if this is a company situation, get the company's computer support person to make the changes.

The second reason is that periodically the software company will issue a new, improved version. Sometimes this is actually an improvement. Other times it is merely an excuse to separate you from some cash. Think carefully before you send away for that new version. Ask yourself whether the new features the manufacturer is making such a big deal about actually matter to you. If they don't, skip it and save your money.

If you have ignored the previous upgrade notice from your favorite friendly software company and are now a full revision behind, you might want to consider getting the update the next time they do a major upgrade. Otherwise you run the risk of getting so far behind that they won't support the older version. Then when you buy a new printer you might not be able to run it using the older software. But never bother updating software you don't use.

☞ See "Program Versions—What Do All Those Numbers Mean?" in Chapter 2 for help in deciphering upgrade numbers.

Shareware—
The Try Before You Buy Software

One kind of software is designed to be tried out before you buy it. This is called *shareware*. The idea is that you get it from someone who already has it and try it out on your machine, doing the tasks you intend to use it for. If you like it, then you "register" your copy by sending a check to the person who wrote the software in the first place. In return, you usually get a printed version of the manuals, access to a support line, and frequently some additional features or upgrades.

This is a great idea, and some of the software is very good. Most of it comes from smaller companies that don't have access to the distribution channels of the big guys. The quality of the software ranges from very professional to horrible though, so it is a lot like going to a garage sale. Sometimes you find a gem, but just as often you find junk. On the other hand, you only have to pay for the stuff you actually use.

Finding shareware can be a catch-as-catch-can proposition, but you can

1. *Ask any computerphiles you know.*

2. *Go to the funkiest computer store around and look for bins of shareware, catalogs, and magazines.*

3. *Go to a bookstore and look for the SYBEX Shareware Treasure Chest series. Some very cool programs are available in this series, and the accompanying text and pictures give you a good idea of what you're getting before you lay out much dough.*

Chapter 13

CARE AND FEEDING OF YOUR HARD DISK

Schnur's Rule of Hard Disks: No matter how large the hard disk, the need for space will always exceed the available space by ten percent.

WHOLE BOOKS HAVE been written about taking care of hard disks, which is nice if you have nothing better to do with your life than read about hard disks. But even those of us with lives to lead need to understand some basics about our hard disks, since this is where all the work we do on our computers is stored.

In this chapter, you will learn what a directory is and why it is sometimes called a subdirectory. You will learn how to find your way around on your hard disk and how to check the health and happiness of your hard disk.

Directory Assistance—Not 555-1212

Think of a directory as a box to put things in. You can have big boxes or little boxes. And each box can contain things (files) or more boxes (directories), or a combination of the two. The name of the directory is like the label on the outside of the box. It *should* tell you something about what is in the box, but if it doesn't, the only way to see what is inside is to open it up and take a look.

Your hard disk, then, is like a big box that has all the other boxes in it. How many other boxes and how many boxes inside boxes inside boxes you have is mostly a function of how compulsive you are about organizing. A certain amount of organizing is essential, but don't get carried away with it.

What Is a Root Directory?

The *root directory* is really the big box in which all other boxes fit. Every disk has a main directory called the root directory. It is identified by the leading backslash character (\). To change to the root directory of the drive you are on, type

    CD \

☞ *For more information on the CD (Change Directory) command, see "Changing Directories" in Chapter 1.*

☞ *When you are in a directory, you are* **logged** *to that directory. If you change drives, your current directory on the old drive doesn't change.*

☞ *The root directory has a tendency to get cluttered up with all sorts of files that don't belong there. If you can't find a file in the directory where you thought you left it, check the root directory.*

If That's a Directory, Then What's a Subdirectory?

There really isn't a difference between a directory and a subdirectory. All directories are subdirectories, except the root directory. A directory is a subdirectory of another directory if it is contained within the other

About DOS—Nerd Notes You Can Ignore

Each subdirectory contains two place holders in it called . and .. (pronounced *dot* and *dot-dot*). Dot is shorthand for the current directory (whatever it is) and dot-dot is shorthand for the current directory's parent. So, if you are working on your 1994 budget projections, and your current directory is

    C:\QPRO\BUDGET\1994

then all you need to do to change directories to your main BUDGET directory is type

    CD ..

directory. The subdirectory of a directory is called a "child" directory. Just as there can be many smaller boxes inside a larger one, there can be more than one child of a parent directory.

So, for example, you could have a QPRO directory that has all your Quattro Pro files in it. That directory could then have a child directory called BUDGET, which could then have subdirectories for 1993 and 1994. In this structure, BUDGET is both a child (of QPRO) and a parent (of 1993 and 1994). Then, in the 1993 directory, you would have your actual worksheets—JAN.WQ1, FEB.WQ1, and so on.

☞ *Subdirectories are also spoken of as being "under" another directory. This is because drives are often shown as a sort of upside-down tree with the root directory on top and the directories and subdirectories branching out below.*

☞ *The DOS Shell provides a good visual representation of the directory structure of your hard disk. See Chapter 4 for help on opening up the DOS Shell and poking around inside.*

The Name Game—Directory Edition

Directories follow the same naming rules as file names. They can be up to eight characters long, plus up to three characters for an extension. Don't use the extension when you're naming directories, because it makes directories look too much like files.

Hard Disk

☞ *Directory names should be kept as short as possible, but they should be descriptive. It is easier and quicker to type*

CD \UTIL

than

CD \UTILITY

but they both are equally descriptive. A directory name of UT, however, is carrying this a bit far.

☞ *For details about allowable names for files and directories, see "Naming Files (and Directories Too)" in Chapter 15.*

How Do I Tell If It's a File or a Directory?

When you use the DIR command you will get a list of files that also includes directories. For example, if you are at the root directory of the C drive and type in

DIR

you will get a list that includes all the files in the root directory plus all the directories. The directories will have a date and time next to them like the files, but will be marked as <DIR>.

If you use the command

DIR /W

the directories will be harder to distinguish because they are not marked as <DIR>. Instead, they have brackets around their names.

How to Get a List of Directories Only

If you have DOS 5 or 6, type in the following at the prompt:

DIR /AD

This is asking DOS for a list of "files" with the **A**ttribute of **D**irectory. Even hidden directories will show up in the listing.

If you have an earlier version of DOS, try typing in

C:\DIR *.

This will give you a list of everything that doesn't have an extension in that root directory. If you have any actual files without an extension, you can tell them from the directories because the files will not have that telltale <DIR> designation.

☞ This is yet another reason to either upgrade your DOS or make sure your directory names don't have extensions and your file names do.

Making a New Directory

Making your very own directories to stuff stuff into couldn't be easier. If you want the directory to be in the root directory of your disk, go to the root directory and type in

        MD *name*

MD stands for **M**ake **D**irectory, of course. And *name* is whatever you want to name the directory.

If you want to put the directory inside another directory as a subdirectory, include the path in the command. For example, if you want to make a directory called POEMS in your main WORD directory, just type in

        MD \WORD\POEMS

Now when you are using WORD for DOS you will have a POEMS directory in which to save your work.

Finding Your True Path

A *path name* is a like a road map telling DOS how to find a particular location on your hard disk. A full path name starts with the drive and proceeds through every layer of directory to get to a specific spot.

For example, if you have a file called TREES.DOC in your POEMS directory under your WORD directory on your C drive, the full path name for this treasure would be

        C:\WORD\POEMS\TREES.DOC

This would be enough information for DOS or any DOS program to locate the file. That's

C:	Drive name
\	Root directory
WORD	Directory in the root directory
POEMS	Subdirectory inside the WORD directory
TREES.DOC	File inside the POEMS subdirectory

Path names can get very long, so take the time to type them in carefully and check your typing as you go. You don't have to include the drive name if you're logged to that drive, but it's a good idea to include it at least *mentally*, so you're sure where you're going.

If you are specifying a path to a directory under where you are, you don't need to include any directories above your location. For example, if you're already in the WORD directory and you need to specify a path to the same file as above, you can type in

```
POEMS\TREES.DOC
```

☞ *If you get the error message "Path not found" you probably made a typing error. Check to be sure you're on the right drive and try again.*

The PATH Command

In your AUTOEXEC.BAT you probably have a line that starts with the PATH command. When you are instructed to put something in your PATH or some wiseguy asks "Is that program on your PATH?" this is what they're talking about.

When you type in the name of a program at the DOS prompt, DOS looks for that program (a file with the .COM, .EXE, or .BAT extension), first in the current directory and then along the PATH. The PATH statement in your AUTOEXEC.BAT file may say something like this:

```
PATH C:\;C:\DOS;C:\WORD;C:\UTIL;
```

So if you were to type in the name of a program at the prompt, DOS would look for that program first in the directory you're in, whatever that is. If it didn't find the program there, it would start down the PATH, looking first in the root directory of drive C (C:\). If the program is not to be found there, the search continues in the DOS directory, followed by the WORD directory, followed by the UTIL directory.

If the program name is not to be found in the PATH, you will get the dread "Bad command or file name" error message. If a program you use a lot doesn't add itself to your PATH statement, you'll want to add it. To add a directory to your PATH, open the AUTOEXEC.BAT file using DOS EDIT. Move the cursor to the end of the PATH statement. If there's not a semicolon at the end, add one. Then type in the drive and directory name and a semicolon. For example to add WP51 to the above PATH, I'd type in

```
C:\WP51;
```

so the whole PATH would look like this:

```
PATH C:\;C:\DOS;C:\WORD;C:\UTIL;C:\WP51;
```

☞ *See "Using DOS EDIT to Change Your Files" in Chapter 11 for information on editing the AUTOEXEC.BAT file.*

☞ *DOS goes through each directory looking for a file with the name you specified and with the extension .COM, .EXE, or .BAT (in that order). So if you have both a Q.EXE and a Q.BAT in the same directory, Q.EXE will be found first.*

☞ *If you have two programs with the same name on your drive, DOS will execute the one earliest in the PATH statement.*

☞ *A PATH statement is limited to 127 characters. A semicolon separates each directory being searched.*

☞ *No matter what anybody tells you, it doesn't really matter whether a directory is at the front or at the end of the PATH statement. On old, slow computers it might take a millisecond longer for DOS to find a program in a directory at the end of the PATH, but who cares?*

Moving around in Directories

If your prompt doesn't tell you what your current directory is, type in the **C**urrent **D**irectory command:

CD

If you want to change directories, the same command magically becomes **C**hange **D**irectory. Just add the name of the directory you want to change to. So if you want to go to the root directory, type in

CD \

If you want to go to the POEMS subdirectory under your WORD directory, type in

CD \WORD\POEMS

☞ For more information on changing directories, see "Changing Directories" in Chapter 1.

☞ For more on paths, see "Finding Your True Path" above.

How Much Room? The CHKDSK Command

CHKDSK, short for **CH**ec**K** **D**i**SK**, gives you a lot of information about your disk.

To run CHKDSK, exit Windows or the DOS Shell so you are at the DOS prompt, and type in

CHKDSK

The primary function of CHKDSK is to report on the health of your hard disk. It looks for stray pieces of files that somehow got lost (unattached clusters), or attached to more than one file (cross-linked), or any of several other problems. Most of the problems aren't very serious and are generally the result of rebooting the computer or turning the power off without first exiting the program you are working in.

Figure 13.1 shows an example of a CHKDSK report. If the disk was given a volume name at the time it was formatted, the first lines will show that name plus the date it was formatted. Next comes the serial number of the disk and five lines of information about the total

FIGURE 13.1:
CHKDSK gives you a lot
of information.

```
C:\>CHKDSK
Volume Serial Number is 199F-70FB

170266624 bytes total disk space
  8032256 bytes in 4 hidden files
   634880 bytes in 147 directories
137801728 bytes in 3047 user files
 23797760 bytes available on disk

     4096 bytes in each allocation unit
    41569 total allocation units on disk
     5810 available allocation units on disk

   655360 total bytes memory
   446336 bytes free

C:\>
```

amount of disk space, the number and total size of hidden files, the number and size of directories, the number and total size of the regular (user) files, and the amount of free space left on the disk. It then gives you three lines of essentially useless information about the allocation units on the disk, and finally it tells you exactly how many bytes of total DOS memory you have and how many of those are available for use (free).

☞ *Don't run CHKDSK from the DOS Shell or from inside Windows. You should only run CHKDSK from the bare DOS prompt.*

☞ *If CHKDSK reports "File allocation table bad…" or some file "is cross-linked," proceed immediately to "Scrambled FAT" or "CHKDSK Says I Have Cross-Linked Files!" in Chapter 17.*

Run CHKDSK— Nothing to Lose but Your Chains

You should run the CHKDSK command once a week. If you have a problem with your hard disk, CHKDSK can sometimes give you an early warning. If you get no error message, but just a report back like that in Figure 13.1, then you can relax. If, however, you get an error message about lost allocation units or unattached clusters, chances are you turned the computer off without exiting the program you were in. This results in bits and pieces of files being strewn about the landscape of your hard disk. Usually this is *not* serious.

Hard Disk

When this happens, CHKDSK will report that it was unable to fix the problems it found and that you need to run CHKDSK with the /F switch. Go ahead and do this by typing in

```
CHKDSK /F
```

That's F for **F**ix. This time, when you get the question "Convert lost chains to files?" press Y for Yes. This will create one or more files in the root directory of your disk called FILE0001.CHK, FILE0002.CHK, and so forth. Sometimes DOS gurus and DOS books will lead you to believe there is something you can make of these files. This is a cruel hoax. Unless the only copy of your doctoral dissertation has somehow disappeared, go ahead and delete the files. Type in

```
DEL \FILE*.CHK
```

If, however, you have good reason to believe that your masterwork is among those clusters, get help before you delete anything.

DEFRAG This, Jack!

When DOS writes a file to your disk, it tends to put it pretty much anywhere it finds room. Which would be fine, except that it tends to put a piece of the file here, a piece there, and pretty soon you have files spread all over your hard disk.

Now this isn't a problem for DOS. It can find the pieces pretty easily, since it knows where it put them. But it is a problem for you. Since DOS has to go to several different places on the hard disk to get the file, it takes longer than if it could just read it in one big piece, all from the same section of the hard disk. When you have a file spread over multiple places on your hard disk, the file is said to be *fragmented*. The more fragmentation of files you have, the slower your hard disk will run.

With DOS 6, Microsoft includes a disk defragmentation program called DEFRAG. To run DEFRAG, exit Windows or the DOS Shell so that you are all the way out to the bare DOS prompt. Then simply type in

```
DEFRAG
```

and you are on your way. Select the C drive as the one you want to optimize, click on OK, then click on the Optimize button when you get

Hard Disk

Read This If You Don't Have DOS 6

In earlier versions of DOS, you had to buy a third-party utility to *compress* or defrag your hard disk. All the major utilities packages included a defragger, so if you have PC Tools, Norton Utilities, or any of several other packages, you can use one that came with your utility package. With PC Tools, it is called COMPRESS, and with Norton it is called SPEEDISK or SD. They all work pretty much the same, though each has a slightly different look or feel.

the chance. For those of you with an insatiable need to tinker, you can mouse around in the menu and change the sort order of your files and other options. For the rest of the rational world, just take the defaults.

☞ *You should run DEFRAG at least once a week if you use your computer very much at all. Your hard disk will work faster and it will be much more likely that you can recover your data in the event of a disaster, since each file is stored in one lump.*

Double Your Hard Disk, Double Your Fun

An outstanding addition to DOS that came along with DOS 6 is Double-Space, a program that lets you double the space on your hard disk (well, almost double) without spending a dime on new hardware.

The disadvantage of DoubleSpace, like so many things in life, is once you've done it, you can't undo it.

To run DoubleSpace, just leave Windows or the DOS Shell, go to the DOS prompt, and type in

    DBLSPACE

You'll get what's called a Welcome screen. Just press Enter. You'll then get a chance to choose between Express and Custom setups. Choose Express and press Enter again.

You'll get a confirmation screen. Press C to choose drive C as the object of DoubleSpace's attention. DoubleSpace will do its thing, and when it's finished, you will have a much bigger drive C and a new drive that contains all the magic files that make this much bigger drive C possible. The new drive will also contain any files that could not be compressed, either because they contain some sort of error or because they will not work on a compressed drive. Don't fiddle with any of the files on this new drive.

☞ *Be sure to quit all other programs before running DoubleSpace. You can't run it from the DOS Shell or from Windows.*

☞ *You need at least 1MB of free space on your hard disk to run Double-Space. Run CHKDSK (see "How Much Room? The CHKDSK Command" earlier in this chapter) to make sure you have this much available.*

☞ *If your hard disk is very big, pretty packed with data, or sort of on the elderly side, this process may take up to several hours. So don't run DoubleSpace when you're facing a deadline.*

☞ *If your computer already has a compressed hard drive or some sort of unusual configuration, get help with running DoubleSpace.*

Chapter 14

AN OUNCE OF PREVENTION

Britton's Lament: The likelihood of a hard disk crash is in direct proportion to the value of the material that hasn't been backed up.

MOST DISASTERS THAT can happen to your computer are avoidable. And those that aren't can be recovered from *if you take protective measures beforehand*. If the work you do on the computer is important to you and you would feel seriously perturbed if you lost any of it, then read this chapter.

Protecting Your FAT

The *File Allocation Table* (charmingly known as the *FAT*) is how DOS keeps track of all the files on your hard disk. In the FAT is each file's name, some useful information about the file such as its size and whether it has been backed up, and an address for where it is stored on the hard disk. This way, when DOS needs to read a file or write to it, it doesn't have to search through every file on your hard disk. All DOS needs to do is read the FAT. When DOS finds the name of the file it wants, DOS can go directly to the file.

If something should happen to damage the FAT, however, it becomes impossible for DOS to find the file. If you have DOS 5, you have MIRROR, a utility that can make a copy of your FAT and put it all the way at the opposite end of your disk, out of harm's way. This way, if one version of your FAT is lost, MIRROR's version will be available.

To make a copy of your FAT, use EDIT to add the following line to your AUTOEXEC.BAT file (you can put it anywhere):

```
C:\DOS\MIRROR
```

If you have DOS 6, you don't have to worry about this because the MIRROR utility is automatically run any time you format a drive. So your FAT is safe. (Doesn't that make you feel better?)

☞ *For help with DOS EDIT, see "Using DOS EDIT to Change Your Files" in Chapter 11.*

☞ *If you do find yourself with scrambled FAT, you will need help. A DOS guru armed with the Norton Utilities or a similar package may be able to redeem the situation, at least partially.*

Backups and Why You Really Should Do Them

The most important thing you can do to protect your work is to back up your hard disk. If you do this often, the worst that can happen is that you will lose any work since the last time you did a backup. Every single computer book tells you to do backups. Most people ignore this advice. Sooner or later, they regret it.

Minasi's Maxim: There are only two kinds of computer users. Those whose hard disk has crashed and those whose hard disk hasn't crashed—yet.

Backing Up—It Only Hurts the First Time

With DOS 6, Microsoft has provided a backup program that is simple, friendly, and effective. If you don't have DOS 6, upgrade. Or you can buy the same technology directly from Symantec because the backup program in DOS 6 is a modified version of Norton Backup. Other popular and friendly backup packages are Central Point Backup and FastBack.

The directions for backing up in this section assume you are running MSBACKUP from DOS 6, but they are essentially correct for any of the other backup utilities discussed above, though the individual steps will vary. It really doesn't matter which backup method you use. What matters is that you do the backup.

Prevention

Teaching MSBACKUP about Your Computer

The best way to get started with MSBACKUP is to get someone to help you set it up the first time. The whole process can be a bit intimidating, though it isn't really difficult. But if getting someone else to do the setup is not feasible, or you really want to do it yourself, here is what's involved.

Walker's Rule of Procedures: Before you do anything, you have to do something else first.

The first time you run MSBACKUP, you need to teach it about your computer. MSBACKUP handles this pretty automatically. All you need to do, usually, is press the Enter key periodically and swap a couple of floppies in and out of the drive. The process involves several steps, and even does a small backup to make sure that everything works as expected. Before you start, you will need two floppy disks of the same size as you will be using for backups. If you can, use high-density, $3^{1}/_{2}$-inch disks, since they take up less room and are less subject to physical abuse, but any floppies will do. When you are ready, type

    MSBACKUP

to begin. Since this is the first time, you will see a dialog box that says "Backup requires configuration for this computer" and offers you two choices: Start Configuration and Quit. Select Start Configuration, and you're on your way.

Next it will offer you a chance to configure your mouse and video screen. Just accept the default settings. MSBACKUP will put up another dialog box telling you to remove any floppies from your drives. Do so, then select Start Test.

MSBACKUP will run through even more tests, asking you for your input periodically. Just keep taking the defaults. The only exception will be if it chooses the wrong drive in the Backup To window. If it selects A and you want B since that is your $3^{1}/_{2}$-inch drive, just select B: followed by OK.

When the program is all ready to begin, it will prompt you to insert your first disk in the drive you selected and choose Continue. Stick the floppy in, hit Enter, and off it goes, merrily backing up files from your DOS directory to the floppy. If the disk you put in already has files on it, you will be warned and asked if it is OK to overwrite the files.

When the first floppy is full, MSBACKUP will beep at you and prompt you to put the second floppy in. This is the one time you don't need to wait for the light to go out. MSBACKUP, like virtually all high-speed backup programs, is smart enough to figure out how to handle the floppy drive without turning off the light. Just pop the first disk out and put the second one in. MSBACKUP will continue on its own.

At the completion of the backup, you will see an informational window that tells you how many files were backed up and how long it took. There is also a cheeky little line that tells you how long MS-BACKUP had to wait for you. The nerve. Anyway, once you acknowledge that, MSBACKUP will prompt you to put the first floppy in so it can compare the files on the floppies to the ones on your hard disk.

Follow the bouncing prompts some more, and when all is done, you will get another one of those cheeky little information boxes. This one tells you how well the files on the floppies compared to the originals on the hard disk. Press the Enter key a couple more times, and MSBACKUP should know all it needs to know about your system. Now you are ready to do a real backup.

Doing the Backup

When you finally finish the configuration the first time, you are faced with MSBACKUP's main menu. This is also the menu you'll see after typing

    MSBACKUP

when doing subsequent backups. Either way, click on Backup to start the backup.

Now you are at the Backup screen, which looks like Figure 14.1. From here you select drives and files to back up, which drive to back up to, and various options. I suggest that you get help from your computer

Prevention

FIGURE 14.1:

The Backup screen

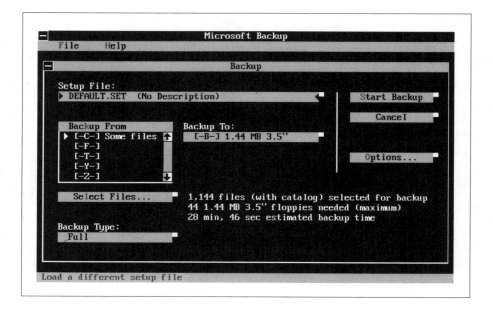

supervisor or a friendly nerd to set up your regular backups, but if that's not possible, you can do it yourself.

The important areas of the Backup screen and their functions are as follows:

☞ *Setup File* lets you choose from a list of predesigned backups.

☞ *Backup From* lets you choose which drives are included in your backup. Highlight the drive letter and press the Spacebar to select all the files on the drive.

☞ *Select Files* lets you choose which files from the currently selected drive you want to back up. Click on Select Files and press Enter. Use the arrow keys to highlight files and the Spacebar to select or deselect individual files.

☞ *Backup Type* lets you choose what type of backup to do: Full, Incremental, or Differential. A full backup is everything, an incremental is all the files that have changed since the last incremental or full backup, and a differential backup is all the files that have changed since the last full backup.

☞ *Backup To* lets you choose which drive and type of floppy to save the files on.

☞ *Backup Statistics* predicts the amount of time and number of floppy disks required for the current set of files. This prediction is usually on the high side of reality.

☞ *Action Buttons:* Start Backup starts the backup, Cancel exits the Backup window without running a backup, and Options lets you change the defaults. Don't change the defaults unless you really, truly know what you're doing.

Once you have selected the files you want to back up, select Start Backup and put a floppy into the drive.

☞ *Always number the floppies in a backup set as you use them. It's a lot harder later.*

☞ *Store backup disks away from stray magnetic fields, heat, and humidity. See "Do Not Fold, Spindle, or Mutilate" in Chapter 9 for good advice on preserving your floppies.*

Verifying Your Backup

Once you have made a backup, it is a good idea to verify that the floppies match what is on your hard disk. This is especially important the first time you use a set of disks, in case there is a bad disk. To compare the files on the floppies to the hard disk, select Compare from the main MSBACKUP menu. You'll get the Compare window, shown in Figure 14.2, on the screen.

The important parts of the Compare window and their functions are as follows:

☞ *Backup Set Catalog* lets you choose from a list of previous backups to compare.

☞ *Compare From* lets you choose which floppy drive the backed up files are on.

☞ *Compare To* lets you choose whether to compare the files to their original locations or to another drive or to a different directory. Normally you will choose their original locations.

Prevention

FIGURE 14.2:
The Compare window

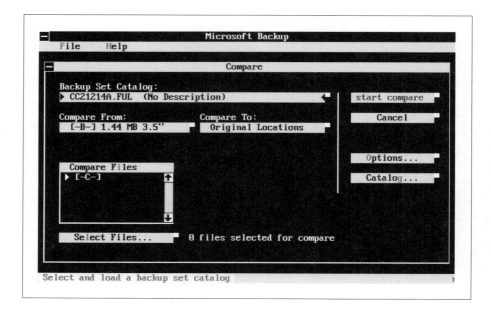

☞ *Compare Files* lets you choose which drives to compare. Normally, you should select all the files on the drive by highlighting the drive and pressing the Spacebar.

☞ *Select Files* lets you choose individual files to compare.

☞ *Action Buttons*: Start Compare begins the comparison, Cancel exits the Compare window, Options lets you decide if you want MS Backup to beep at you and if it should quit after the comparison, and Catalog retrieves a catalog (a list of the files in a backup) from floppy disk if it has been deleted from the hard disk.

Once you have selected the files to compare, highlight the Start Compare button and press Enter. Follow the prompts, and if all goes well, you will have a verified backup that you can feel confident will allow you to successfully recover your files in the event of some disaster.

Using Your Backup—Restoring Files

The real reason you create a backup is in the unlikely event that you need to restore a file or worse, a whole hard disk. If you have had a major disaster and need to restore your entire hard disk, get help.

Go first to Chapter 17, "Now You Need a Nerd," so you can make sure that the source of the disaster has been dealt with before you start restoring your files.

When you go for help, the absolute first thing that person will ask is "Of course, you have a backup, don't you?" This will be said with arched eyebrow and in a sarcastic tone. Then you can blandly look him or her straight in the eye and say, "Of course. I always do backups." This will be the most shocking news this person has ever heard. And you will have earned more moral credit than you can ever use up.

The steps for restoring files from a backup are exactly the same as for comparing them, and the windows look the same, except for saying Restore instead of Compare. Just select the files you need to restore, and then highlight the Start Restore button and press Enter.

☞ *Use MSBACKUP to transfer files between computers. Just back them up onto floppy, and then restore them on the other computer. Choose the Catalog action button, and select Retrieve to retrieve the backup catalog off the last floppy of the backup set.*

Viruses—What They Are and How to Avoid Them

Viruses are programs that are written with the deliberate intent of causing you and your computer grief. They range from the merely annoying to those that will destroy all the data on your hard disk.

If you only buy shrink-wrapped software from commercial outlets, never share disks with *anyone* else, never let anyone else use your computer, don't download programs from bulletin boards, and always wash your hands after using the bathroom, the chances of your getting a virus are very small. But if you work in an environment where computers are shared among several people, your chances of catching one of these bugs is pretty high.

Where Viruses Come From

Viruses are written by computer vandals. Nasty little mole-like creatures whose blighted lives are devoted to making others as miserable as they are. They write viruses and then take the product of their twisted psyches and put it on a bulletin board someplace—usually hidden inside a harmless-looking piece of shareware.

So a common source of computer viruses is a poorly supervised bulletin board. Since bulletin boards, at least the smaller ones, are the province of nerds, you are unlikely to get one this way. But if one of your friends or coworkers hands you a disk and tells you what a great new game is on it, you might want to think twice about accepting the disk. In the first place, if the disk is commercial software, using it would be software piracy. Even more to the point, though, is that you have no idea where that disk has been before you got it. It could well harbor a virus, waiting to destroy your hard disk.

Scott's Seven Rules for Safe Computing

1. Always buy software from a known commercial source.

2. Never share disks with a friend. Once the disk leaves your hands, don't take it back.

3. Always obtain new drivers direct from the manufacturer.

4. If you use shareware, get it direct from the author or from a known commercial source such as CompuServe or the Public Software Library.

5. Avoid small bulletin boards. Stick to the major commercial information services, such as CompuServe, GEnie, and Prodigy. Some small bulletin boards are excellent, but unless you are very sure of the operator, it just isn't worth the risk.

6. Check your computer regularly for viruses, using one of the major virus detectors. These include Microsoft AntiVirus (MSAV) in DOS 6, McAfee's SCAN, Norton AntiVirus, and Central Point AntiVirus.

7. Update your virus detector at least every three months. New viruses appear with appalling regularity.

How to Prevent Infection

The best way to prevent a virus infection is to follow the rules for safe computing above. And if you know that you occasionally violate some of rules one through five, then absolutely follow rules six and seven. If you have DOS 6, then you already have an excellent virus detector called MSAV for Microsoft AntiVirus. Just make sure that you get regular updates, since there are new viruses discovered often. Microsoft includes a coupon for regular updates to MSAV in the package for DOS 6.

The other major players in the antivirus game are Norton, Central Point (which designed Microsoft AntiVirus as well), and McAfee. The first two are available from most commercial software outlets, and McAfee's combination of SCAN and CLEAN is available to be downloaded either directly from their bulletin board or from Compu-Serve. See Chapter 21, "Murphy's Seven Programs That Can Save Your Cookies," for McAfee's address and phone numbers.

Checking for a Virus

To check your computer for an infection using MSAV from DOS 6, type in

```
MSAV  /P  /A
```

at the DOS prompt and press Enter. This will cause Microsoft AntiVirus to check all drives on you computer (*A* for **A**ll), except floppies, and report back the results. Include this command in your AUTOEXEC.BAT file to check for viruses every time you start your computer.

Prevention

To check a floppy to make sure it's safe, insert the floppy into the drive and type

    MSAV A: /P

Substitute **B:** in this command if you are checking a floppy in your B drive.

☞ *See "Using DOS EDIT to Change Your Files" in Chapter 11 for help in adding MSAV to your AUTOEXEC.BAT file.*

☞ *The /P switch above tells MSAV to operate at the command line. If you run MSAV without the /P prompt, you can get to all the menus and options inside MSAV. Trust me, you don't need any of that.*

☞ *For information on switches, see "Command Line Syntax" in Chapter 2.*

OK, That Didn't Work, Now How Do I Get Rid of It?

Should you be unfortunate enough to catch a virus, you will need to take immediate measures to prevent further damage. I suggest you ask your computer resource person or favorite nerd for help, since some of the viruses out there require pretty drastic action. If you have made a backup of your hard disk files, you should be able to recover the vast majority of your work, even if you are dealing with one of the nastiest viruses. The important thing, though, is to ensure that you don't become reinfected or cause others to get infected. If you have recently loaned a file or disk to a coworker or friend, call them up and warn them. If you just got a file or disk from a coworker or friend, they may be the source of your infection. Call them up and let them know, before they spread the virus to someone else.

Most viruses can be successfully removed by using the MSAV program from DOS 6 or any of the other programs described under "How to Prevent Infection." First, however, you need to turn your computer off and let it sit for ten seconds. While you are waiting, get out your original, write-protected DOS disks or your known, safe, antivirus boot disk. Put this disk in your A drive, and turn your computer back on. If you are using MSAV, then you will type, from the A> prompt:

    MSAV

Highlight Detect & Clean and press Enter. MSAV will eradicate any viruses it discovers. In some cases, however, the virus will have fatally mugged one or more files on your hard disk. In this case, you will need to restore the files from your backup. Aren't you glad you do backups?

☞ *For directions on how to make a safe antivirus boot floppy, see "Making an Emergency Disk" in Chapter 16.*

☞ *For help in making backups and restoring them, see "Doing the Backup" and "Using Your Backup—Restoring Files" earlier in this chapter.*

The Ultimate Security against Viruses

If you have DOS 6 you have VSAFE, a program that can provide you with complete protection against viruses. On the plus side, it's in your computer memory all the time on the alert for suspicious activity that would indicate a virus. On the minus side, it's in your computer memory all the time, using up some of your precious conventional memory.

You can type

VSAFE

at the DOS prompt and the program will be loaded into memory, but only for the current session. To have it loaded every time you start the computer, add VSAFE to your AUTOEXEC.BAT file. Using DOS EDIT, open the AUTOEXEC.BAT file and add a line (anywhere) that simply says

VSAFE

The program will now automatically check all files that are potential sources of infection. To remove VSAFE from memory, press the Alt key and the letter *V* at the same time. You'll get a screen of VSAFE Warning Options. Press Alt-U and VSAFE will be unloaded from your computer.

☞ *See "Using DOS Edit to Change Your Files" in Chapter 11 for help in editing your AUTOEXEC.BAT file.*

☞ *After you put VSAFE in your AUTOEXEC.BAT file, you still have to restart your computer for the change to take effect.*

Prevention

☞ *Type*

HELP VSAFE

at the DOS prompt for the explanation of all the options in the VSAFE Warning Options screen. You shouldn't turn anything that's on to off. Be aware that any additional options you turn on may slow your computer's operation noticeably. But don't worry, make a note of what you do, and if the result is a nuisance you can always go back and reverse the procedure.

Like all memory-resident programs, VSAFE can cause conflicts of varying severity in your system. Always unload VSAFE when you are running setup or install programs, or before running DoubleSpace. Run MSAV on installation disks as described in "Checking for a Virus" earlier in this chapter. Restart VSAFE after the program is installed and running OK.

If weird things start happening on your system, unload VSAFE and reboot. If that cures your problem, just run MSAV faithfully and leave VSAFE out of the equation.

Chapter 15

WHITHER FILES?

Jan's Rule of Navigation: If you don't care where you are, you're not lost.

FOR SOME REASON unknown to science, files on computers are often overcome by wanderlust. No matter how nicely you treat them, eventually one or more will stray. So in this chapter you'll get some advice on naming files and directories so they'll be easier to use and find. Later in the chapter there's also information on how to find these ungrateful files and directories when, despite your best efforts, they have unaccountably wandered away.

Naming Files (and Directories Too)

Every file needs a name. When you are staring blankly at a list of names in a directory, you will be glad you gave the file a useful name that conveys some information.

File names can be from one to eight characters long. Every file can also have an extension of one to three characters. The extension is separated from the main name by a period, as shown in the following example:

```
FILENAME.EXT
```

Every file in the same directory must have a unique name. For example, your WORD directory can have only one file called CHAP_ONE.TXT, but you can have as many files called CHAP_ONE.TXT as you have directories on your hard disk.

Unsolicited Advice on Naming Directories

All the rules for naming files apply as well to naming directories. But directories are more or less permanent parts of the landscape, so it's a good idea to make directory names as short and easy-to-type as possible. Avoid putting extensions on directory names. You will quickly find yourself annoyed at having to type in all that stuff all the time.

Legal Names for Files

The first eight characters of a file name can be any letters or numbers. The following names would be OK with the DOS Police:

```
WHATSUP
401
UNCLE
```

File names can also include the following characters from the keyboard:

```
_ ' ~ ! @ # $ % ^ & ( ){ } -
```

If you want to add your own extension, you can. You must specify the period and then add up to three more characters, as in the following examples:

```
WHATSUP.DOC
401.K
UNCLE.SAM
```

☞ *Some programs add their own extensions. You just provide the first part of the file name and the program provides the extension.*

☞ *File names are not case-sensitive. You can enter names in either upper- or lowercase.*

☞ *The extension is normally used to identify file types. It really is more efficient to use the main file name to define the contents of the file and the extension to define the file type. A bunch of file extensions are shown in the Table 15.1.*

You can use whatever extension you like, but beware of using ones that already "belong" to a specific program. The potential for confusion is high. Also, see the section "Dangerous Extensions" later in this chapter.

TABLE 15.1:
File Extensions

Extension	Program
SPREADSHEET	
.WK1	Lotus 1-2-3
.WK3	Lotus 1-2-3 version 3.x
.ALL	Allways (1-2-3)
.FMT	Impress (1-2-3)
.WQ1	Borland Quattro Pro
.WB1	Borland Quattro Pro for Windows
.XLS	Excel
WORD PROCESSING	
.DOC	Microsoft Word (DOS, Windows)
.RTF	Rich Text Format (generic text format)
.SAM	Lotus Ami Pro, Samna
.RFT	IBM Display Write (DCA-RFT format)
.ASC	ASCII text
.TXT	ASCII text
DATABASE	
.DB	Borland Paradox (DOS, Windows)
.DBF	Borland dBASE

Extension	Program
GRAPHICS	
.BMP	Windows bitmap
.GIF	Graphics Interchange Format
.DXF	Drawing Exchange Format (AutoCAD)
.CGM	Computer Graphics Metafile
.WPG	WordPerfect graphics
.ICO	Windows icon file
.TIF	Tagged Image File
.PCX	Paintbrush format
EXECUTABLE AND PROGRAM	
.COM	Command file
.EXE	Executable file
.BAT	Batch file
.DLL	Dynamic Link Library (Windows)
.OVL, .OVR	Overlay file
.SYS	System file
MISCELLANEOUS	
.HLP	Help file
.INI	Program initiation (configuration information)
.PIF	Program Information File (Windows)
.CFG	Configuration file
.BAK	Backup file
.NET	Network file
.BIN	Binary file
.DAT	Data file
.ZIP	Compressed file (PKZIP)
.LZH	Compressed file (LHARC)

Illegal Names for Files

DOS has strict rules about what you can and cannot use in file names. If you try to use any of the following characters in a file name, you will

> ### *Dweeb Alert! Making Up Truly Weird File Names*
>
> The so-called extended ASCII code has all sorts of weird characters that you can include in your file names if you are so inclined. For example, if you want a file with the name MY STORY, you can get the space by pressing the Alt key, and while holding it down press 255 on your numeric keypad. This means the actual "keyboard" name is M, Y, Alt-255, S, T, O, R, Y.
>
> Or if you wanted a file called I¥4U, you'd type in I, Alt-157, 4, U.
>
> For other characters, look in your DOS manual for a list of the 128 *extended* ASCII characters. You can use any of them in a file name.
>
> This is, of course, inefficient, pointless, stupid, and something you will want to try right away.

be treated rudely:

```
*  +  =  \  ¦  [  ]  ;  :  "  ,  <  >  ?  /
```

In addition to these, you can't use a period except to divide the main name from the extension. All these characters have special meaning to DOS and are not for the likes of you.

Your file also cannot be named any of the following: CLOCK$, CON, AUX, PRN, NUL, LPT1, LPT2, LPT3, COM1, COM2, COM3, or COM4. These are DOS device names, and as you know, it's not nice to confuse DOS.

Dangerous Extensions

Certain file-name extensions are special. Files that end with .COM, .BAT, and .EXE are program files. .SYS describes a system file. .OVL and .DLL are other extensions that DOS recognizes as being for specific types of files. With the exception of .BAT, these are not files that you will be making, so don't use these extensions; otherwise, chaos and madness will rule the earth and it'll be all your fault.

More Files

The DIR Command

The DIR command is used to display a list of files on disk. At the DOS prompt, type in

    DIR

and press the Enter key.

When you see a list of files after typing DIR, the information is in five columns. First is the file's name followed by the three-character extension. The extension is part of the file's name, though not all files may have an extension. Next is the file's size in *bytes*, or characters, followed by the date and time the file was created, or if it's been changed, the date and time of the most recent change.

To see a list of files in another directory on the same disk, specify the directory path name after the DIR command:

    DIR \WORD\POEMS

Press Enter and you will see all the files in the POEMS directory.

To see only a particular group of files, use the DIR command with the * wildcard. For example, to see all the files with the extension .BAK, type in

    DIR *.BAK

To see all the files that begin with the same letters, use the * wildcard again. So to see all the files that begin with the letters *MEMO*, type in

    DIR MEMO*

☞ For information on directories and path names, see Chapter 13, "Care and Feeding of Your Hard Disk."

☞ See "Legal Names for Files" earlier in this chapter for rules on file names and extensions.

☞ For definitions for and uses of wildcards, see "What's a Wildcard?" later in this chapter.

Displaying a Sorted DIR

The display of files you get when using the DIR command is not usually in any order that's helpful. To get the DIR command to sort the files for you, you need to use the O (for **O**rder) switch. The /O switch has several variations, as follows:

/ON	Sorts alphabetically by **N**ame
/OD	Sorts by **D**ate, earliest first
/OG	Sorts with directories **G**rouped before files

So, for example, to get an alphabetical listing of files on your A drive, you'd type in

```
A: DIR /ON
```

There's a space between the DIR and the /, but none between the rest of the characters.

More Ways to Look at DIR

The DIR command has several switches in addition to the sort options above. You can include one or more of the following to the DIR command:

/A	Includes all the files in the directory, even the system files and hidden files
/AD	Displays **D**irectory names only
/B	Lists only **B**are file and directory names
/P	Displays one **P**age at a time
/S	Displays all the files as well as the contents of all **S**ubdirectories
/W	Displays in **W**ide format, five columns across the screen

Put a space between switches, but not within the switch. So, for example, to see all the files on drive C, sorted alphabetically, one page at a time, you'd type in the following at the DOS prompt:

```
DIR /A /ON /P
```

More Files

The order of the switches doesn't matter, so you could just as easily type in

```
DIR /P /A /ON
```

☞ For information on switches, see "Command Line Syntax" in Chapter 2.

Finding Files That Have Wandered Away

Files do have a knack for wandering around. Sometimes you inadvertently save them to the wrong directory. Or you make a typing mistake while saving or while trying to retrieve. To find a file, you have to know all or part of its name.

If you have DOS 5 or DOS 6, open the DOS Shell and select Search from the File menu. Type in the name of the file and click on the OK button. DOS Shell will search the entire disk for you without a whimper and report its findings in the Search Results window. Press Esc to return to the DOS Shell file list window. If you don't know the whole file name, see "Finding Files You Don't Know a Lot About" below.

If you want to search from the DOS prompt, first try looking in the directory where you think it might be. Type

```
DIR /P
```

This will give you a page-at-a-time listing of the directory contents. If it's not in the directory you expected, you can search the entire disk. So, for example, if you're looking for a file called MR_PBODY, you'd type in

```
DIR \MR_PBODY /S
```

Press Enter. The /S switch tells DOS to include **S**ubdirectories in the search. If DOS locates the file, you'll see it on the screen, as in Figure 15.1.

The file MR_PBODY has been found in the WAYBACK directory. Use the CD command to move to that directory and you can get at the file.

FIGURE 15.1:
You can use DIR /S to find files from the DOS prompt.

```
C:\>DIR \MR_PBODY /S

  Volume in drive C has no label
  Volume Serial Number is 199F-70FB

Directory of C:\WAYBACK

MR_PBODY            27 01-13-93  11:50a
        1 file(s)            27 bytes

Total files listed:
        1 file(s)            27 bytes
                       23678976 bytes free

C:\>
```

☞ *Unfortunately, before DOS 5 there wasn't a useful DOS Shell, and the DIR command wouldn't let you search subdirectories. Another good reason to upgrade. But for those who cling to their older versions of DOS, check out Chapter 20, "Murphy's Eleven Favorite Pain-Relieving Programs," for programs that will help you do any kind of search in a jiffy.*

Finding Files You Don't Know a Lot About

It's always easier to find a file if you know its exact name, but of course, that's often not the case. You know *something* about the file name, but not everything.

If you're not sure if the file has an extension, type in

    DIR \MR_PBODY.* /S

If you're not sure how you spelled the file name, type in

    DIR \MR* /S

and you'll get a list of all the files that start with *MR*.

If there are lots of files that start with *MR*, add a /P to the above command so you can look at the files a page at a time.

If you search in the DOS Shell, type in

    MR_PBODY.*

More Files

or

```
MR*
```

and click on the OK button. DOS still searches the entire disk, but you don't have to enter any switches or commands to get the job done.

If you're not sure at all of the name, but think you'll know it when you see it, you're going to have to wander from directory to directory using the CD and DIR commands until you find what you're looking for. Sad, isn't it?

☞ For information on wildcards, see "What's a Wildcard?" later in this chapter.

☞ For navigation help, see Chapter 1, "Basic Training," for help with changing drives and changing directories.

☞ See Chapter 4, "The DOS Shell," for all you need to know about running DOS Shell.

☞ Chapter 20, "Murphy's Eleven Favorite Pain-Relieving Programs," has suggestions for programs that can make all this searching a lot less of a pain.

Finding Lost Directories

Lost directories are easy to find in DOS 5 or DOS 6. Just open the DOS Shell and select Single File List from the View menu. Next to the directory names in the Directory List will be a plus sign (+) if that directory has subdirectories. Click on the plus sign to see what's there. You can easily check every directory on the disk in a minute or less to find the subdirectory you're looking for.

If you insist on doing this from the command line, then type in

```
DIR \*.* /AD /S /P
```

The translation of the above command is something like this:

DIR	Get me a directory,
\	starting in the root directory
.	of all the files, regardless of name,

/AD	that have the directory attribute.
/S	Include all the subdirectories
/P	and do it a page at a time.

You'll get a page-at-a-time display of all the directories and subdirectories on your drive. When you see the one you want, press Ctrl-C to halt the search. Use CD to go to the location of the subdirectory.

☞ This only works in DOS 5 and 6. If you still have an older version of DOS, Chapter 20, "Murphy's Eleven Favorite Pain-Relieving Programs" lists several programs that can help.

☞ See Chapter 4, "The DOS Shell," for information on running DOS Shell.

☞ Chapter 2, "The DOS Prompt," has information on switches and command line syntax.

☞ The CD command is covered in "Changing Directories" in Chapter 1.

What's a Wildcard?

DOS has two wildcards—characters that stand in for other characters. One is the * (usually referred to as the star, even though we both know it's really an asterisk) and the other is the ? (referred to as the question mark, even though we both know it's really a question mark).

The * stands for any group of valid DOS characters and the ? stands for any single character. But the ? wildcard is strictly for those who do things just to prove they can. Stick with * and save ? for the pocket-protector crowd.

Wildcards work in many programs as well as in DOS commands.

Using the * Wildcard

You can use the * wildcard to stand in for one or more of characters in a file name. The best way to understand the use of the * is to see some examples.

The wildcard file name *.* matches *all* files.

The wildcard file name *.WK1 matches all files with the extension .WK1.

The wildcard file name SHERMAN.* matches all files that start with SHERMAN regardless of extension, including SHERMAN.DOC, SHERMAN, and SHERMAN.BAK.

The wildcard file name SHER*.* matches all files that start with SHER regardless of how they finish up. This would include all of the SHERMAN files above, plus the files SHERWOOD.DOC and SHERYL.RES.

One truly weird limitation of the star wildcard is that you can't use it in the middle of a name. For example, if you typed in

```
C*L.DOC
```

in an attempt to find all your files that start with C, end with L, and have the extension .DOC, you would instead get a listing of all the files that start with C and end with the extension .DOC. All of them. This is because once DOS sees the *, it ignores all the characters to the right until it reaches the file extension.

4

When you suddenly feel Fear, Loathing, Uncertainty, and Grief combined with the certain knowledge that things have gone horribly wrong, you're FLUGGED. This part will come to your rescue with things you can fix, things you need an expert for, plus error messages from hell and how to deal with them.

I'M FLUGGED!

How to Get UnFLUGGED

Chapter 16

THINGS YOU CAN FIX

Masters's Maxim: Anything can be made to work if you fiddle with it long enough.

Masters's Mom's Maxim: If you fiddle with something long enough, you'll break it.

SOME OF THE things that go wrong at the computer are problems you can protect against. Chapter 14, "An Ounce of Prevention," deals with the sort of things you can do to forestall disaster. At the other end of the scale are the truly perplexing hardware and software problems that cry out "Now You Need a Nerd!" (Chapter 17).

But for lots of everyday annoyances, you won't need help. Some problems may look scary initially, but you can handle them yourself.

These include the following:

☞ Your computer stops in the middle of the boot process and won't go any further. See "How to Make a Boot Floppy and What to Do with It."

☞ You lost a file, and you think it may have been accidentally deleted. See "Where Is That *&^%# File?"

☞ You type in the command for your new program, but it doesn't work. See "What Do You Mean 'Bad Command or File Name?'"

☞ The command you have been using to start your word processor (or whatever) suddenly stops working. See the section "It Worked Yesterday."

☞ You suddenly have an irresistible urge to type **FORMAT C:** and you succumb to it. This one is a toughie, but if you act *immediately*, you have a chance. See "Format C:—How to Unformat" later in this chapter.

☞ Thinking you are simply cleaning off all the files on a floppy disk, you type **DEL *.*,** only to find you are actually in the directory where your doctoral thesis was stored. See "Del *.* and How to Recover from It—The UNDELETE Command."

How to Make a Boot Floppy and What to Do with It

When you make changes to your computer, there is one bit of preventative medicine you should do *before* you start. Make a current boot floppy. This is a floppy disk that will let you boot your computer and restore your currently working configuration after you have done something really dumb.

There are actually two kinds of boot floppies, and you should have both. The first is what I call an OOPS disk. It is simply a copy of your current configuration on a bootable disk. Its sole purpose is to let you boot the computer and copy your CONFIG.SYS and AUTOEXEC.BAT back onto your hard disk. You should update this floppy every time you permanently change your CONFIG.SYS or AUTOEXEC.BAT.

What Makes a Disk Bootable and Do I Care?

When your system starts up, it looks for a disk first in drive A. If none is there it goes to drive C. The computer examines the first disk it finds to see if it contains the *system* files. When a disk with system files is found, the computer uses that disk's information to start the system running. If a disk with system files is in drive A, that disk will be used to tell the computer about itself. Computers can normally be booted only from drive A or drive C.

A bootable disk is a disk your computer can use to get itself started. By definition, your hard disk must be a bootable disk for things to work. But a floppy can also be made bootable.

The second kind of boot floppy could be called your Emergency disk. It has the programs on it you might need to recover from a problem more serious than screwing up your configuration.

Making an OOPS disk

Take a floppy that doesn't have anything on it that you want to save, put it into your A drive (and no, this time the B drive isn't good enough), and type

```
FORMAT A: /S
```

The *S* in the above command copies your system files to the floppy. When it's done formatting, you can copy your current CONFIG.SYS and AUTOEXEC.BAT to the OOPS disk. Type

```
COPY C:\CONFIG.SYS A:
```

When that's done, type in

```
COPY C:\AUTOEXEC.BAT A:
```

There, that was pretty easy. Now you can make any changes you want to the AUTOEXEC.BAT and CONFIG.SYS files on your hard disk. (See "Using DOS EDIT to Change Your Files" in Chapter 11 for help doing this.) If something goes wrong in your edit that causes your computer not to boot up properly, simply put this floppy in your A drive and restart the computer. When it has booted up and you're still at the A> prompt, type

```
COPY *.* C:\
```

This will copy your *original* AUTOEXEC.BAT and CONFIG.SYS files back to your hard drive. You can remove the floppy, reboot your computer, and you are back to where you started.

☞ See "Reset, Reboot, and the Fine Art of Ctrl-Alt-Del" in Chapter 1 for more on booting.

☞ See Chapter 11, "Your System Defined," for all kinds of stuff on AUTOEXEC.BAT and CONFIG.SYS.

☞ For help formatting a floppy, see (oddly enough) "How to Format a Floppy" in Chapter 9.

Making an Emergency disk

This is the disk for more serious problems. It will include programs to undelete files, unformat disks, and repair virus damage.

Before you create this disk, run a virus scanner to make sure you don't have a virus anywhere on your computer. If you have DOS 6, you can use MSAV for this. See "Checking for a Virus" in Chapter 14 for details.

After you've made sure your system is virus-free, put a fresh, unformatted floppy in the A drive (again, B won't do, it must be A) and type

```
FORMAT A: /S
```

Then, with DOS EDIT, create a CONFIG.SYS on the floppy by typing

```
EDIT A:\CONFIG.SYS
```

Type the following lines in this file:

```
FILES=30
BUFFERS=30
```

Select Save from the File menu. After the light goes out on your drive A, select New from the File menu. Type in the following lines:

```
PATH=C:\DOS
PROMPT $P$G
```

Select Save from the File menu. In the file name box that appears, type in

```
A:\AUTOEXEC.BAT
```

and press Enter. Select Exit from the File menu.

You've just made an AUTOEXEC.BAT and a CONFIG.SYS file on the floppy in drive A. These files have in them the minimum you need to operate should you need to use them.

Next, to copy the other files you'll need to the floppy, type in the following lines at the DOS prompt, pressing Enter after each line.

```
C:
CD \DOS
COPY UN*.* A:
COPY MSAV*.* A:
```

There, you've created your Emergency disk. Write-protect the disk, stick a nice, distinctive label on it, and store it where you can find it, if and when you need it.

☞ See Chapter 3, "Files and the Things You Do with Them," for all the variations on copying files.

☞ "Using DOS EDIT to Change Your Files" is in Chapter 11.

☞ Information on write-protecting floppies is in "Write-Protecting Floppies" in Chapter 9.

Where Is That *&^%# File?

OK, you have looked everywhere, and you can't find a file you *know* you had yesterday. You have tried everything in Chapter 15, "Whither Files?" and you suspect you have accidentally deleted the file. After you are done panicking, try the following.

Change to the directory where you *think* you left the file. If you are pretty sure the file is called STANLEY.DOC, then type in

```
UNDELETE STANLEY.DOC
```

You'll get a bunch of strange stuff on the screen that will look like Figure 16.1. At the bottom of the screen is the line you're looking for.

```
C:\>UNDELETE STANLEY.DOC

UNDELETE - A delete protection facility
Copyright (C) 1987-1993 Central Point Software, Inc.
All rights reserved.

Directory: C:\
File Specifications: STANLEY.DOC

    Delete Sentry control file not found.

    Deletion-tracking file not found.

    MS-DOS directory contains     1 deleted files.
    Of those,     1 files may be recovered.

Using the MS-DOS directory method.

    ?TANLEY  DOC        16  2-15-93 11:28a  ...A  Undelete (Y/N)?Y
    Please type the first character for ?TANLEY .DOC:
```

First you're asked if you want to undelete the file. Resist the impulse to shout "NO, I was just typing in UNDELETE for my HEALTH!!" and enter Y for Yes. Then you need to provide the "missing" first letter in the file name. Just do it and you'll get your file back.

If you are not absolutely sure of the file name, change to the directory where you think the file ought to be and type

    UNDELETE /LIST

This will give you a list of all the files in the current directory that DOS knows have been deleted. The first letter of each file will be shown

UNDELETE: So What's the Scoop on That Missing First Letter?

When you use DELETE, the file is in fact, not deleted. It disappears from view because DOS changes the first letter of the file name into a small Greek letter sigma (σ) so it no longer shows up in any of your file listings.

When you use UNDELETE, DOS goes looking for the file name you supply—minus the first letter. That's why DOS has to ask for that first letter. You provide a letter, DOS uses it to replace the sigma, and presto! The file is back from the dead.

as a ?, so our file STANLEY.DOC will appear as ?TANLEY.DOC. If the list is long and scrolls by too fast to see it all, type the command

```
UNDELETE /LIST | MORE
```

which will let you see a page at a time. That's UNDELETE followed by a space, then a forward slash and LIST. This is followed by another space, the pipe symbol (usually on the same key as the backward slash), another space, and MORE.

If you see something that looks like it might be the file you are looking for, great. Write down the name and type in the UNDELETE command again, this time with the correct name. If the name doesn't appear here, then try changing to the root directory and typing

```
UNDELETE /LIST | MORE
```

to see if it got left there somehow.

☞ There's more on UNDELETE in "Undeleting a File" in Chapter 3.

When UNDELETE Won't

Someday you will try UNDELETE and get the message "Not recovered. The file's data space is being used by another file." This means part or all of your file has been overwritten by another file.

If this is a file you cannot *live* without, don't do another thing until you rush out and buy Norton Utilities (any version). With UnErase, a program that is part of Norton Utilities, you can "manually" unerase a file that has been partially overwritten. Get a more experienced pal to help you if you can. However, you can do it yourself if you carefully follow the instructions that come with Norton Utilities.

☞ If you find this happening to you with some regularity, see "Undeleting a File" in Chapter 3 for information on how to increase the protective capacity of UNDELETE.

What Do You Mean "Bad Command or File Name?"

OK, so you installed this neat new program, followed all the directions, and you just took the last floppy disk out and you are ready try it out. The program's manual says to just type **NEAT** to run their neat program, so you do, and DOS says

```
Bad command or file name
```

Wait a minute here! You did everything right, why won't it work? The answer is that you probably need to reboot your computer and try again. Many programs make changes to your CONFIG.SYS or AUTOEXEC.BAT file, and in order for these changes to take effect, you need to reboot your computer. Installation programs often modify your PATH so that DOS can find your new program.

☞ If the program didn't plop itself into your PATH and it's a program you expect to use a lot, maybe you should add it yourself. For more on the PATH command, see "The PATH Command" in Chapter 13.

☞ For more on rebooting, see "Reset, Reboot, and the Fine Art of Ctrl-Alt-Del" in Chapter 1.

☞ For more information about your CONFIG.SYS and AUTOEXEC.BAT files, see Chapter 11, "Your System Defined."

It Worked Yesterday

One of the most frustrating things that can happen is to have a program or command that you use every day suddenly stop working. Usually, the explanation for this is simple, and you just need to work through a few things to see what caused it. But before you start straining the brain, first try doing a cold boot of your computer. Turn the power off, wait ten seconds or so, remove any floppy disks from your drives, and then turn it back on. Perhaps 90 percent of all problems can be fixed this way.

If this doesn't work, then the first question to ask yourself is "Did *I* change anything in the last day or two?" Specifically, did you

☞ Install a new program?

☞ Delete some files, especially in the root directory of your hard disk?

☞ Add any new hardware that might have changed your system or the location of files on it?

☞ Move some files from hither to yon?

If the answer to any of these questions is yes, then you have a pretty good idea of where to look for the problem.

If you installed a new program, the program itself may have modified your CONFIG.SYS or AUTOEXEC.BAT file. Most programs that do this save a copy of the old file, usually with an extension such as .BAK, .SAV, .000, or another extension that indicates which program created it. Look for these files in the root directory of drive C by typing

```
DIR C:\AUTOEXEC.*
```

This will give you a list of all the files that start with AUTOEXEC. For CONFIG.SYS, substitute CONFIG.* in the above.

Check the date and time on your AUTOEXEC.BAT file. If the date indicates it has been changed recently (like it has today's date or yesterday's date), then you will need to figure out where the changes are. Compare the file AUTOEXEC.BAT to the file you suspect is the previous version. For example, to compare AUTOEXEC.BAT to AUTOEXEC.BAK, you would use the DOS command FC, which is short for **F**ile **C**ompare. Type in the following at the DOS prompt

```
FC AUTOEXEC.BAT AUTOEXEC.BAK
```

The result of this command looks something like Figure 16.2. It shows the line that is different plus the line before and the line after. This should give you enough information to figure out what got changed and how to change it back. Use DOS EDIT to correct your AUTOEXEC.BAT or CONFIG.SYS and then reboot your computer.

FIGURE 16.2:

Using FC to compare two files

```
C:\>FC AUTOEXEC.BAT AUTOEXEC.BAK
Comparing files AUTOEXEC.BAT and AUTOEXEC.BAK
***** AUTOEXEC.BAT
PROMPT $p$g
PATH C:\DOS;C:\UTIL
SET TEMP=C:\DOS
***** AUTOEXEC.BAK
PROMPT $p$g
PATH C:\DOS;
SET TEMP=C:\DOS
*****


C:\>
```

If this isn't the problem and you installed a new board or another piece of hardware, try removing that board temporarily. If everything works again, call the manufacturer's technical support phone number and work through the problem with them. If things still aren't working, then you probably still need to contact the board's manufacturer, since chances are they made other changes to your system that you haven't yet found.

☞ See "Using DOS EDIT to Change Your Files" in Chapter 11 for help in editing your AUTOEXEC.BAT or CONFIG.SYS file.

A Tirade You Can Safely Skip Over

All too many installation programs these days seem to think they can play fast and loose with your computer. Some will warn you they are making changes, though they won't tell you what those changes are or let you stop them, and others are even worse. They make changes without even warning you! How rude!

If you have problems because of this kind of installation behavior, *complain!* It is quite easy for the program to be set up in such a way that you are told what changes are proposed and allowed to edit them. So don't let them run roughshod over you. Whose computer is it, anyway?

Format C:—How to Unformat

OK, you really did it this time. Even though DOS asked you several times if you were *really* sure, you kept saying yes, and you formatted your hard disk.

Boy, do *you* feel stupid! But stop. Don't compound the error! And don't do *anything* else. Take out your Emergency disk and put it in your A drive. OK, now reboot your computer, and type

```
UNFORMAT C:
```

You will be presented with a suitably strong warning message from DOS, and since you know why and how you got here, you may answer Yes.

After some alarming clicking sounds, your disk will be rebuilt. You will need to restart your system before going on.

☞ *This command often works on a floppy disks too. If the disk was not formatted using DOS 5 or DOS 6, though, you're out of luck.*

If You Have an Earlier Version of DOS

Before DOS 5, recovering from the unintentional formatting of your hard disk was a much less certain process. It is still possible if you touch nothing, but you will probably need help. Don't be shy about asking for help in this case. Call your favorite nerd or computer resource person immediately, and offer them whatever bribe it takes. They will have to use a third-party recovery utility, but there is still a chance they will get it all. And while you're waiting for them, you can either contemplate the error of your ways or go out and buy the DOS upgrade.

Del *.* and How to Recover from It

Sooner or later, you are going to do this one. Even though DOS always warns you and asks you if you are sure, sooner or later you will be sure you are just deleting all the files on a floppy, and find out you are actually deleting all the files in the root directory of your hard disk.

As soon as you get that sick feeling that maybe you weren't so sure after all—STOP! If you immediately issue the DOS UNDELETE command, you should have no problem recovering the files. Just type

```
UNDELETE *.*
```

and DOS will start the process of saving your cookies. First, it will display a file name, except the first letter will have been replaced with a ?, and ask you if you want to undelete the file. If you do, respond Y for Yes and then type in the first letter of the file name. If you can't remember, just fake it. You can always rename the file later when you figure out what it should have been.

This process will be repeated, one file at a time, until all the files are recovered.

A Cautionary Note for Those with Older DOS Versions

UNDELETE was a command introduced in version 5 of DOS. So if you haven't upgraded, you don't have this available. However, there are a number of excellent third-party utilities out there that will do the same thing, and the chances are your favorite nerd has one of them. So, even if you have an older DOS, you can recover from inadvertently deleted files. But you will need to call for help. Do it immediately, and you will have an excellent chance of complete recovery.

Drivers and How to Get Them

As new programs are created, they tend to push the envelope just a little bit farther, trying every trick they can to squeeze just a little more speed or functionality out of your system. And as they do this, they also tend to create problems for you. For example, a mouse driver that worked perfectly on your EGA video system just won't cut the mustard on your new Super VGA system. Some of your software may work fine, but some will cause all sorts of weird things like a mouse arrow that completely disappears.

So what is a poor soul to do? Get a new driver for the mouse, of course.

There are basically three ways to get new drivers for your existing hardware so that it will work with newer software programs. The first is the easiest. Many programs ship with updated drivers that are known to work with the more common hardware out there. So, for example, when a new version of Windows comes out, it will also include new versions of many of the drivers that are necessary to make it work. Great, but that only applies to programs that ship their own drivers, and even then there are updates and "fixes" that come after you buy the software that you may need.

The second way to get a new driver is to contact the manufacturer of either the software or the hardware and ask them to send you a copy. Most will charge you only a small fee to cover the cost of making and sending you the disk containing the driver, but this takes time and it is a pain.

The third way is to download the new driver from either the manufacturer's electronic bulletin board, called a BBS, or from one of the large, commercial information systems such as CompuServe. This is a great way to get the latest and greatest, but it requires a modem, software, and a fairly high level of comfort with both of them. However, there is a usually reasonable workaround. There's bound to be someone in your company or someone you know outside the company who is a BBS or CompuServe user. Ask them to download the latest driver and give you a copy. In fact, in many companies, this will be handled semi-automatically by someone in the MIS department, so ask around. This is by far the fastest and cheapest way to get new drivers.

Before you copy the new driver on top of the old driver, make a copy of the old driver just for safety's sake. Then use the COPY command to copy the new driver into the appropriate directory. I can't tell you what the new directory is; it's wherever the old nonfunctioning driver is. Then reboot your computer and test the new driver to see that it works as it's supposed to. Only after you've thoroughly tested the new driver should you throw out the old driver.

Dunn's Rule for Success: If at first you don't succeed, try, try again. Then quit. No use being a damned fool about it.

Chapter 17

NOW YOU NEED A NERD

Varadan's Verity: An expert is a person who avoids the small errors while sweeping on to the grand fallacy.

COMPUTERS ARE FAIRLY predictable beasts. Once they are working properly they'll just keep percolating along. But sooner or later your computer is going to do something really peculiar. After you've checked Chapter 16 for things you can handle yourself, look here for problems that probably require an expert.

It's Just DEAD!

One morning you arrive at your computer, humming a happy tune, and when you turn the thing on...NOTHING! In computers there are, however, different degrees of deadness, so let's try them one at a time.

Totally dead—no sound, no action

Is it plugged in? Your main computer box is probably plugged into some kind of power strip. Is the power strip switched on? Is the power strip, in turn, plugged into an outlet? Check the outlet to make sure it has power. If all this checks out OK, then chances are you have a bad power supply or a grounded something inside the computer box. This isn't usually a big deal, in that you haven't lost any data, but you will have to get some help deciding if the problem is the power supply itself or one of the boards inside your computer box.

Partly dead—it's on, but it doesn't work

So you turn on the computer, it makes all the customary sounds, but you get no action.

No picture	Is the monitor plugged in? Is it turned on? Check the brightness knob. Is there a screen saver on? Move the mouse or press a key to turn a screen saver off.
Keyboard doesn't respond	Is the keyboard plugged in? (If it's not, don't plug it back in while the computer's on.) Is the keyboard locked? (There's a keylock on the front of most PCs. It has be in the ON or UNLOCK position for the computer to work.)

Mostly dead—it's on but it says weird stuff

The bad-news messages you can get when starting up your computer that refer to hardware include

☞ *Non-System disk or disk error:* If you are lucky, this just means you accidentally left a floppy in your A drive. Remove the floppy and try again. If you aren't lucky, something is wrong with your hard disk and you will need to get help.

☞ *Keyboard error Press <F1> to RESUME:* And how are you supposed to press F1 if the keyboard isn't plugged in? Turn the power off, and make sure that both ends of your keyboard are plugged in (some keyboards only have a plug at the computer-box end). Then turn the power back on, and if you get it again, try pressing the F1 key. If it continues its boot-up process, chances are something is getting a bit iffy about your keyboard, and you will want to think about a new one. They run from about $45 to $145, so now is a good time to get the one you really wanted.

☞ *Parity error:* This means that at least one of your memory chips is getting flaky. Frequently, you will be able to run some programs, but certain others will have trouble or crash with this error message. The problem, however, is in the hardware.

☞ *NO ROM BASIC SYSTEM HALTED:* This one is my personal favorite. Just turn it off and call your repair person to make an appointment. For reasons beyond either of us, your hard disk has disappeared.

These are all hardware-related problems, and except for the first two, they will almost certainly require opening up the computer box and poking around in the guts. If you have a friend who fancies him or herself an expert, you can let them take a look. But if they don't come up with something obvious, you are going to have to get serious help.

Mayor Daley's Advice to Murphy: Save early, save often.

Strange Behavior

Sometimes your computer seems to be working, or at least all the parts come on, the screen works, and so on, but when you run a certain program, it behaves oddly. Maybe you get a message like "Divide by 0," "Divide Overflow," or "Stack Overflow," and you are unceremoniously dumped out all the way out to DOS from the inside of the program, or

Ask for Help

worse, the error message ends with "SYSTEM HALTED," and the only thing you can do is power off and power back on.

The first problem is that you have lost whatever you were working on when this happened. This is not good, and tends to remind one of why one hates computers. The second problem is you don't really know *why* it happened, and the error message provides little help for that.

Software problems like these are most often caused by the interaction of two or more programs or by a hidden hardware incompatibility with new software. They are a pain to track down, but it can be done. If it happens in lots of programs, you may have a virus. Run MSAV to make sure that you haven't gotten a sudden case of computer flu.

If the problem is only with a specific program, then try calling their technical support line. Don't let the tech support engineer intimidate you. Be patient with him or her, and she or he will be patient with you. If they say something you don't understand, stop them. Ask them to back up and make sure you understand before you let them go on. Don't be afraid to say "I don't understand." They have access to a huge amount of knowledge about their program and how it interacts with other programs, so the chances are good that they can help you find the source of the problem.

If none of this helps, summon a local guru because you may well have a hardware problem.

☞ For information on viruses and how to get rid of them, see Chapter 14, "An Ounce of Prevention."

Fail On INT 24

Here's a truly informative message. You get this error message usually when you have responded to "Abort, Retry, Fail" by saying "Fail." What it means is that, for whatever reason, DOS was unable to read the disk. If it's your hard disk, get out your Emergency disk and boot from it. If you can now read your hard disk, do a backup immediately using MSBACKUP or whatever backup software you have. Something is unhealthy about your hard disk, and you need to take immediate protective measures. Then call for help to try to find the source of the problem.

If it is on a floppy, and there is no data on the floppy that you can't live without, toss the floppy. If you are getting the message fairly regularly with the same drive and different floppies, then you may need to have your floppy drive aligned. Or, if you use more than one computer, you may need to get the floppy drive in the *other* computer aligned. Over time, a floppy drive will sometimes get misaligned, and when this happens it may work perfectly well as long as any floppy in use was formatted on the drive; but when you start sharing floppies between computers, you have trouble. Getting your drive aligned will cost you about the same amount as buying a new one, but there is no guarantee the new one will be correctly aligned either, so it is probably worth getting your current one cleaned and aligned.

☞ For help with MSBACKUP, see Chapter 14, "An Ounce of Prevention."

The Case of the Disappearing Hard Drive

If your computer suddenly can't read or write to your hard disk or suddenly can't find the hard disk while you are up and running, your computer is trying to tell you something. It may be trying to tell you that your hard disk controller is going (or has gone) bad, or that the computer is running too warm, or that your power supply is getting ready to go belly up, or any of several other equally unpleasant things.

First, turn your computer off completely. Take a look at the back of the computer box, and you will see one or two fans. Try cleaning around them and around any vents in the area. Then let everything sit for a good half hour or so while you review your list of possible resources.

At the end of that time, put your Emergency disk into drive A and turn the power on. If you can read your hard disk, do an immediate backup. If everything seems to work fine but the problem comes back after a while, chances are you have a temperature-related problem. It could be a problem with the power supply, the hard disk controller, or any of several other possible spots. In any case, it is time to call a repair person.

Invalid CMOS Configuration

The CMOS (pronounced *SEE-mahs*) is a special piece of memory that stores information about the hardware on your computer—things like how much regular memory is installed, how many and what kind of floppy drives you have, and the most important one, what kind of hard disk you have. In order to remember all this, there is a battery connected to the CMOS that keeps it from losing its little mind. If this battery dies, your computer will forget everything it knows about itself.

If you add memory to your computer, change or add hard drives, or make other alterations, you will probably have to change your CMOS configuration. If you add memory, for example, you will get an "Invalid CMOS Configuration" error message, and it will immediately offer to run the Setup program or suggest that you do so. If you get this because your battery failed, you will need help to get it going.

Most newer computers have the Setup program in ROM memory where it can be run even if you can't do anything else. On some computers, the procedure is to press the Del key as the computer is booting up, and this takes you to the Setup utility. This is not for the faint of heart, since if you make a mistake, especially with the hard disk type, you will have serious problems. So get some help before you run the Setup program.

☞ *Both Norton Utilities and PC Tools include special programs that can make a copy of your CMOS configuration and will walk you through the process of restoring it. See Chapter 21, "Murphy's Seven Programs That Can Save Your Cookies," for more information.*

☞ *Next time you have your favorite nerd helping you, get him or her to tell you what your hard disk type is (it's a one- or two-digit number) and write it down where you won't lose it. This can make life much easier for both of you if your battery suddenly dies.*

☞ *Batteries have a limited life. Some will last several years; others don't seem to make it past the warranty period on the computer. Next time the cover on your computer box is open for some other reason, get someone to show you where your battery is and how to replace it. Sometimes you'll simply have a pair of alkaline AA batteries, others will have special lithium batteries. In either case, if you know what kind you need, you can easily replace it yourself. Take the cover off and power up the computer, and then with the power on, replace the battery. This way, your CMOS won't lose its little brain. This should probably be done every couple of years, but if you are uncomfortable with it, by all means get help.*

Signs of Imminent Hard Drive Death

There are several indicators of an impending hard disk death. Some are subtle, others pretty obvious. If you see *any* of these, do a backup as soon as possible, and keep all your important work backed up.

One of the more obvious signs of imminent death is any sort of "read error," "write error," or "seek error" messages related to your hard drive. If you start getting *any* error messages related to your hard drive, get concerned. Try to analyze the messages to see if there is a pattern. Do they always happen when you first fire up the computer in the morning, and then go away as the day goes on, or is the opposite true? In either case, you are showing signs of temperature-related problems. Make sure you have a current backup and that you keep it current.

If it sometimes seems like your hard drive takes a really long time to do something that used to be pretty quick, you may be seeing a warning sign. First, of course, do a backup. Then, if you have DOS 6, run the DEFRAG program.

☞ *For help with DEFRAG, see "DEFRAG This, Jack" in Chapter 13.*

☞ *Spinrite can sometimes help, even with those drives that can't be low-level formatted. (See "Only Nerd Wannabes Need to Read This" below.) Also, Norton Utilities has a program called Calibrate that does some of the same things that Spinrite does. See Chapter 21, "Seven Programs That Can Save Your Cookies".*

> ### Only Nerd Wannabes Need to Read This
>
> What exactly is a "low-level format?" A low-level format, as opposed to DOS's FORMAT command (sometimes called a high-level format), is what actually defines the sectors on your hard disk. The majority of hard disks in computers today are of the IDE (Integrated Drive Electronics) type, and are shipped from the factory with the low-level formatting already done. Older drive types, and SCSI drives, can be low-level formatted.

Scrambled FAT

One of DOS's least friendly error messages is "File allocation table bad." This means that something has scrambled your FAT, which is about as serious as scrambling eggs, in that once they're scrambled it's hell to unscramble them. However, it may be possible to recover from this with the proper tools. Stop what you are doing and immediately call for assistance. A DOS expert may be able to help.

CHKDSK Says I Have Cross-Linked Files!

When CHKDSK reports that files are cross-linked, it means that two files are trying to use the same piece of disk space. To try to recover from this, first copy the two files that DOS reports as cross-linked to a new location, then delete the originals. With luck, one of files will be OK and the other will be dinged but you will still have part of it.

Cross-linked files are usually the sign of serious software misbehavior. The most common cause is a disk cache program that is interacting with some other software in a less than felicitous manner. You will need to get help with this to find out where the bad vibes are coming from.

How to Cultivate a Nerd

In several places in this book I suggest that you should get help from a nerd or an expert. (The two are not necessarily the same, though there is a substantial overlap.) That's good advice, but how do you go about finding a nerd, and having found one how do you cultivate her or him?

Finding one is easy. Virtually every department in every major company has at least one person who thinks she or he knows a bit more about computers than the average person, and who actually *likes* the stupid things. This last part is the critical factor for nerddom.

So, having found the nerd, how does one cultivate it? Virtually every nerd will help you if you ask, but nerds are, in some limited ways, just like people. If you treat them right, they will go a lot farther to try to help you, and if you are in desperate straits, they will pull out the stops and do their utmost to save your cookies. And all the wonderful disaster recovery programs in the world pale in comparison to a nerd in full attack mode!

Dr. Backer's Nine Rules of Nerd Cultivation

1. If the problem is caused by something you did, 'fess up. It makes the job of recovery a *lot* easier if the nerd knows what caused the problem in the first place. So just say "I typed **DEL *.***. I thought I was in the A drive but it turned out to be the C drive." Don't try to pretend that all those files just "disappeared" on their own.

2. Bribes are good. When the nerd comes to help, have a fresh cup of coffee or a favorite soda waiting. It costs next to nothing, but shows that you care.

3. Reciprocate. Be willing and even eager to use your area of expertise to help out the nerd.

4. Do backups. Absolutely *nothing* will make a nerd more willing to help than knowing that you have a recent backup. First, it lets them try things that they would be leery of without a backup, plus it lets them know that *you* care enough to do your part.

5. Don't keep asking the same question over and over. If you have trouble remembering how to do something, write down the answer. Keep a little log book next to your computer or something. By the time you're asking the same question the fourth or fifth time, you're pushing your luck.

6. When describing your problem to the nerd, try to be more specific than "It's just BUSTED." If you can remember what you did before the problem came up or any error messages DOS gave you, it makes the nerd's job that much easier.

7. If it isn't a disaster recovery situation, try to solve the problem yourself first. If your nerd knows you only call when things are serious, you'll get a much better response.

8. Don't play the field. Nerds are delicate social animals, and if your nerd thinks you're getting computer fixes from other nerds, you'll hurt its feelings.

9. "Stroke" your nerd! Nerds respond to praise much better than criticism. An occasional "WOW! That's amazing!" is also appreciated.

Chapter 18

ERROR MESSAGES YOU LOVE TO HATE

Gaus's Gotcha: Whatever goes wrong, there's always someone who knew it would.

DOS ERROR MESSAGES are either vague or apocalyptic. But even the most dire-sounding are not usually as bad as they first appear, and most errors are totally harmless. Fortunately you are unlikely to come across more than a couple dozen DOS error messages in your whole life. This chapter lists the most common error messages and tells you what they mean.

Abort, Ignore, Retry, Fail
Abort, Ignore, Fail

Means: DOS can't find a device you've sent it to. You'll get a line of text preceding this error telling you where the problem is. Usually it means that the floppy drive doesn't have a disk in it or the drive door is open. You can also get this message if the disk in the drive isn't formatted.

To Fix It: Put a floppy in the drive, close the door, and press R for Retry. If you don't want to do that, press A for Abort to call the whole thing off. You can also try F for Fail, but don't press I for Ignore.

Access Denied

Means: You're trying to mess with a file you shouldn't. The file has been marked by DOS as read-only. There's usually a very good reason for this. Such a file can't be renamed, deleted, or altered in any way. You can also get this message if you're trying to command a directory to do something only a file can do.

To Fix It: Leave the file alone. If you are absolutely sure you want to change or delete the file, see "Bad Guests—Files That Refuse to Leave" in Chapter 3.

Bad command or file name

Means: DOS looked for something and couldn't find it under the name you gave. One or the other of the following happened:

☞ You misspelled the name of the file or typed in an incorrect path name.

☞ You tried to a run a program that's not in the current directory or not in a directory on your PATH.

☞ You tried to run a program that's not a program. For example, you typed in the name of a document file and pressed Enter.

To Fix It: Check the spelling of the command or path name. Use the CD command to see if you're in the directory and drive you thought you were. See Chapter 13 for information on paths and finding your way around directories.

Bad or missing Command Interpreter

Means: DOS can't find COMMAND.COM where it expects it to be.

To Fix It: First try rebooting. Press Ctrl-Alt-Del to restart your system. Make sure there isn't a floppy disk in your drive A.

If that doesn't help, call someone with DOS smarts. They will undoubtedly use your bootable floppy to copy COMMAND.COM back to the root directory of your hard disk. (In order for a floppy to *be* bootable, it has to have COMMAND.COM on it.) This of course, assumes that you have a bootable disk (see "How to Make a Boot Floppy and What to Do with It" in Chapter 16).

Drive not ready
Drive not ready. Drive door may be open.
Not ready reading drive X

Means: You're trying to use a floppy drive that's not ready—either because there's no floppy in the drive or the drive door is open.

To Fix It: Put a disk in the drive and close the door. Press R for Retry. If you get this message about your hard drive, call for help because your hard drive is trying to tell you it isn't a happy camper.

Duplicate file name or file not found

Means: You tried to rename a file using REN (RENAME) and either

☞ You tried to rename the file to a name that already exists.

Error Messages

☞ You misspelled the name of the file you were trying to rename, so DOS couldn't find it.

To Fix It: Check your typing and try again.

Fail on INT 24

Means: Sort of a general throwing-up-of-hands by DOS. This message usually follows an "Abort, Ignore, Retry, Fail" message.

To Fix It: Press A to cancel. If that doesn't work, try F for Fail. As a last resort, reboot. If you are getting this message on a regular basis, see "Fail on INT 24" in Chapter 17.

☞ See "Reset, Reboot, and the Fine Art of Ctrl-Alt-Del" in Chapter 1 for information on rebooting.

File not found

Means: DOS couldn't find the file that you specified.

To Fix It: Check your typing to make sure you have the file name and path correct. Use DIR to check that you're in the directory you want to be.

General failure reading (or writing) drive X

Means: DOS has thrown up its hands again. This usually means that you're trying to read an unformatted (or improperly formatted) floppy, but it could also mean the drive itself is flaky. This message may precede or follow the "Abort, Ignore, Retry, Fail" message.

To Fix It: Replace the floppy with a correctly formatted disk and press R for Retry. If you want to call the whole thing off for now, press A for Abort. (See Chapter 9 for information on correct formatting of floppies.) If the drive is your hard drive, call for help since your hard drive may well be getting flaky.

Incorrect DOS version

Means: You're trying to mix different versions of DOS. For example, you've tried to move some DOS 6 programs to a system running DOS 5. Or you booted off a floppy that was formatted on a different version of DOS from what is on the hard drive.

To Fix It: Don't try to run the DOS program on the system where it doesn't match. No getting around this error. If you booted from a floppy, remove the floppy and reboot your system.

Insufficient disk space

Means: The disk is full. You can't add any files.

To Fix It: You need to delete one or more files from the current disk or insert a disk that has free space.

Invalid directory

Means: You've specified a directory that doesn't exist. It's also possible that you've made a mistake in typing in a path name.

To Fix It: Check your typing and try again. See "Finding Lost Directories" in Chapter 15 if your directory appears to have wandered away.

Invalid drive specification

Means: You've called for a drive that DOS knows nothing about. You'll get this message if you have drives A, B, and C and you enter **D:** at the prompt.

To Fix It: Change to a valid drive and redo the command.

☞ If you get this error message regarding your hard drive it means that DOS has lost track of where your C drive is. See Chapter 17, "Now You Need a Nerd," for help.

Invalid media, track O bad–disk unusable

Means: The disk you're trying to format is physically damaged, or you are trying to format a low-density disk as a high-density disk.

To Fix It: Throw away the disk and try another. Make sure that the disk in the drive is a high-density disk, not a low-density one.

Invalid number of parameters
Invalid parameter combination
Invalid parameter specification
Too many parameters

Means: The switches you added to a command are too many, too few, incompatible, or nonexistent.

To Fix It: To get the correct syntax, go to the DOS prompt and type in

command /?

That's the name of the command followed by a space then a forward-slash and a question mark. Press Enter to get more help than you could ever need. See "Command Line Syntax" in Chapter 2 for an explanation of switches (parameters) and how to use them.

Invalid path

Means: Your last path name was too long, contained invalid characters, or (more likely) was mistyped.

To Fix It: Check your typing and try again. Use the DIR command to check that you have all the names right in your path name.

Non-System disk or disk error

Means: You've started up the computer with a disk in drive A and the disk is not bootable. The bootstrap program goes first to the disk in drive A for DOS files, then to the hard drive. If it finds a disk in A without DOS system files it gives you this message.

To Fix It: Remove the floppy from the drive (or just open the drive door) and press any key to restart the boot process.

☞ See "Why is a Boot Called a Boot?" in Chapter 1 for more on the boot process.

Not ready

Means: You sent a command to a floppy drive or to a printer and DOS didn't find what it was expecting.

To Fix It: Put a floppy in the drive and close the door. If you're sending a command to a printer, turn the printer on.

Path not found
Path too long

Means: Probably that you've made a spelling error or used illegal characters.

To Fix It: Check your typing and try again. Use DIR command to make sure you're where you think you are.

Unable to create destination

Means: While using the MOVE command (DOS 6) you have specified a destination that doesn't exist. Either you have mistyped the path or tried to use an existing file name.

Error Messages

To Fix It: Check your typing and try again. Use CD to verify the directory names you need to use.

Unable to create directory

Means: DOS can't create the directory you specified because

☞ You tried to create a directory with the same name as a file in the current directory (you can prevent this by always using extensions in file names and never using them in directory names).

☞ You specified an invalid path name.

☞ You used an illegal character in the directory name.

To Fix It: Check your spelling, typing, and the path. See "Naming Files (and Directories Too)" in Chapter 15 for information on naming directories.

Unable to open source

Means: You have specified a directory name or an incorrect file name while using the MOVE command.

To Fix It: Check your typing and try again.

Write protect

Means: You are trying to write to a disk that is write-protected.

To Fix It: Remove the disk from the drive. If you are sure you want to write on that particular disk, remove the tab (from a 5$\frac{1}{4}$-inch disk) or move the write-protect switch (on a 3$\frac{1}{2}$-inch disk). Put the disk back in the drive and press R for Retry. Or use another disk that's not write-protected. See "Write-Protecting Floppies" in Chapter 9 for more.

5

A delectable listing of great programs that can save anything from your time to your life, things not to do, and all the DOS commands you can stand. Plus, learn how to fake nine popular programs well enough to fool the average boss.

MURPHY WAS AN OPTIMIST

How to Stay Afloat

Chapter 19

MURPHY'S DIRTY DOZEN
(Twelve Things NOT to Do)

Lattinville's Lament: You can't win them all, but you sure can *lose* them all.

THERE ARE, OF course, lots of things you shouldn't do to a computer, including stuffing silly-putty into the disk drives or using the monitor as a backboard for handball. I trust you can figure such things out for yourself. In this chapter, though, I cover a baker's dozen of serious errors that you might not immediately recognize. Every item is something that you should know about.

Don't Remove a Floppy While the Light Is On

DOS turns the floppy drive light on to tell you that it's busy reading from or writing to the floppy. If you remove it when the light is on, you can cause errors in the file and possible data loss. There is an exception to this though. MSBACKUP and most third-party backup programs control the floppy drive more directly, and to increase the speed at which they operate, they will leave the light on the entire time you are running the backup or restore operation. In this case, follow the prompts.

Don't Turn Off the Computer with the Hard Drive Light On

This goes right along with not removing the floppy from the drive while the light is on. The light is on to let you know that your computer is busy right now. So be nice and wait patiently for the light to go off. Besides, I thought we had decided to leave the computer on all the time, anyway.

Don't Use Your Computer without a Surge Protector

Really, it only takes a single power "oopsie" and your computer just became an expensive piece of junk. The worst part is, you won't always know right away. Hard disks are notorious for seeming to have survived, but doing a crash and burn a few days later. Also, most surge protectors have a limited life span. They protect your computer by slowly destroying themselves. You probably ought to replace yours every couple of years.

Don't Answer Yes to Any Question You Don't Understand

This is a good rule in life as well. If you are suddenly faced with an "Are you sure (Y/N)?" question from DOS, and you have *any* doubts at all about what it means if you say yes, then just say no. Please.

Don't Plug Anything into the Computer When It's Turned On

When the computer is on, plugging something into it can cause an electrical surge that will fry some ridiculously small and overpriced little part on the inside whose sole purpose in life is to protect that 50-cent fuse. Don't do it.

Don't Format a High-Density Disk to Low-Density

You can do this, and you will even think you got away with it in some cases, but the disk will be unreliable and will almost certainly not be readable by a low-density drive. Besides, high-density disks cost more than low-density disks, so why would you want to waste a perfectly good high-density disk?

Don't Format a Low-Density Disk to High-Density

Here you might think you are saving a few pennies, but the is it worth it? After all, the whole reason for having floppies is to preserve all the work you did in a safe place. Formatting a low-density disk into a high-density one gives you an unreliable disk that can't be trusted. This is a bad economy.

Don't Do This!

Don't Turn Your Computer Off and Immediately Back On

This can send a nice, fat little spike of electrical energy zipping through your computer, just looking for something to destroy. It's true, 99 times out of 100 you will get away with this. But over time, it causes excess electrical stress on delicate and expensive components, resulting in premature and catastrophic failure. In other words, it will fry something right in the middle of the project your boss said absolutely has to be on his desk in the morning or you're history.

Don't Keep the Only Copy of an Important File on Floppy

You might think that this is the safest place for a really critical file, but the exact opposite is true. Hard disks almost never fail anymore. Most hard disks have a expected life of greater than 11 years of continuous use (100,000 hours) without a failure, while floppies are subject to all sorts of potential disaster, from your accidentally spilling coffee on them to the dog's deciding that they would make a good chew toy. The best place to keep your most important files is on your hard disk. Keep a copy on a floppy for backup.

Don't Store Floppies near Magnets

Lots of things act like magnets. The monitor, especially near the back end, electric pencil sharpeners, those little paper clip things that sit on your desk, many employee badges, and any motor can erase the data on your floppy in a flash. So make a place to store your floppies that is clean, dry, and away from any magnets. Then leave them there except when you actually need them.

Don't Quit Your Application by Rebooting the Computer

This sometimes seems the easiest way out, but it can corrupt your hard disk and leave all kinds of little problems lying around. Try all the tricks in "Let Me Out!" in Chapter 1 first. If you have tried all of them, and you still can't figure out how to exit from the program, and the manual isn't available, then ask someone. The only exception to all this is when the program absolutely stops responding to the keyboard at all.

Don't Use These DOS Commands

☞ *FORMAT C: (or any drive other than A or B):* This one is pretty obvious. I don't care how mad you are at the computer, there really isn't anything that formatting your hard disk will make better.

☞ *FDISK:* This is one of those little-known commands that very much deserves to stay that way. Its sole use is to prepare your hard disk for formatting. Definitely the purview of nerds, not humans. If you use this command on an already formatted drive you will destroy any data on that drive.

☞ *DELTREE:* This lovely new command was introduced with DOS 6. It will remove an entire directory, including all its files and subdirectories, in one horrible and irrevocable swoop. UNDELETE will not come to your rescue in this case. A third-party utility, such as Norton Utilities' UNERASE, may be able to piece together your missing files, but it's far from certain.

☞ *RECOVER:* This one sounds so innocuous, doesn't it? In fact, it almost sounds like the sort of command you should be using all the time, right? Wrong. If you use this command, you will end up with all your files reduced to funny names like FILE0000.REC, and all your directories gone as well. Not a pretty sight.

Don't Do This!

☞ *CTTY:* This is one of those little DOS commands that almost no one uses, but which can get you totally screwed up. The intent is to let you connect to your computer from a serial port instead of the keyboard and monitor. So, if you use this command, DOS stops paying any attention to your keyboard. The only way out is to press the reset button or turn the power off and back on.

☞ *DEBUG:* No, this won't get rid of the bugs in the software program you just bought. And it certainly won't kill the cockroaches either. This one is strictly for programmers, and it lets them do horribly arcane and brutal stuff directly to the computer, bypassing DOS. Not for the likes of you and me, gentle reader.

Never Show Fear

Never show fear around your computer. It will sense this and go straight for the kill. Seriously, there is nothing to be afraid of. Armed with this book and your own native intelligence, you can make your computer a useful and productive tool. But you are still the boss, and the computer will only do what you tell it to do.

Nick's Rule: It's a mistake to allow any mechanical object to know you're in a hurry.

Chapter 20

MURPHY'S ELEVEN FAVORITE PAIN-RELIEVING PROGRAMS

Eddy's Pronouncement: If it's worth doing, it's worth hiring someone who knows how to do it.

DOS IS A remarkable operating system. It has spanned over ten years and gone from 8-bit processors all the way to 64-bit processors, and it's still viable and useful. But it does have its quirks and foibles, and here are some suggestions for programs whose sole purpose in life is to make it easier to get your job done, without requiring you to be terribly nerdy about it.

COPYQM

DOS includes a program to make a copy of a floppy disk called DISK-COPY. This program was perfectly adequate in the days when all floppies were low-density 5¼-inch disks. But with any floppy bigger than that, it takes forever to work, and you have to repeatedly swap the original and target floppies in and out of the drive. A royal pain in the wazoo.

This little shareware program, for which the registration cost is $15, is a wonder. COPYQM lets you make one or a hundred copies of the same floppy, without ever having to put the original back in. It also formats as you go so you don't have to preformat the disk you're copying onto. When you're finished, you have an exact copy of the original disk, including the volume label and any hidden files. This is what DOS's DISKCOPY *should* have been. Available directly from

> Sydex
> P.O. Box 5700
> Eugene, OR 97405
> Voice: (503) 683-6033
> Fax: (503) 683-1622

DOS 6

DOS 6 can make your life much easier indeed. DOS 5 was an upgrade that focused on data-integrity issues with the addition of UNDELETE and UNFORMAT. DOS 6 focuses on user functionality. It adds utilities that *should* have been in DOS all along, but which either weren't or were there in pretty unfriendly forms. But the addition of MSBACKUP, MSAntiVirus, and DoubleSpace are worth the cost of the upgrade in and of themselves, if you don't already have versions that do much the same thing or better.

LIST

LIST is one of those programs that I take for granted, I have used it for so long. LIST is available in two versions, a shareware version called LIST Plus, which has a registration fee of $39, and a commercial version called LIST Enhanced, available shrink-wrapped at your favorite software store. The list price on LIST Enhanced is $99. Both are available directly from the author, Vern Buerg, at

Buerg Software
139 White Oak Circle
Petaluma, CA 94952
Voice: (707) 778-1811
Fax: (707) 778-8728

Oh, I forgot to tell you what it does. LIST is a file viewer. It lets you read a file or group of files by paging through them. You can scroll up or down, a page at a time or a line at a time, or have it scroll continuously, at a pace you control. You can search for text within the file, or print part or all of it.

Norton Commander

The Norton Commander is another way of getting away from that darned command line prompt. It's a file manager with editing capability. You can do all the usual file stuff: moving, copying, deleting, plus the look of the program is friendly and easy to figure out. This is not a personal favorite of mine, but I have otherwise sensible friends who swear by it.

Norton Desktop for DOS

Some users will find Norton Desktop for DOS a bit intimidating at first, especially to set up, but once you have it up and running, it is hard to beat for an easy-to-use, mouse-aware desktop. Norton Desktop for DOS provides a menu system to make running your programs easier, a whole raft of utilities, and a really cool screen saver. Buy it for the screen saver and it will help overcome Windows-envy on your older, slower PC. Some of the goodies in here include

☞ *Norton Backup for DOS:* This is the full-featured version of the somewhat limited MSBACKUP program in DOS 6.

☞ *Norton Speed Disk:* The full-featured version of the DEFRAG program that is included with DOS 6.

Pain Relievers

☞ *Norton AntiVirus:* An excellent antivirus program.

☞ *UnErase and UnFormat:* Norton disaster-recovery programs that can do lots more than DOS UNDELETE and UNFORMAT.

☞ *NCache:* A disk-cache program that can speed up your computer noticeably.

☞ *Norton Menus:* An easy-to-use way to create menus for all your programs. It's smart enough to recognize and automatically install most common programs.

☞ *Norton Scheduler:* The program that runs the really cool screen saver.

☞ *All sorts of other little goodies:* Including a safe formatter, Norton Disk Doctor (see Murphy's Seven Programs That Can Save Your Cookies), an automatic, easy-to-use MCI Mail program, and an overall interface that makes it very easy to find, copy, move, and delete files without ever having to see a bare DOS prompt.

My only real complaint with Norton Desktop for DOS is that it is quite intimidating to set up. Mostly this is because it will do so many neat things. Get some help with the initial setup if you are easily flummoxed by too many choices. Once set up, though, I think you'll find it pretty easy to use.

Norton FileFind

You can use DOS Shell to find files, and you can use lots of other programs to find files, but when push comes to shove, nothing beats FileFind. If you remember part of the file name, or even if all you remember is a phrase that is in the file, FileFind will find it. This program is included in the Norton Utilities, and a version called SuperFind is included in Norton Desktop for DOS as well. There are other programs that have similar functionality, but this one has been my favorite for years.

Quarterdeck Expanded Memory Manager (QEMM)

With DOS 6, Microsoft included a program to help simplify the configuring of your memory called MemMaker. MemMaker is a big improvement over nothing at all, which is what DOS had before, but it still falls a long way short of what Quarterdeck has managed to provide. With QEMM you can be as nerdy as your heart desires or you can just let QEMM handle it. QEMM will install itself, inspect your system to figure out what kind of video, hard disk, and so forth you have, and then optimize both itself and your memory for maximum effectiveness. And all for a price of around $50 at your favorite software store.

Stacker

No matter how large your hard disk, eventually you will wish it were bigger. With DOS 6, Microsoft included a utility called DoubleSpace that compresses each file as it is written to your hard disk, and then uncompresses it when you need to use the file, all in the background so you are completely unaware of the process. The result is an increase in apparent hard disk space by about 60 percent. But if you don't have DOS 6 get a copy of Stacker. Stacker gives you the ability to fine-tune the compression routine, optimizing for speed, size, or somewhere in between. On today's faster machines, you will notice virtually no decrease in speed from using Stacker, even at its highest compression setting.

Ultravision

This little program from Personics is one of those programs that once you have it, you wonder how you ever did without. If you have an EGA or VGA computer, this gives you complete control over your screen fonts, colors, etc. You can make your computer have bright green characters on an orange background with Old-English–looking characters, if you really want to. Or, more to the point, you can have many of your favorite applications running with more lines and columns per screen than DOS's standard 80 characters wide by 25 lines per screen.

Pain Relievers

This can be especially helpful with spreadsheets. I have my Quattro Pro set up to have 108 characters per line, which I find really helps. In WordPerfect, I use a 94 by 36 screen for a good compromise between seeing more of the page and not getting the characters so small I can't see what is happening. Ultravision also has a laptop version that makes most laptop screens substantially easier to work with.

Windows

Windows can make your life easier? Yes, if you have the horse-power. Windows is a useful and undeniably cute interface, but it is a hog. It needs lots of hard disk space and a substantial amount of memory to make it happy. If you have the computer to handle it, you will find it a useful addition. But if you have an older or less powerful computer, I suggest you stay away from Windows. If you have a hopeless case of Windows-envy because of all the cute screen savers that are available for it, get Norton Desktop for DOS.

XTree

XTree has been around for years, and there are various iterations of it, from XTreeLite to XTreeProGold. All are similar except for all the extras in the more expensive versions. The extras add mainly to the price, not the usefulness. This is still my favorite hard disk file-management tool. I keep dating other file utilities, but after a brief fling, I always come back to this one. Hard to say what the appeal is, since it certainly isn't sexy or particularly cute, but it just gets the job done for me.

Chapter 21

MURPHY'S SEVEN PROGRAMS THAT CAN SAVE YOUR COOKIES

David's Dictum: An ounce of application is worth a ton of abstraction.

SOONER OR LATER, you are going to have a crisis with your computer. It may be something that could be delicately described as "operator error" that causes the problem, or it may simply be the fickle finger of fate. Whatever the source of the problem, there are programs out there that can help you recover.

DOS 6

If you don't have DOS 6, the upgrade is one of the most helpful things you can do for yourself.

With the introduction of DOS 5, Microsoft added several disaster-relief packages, most notably UNDELETE and UNFORMAT. With DOS 6, this is carried an important step further. Now DOS includes both an anti-virus program and a fast and efficient backup utility. If you don't have one of the third-party alternatives, these alone are worth the price of the upgrade.

MSBACKUP makes backing up your hard disk as painless as it can be. And absolutely, positively *nothing* will protect you better than having a current backup. Period.

☞ *If you have DOS 5 or earlier, you are missing some of the great cookie-savers in DOS 6. Central Point Backup, Norton Backup, SCAN and CLEAN, Central Point AntiVirus, and Norton AntiVirus, all of which are described in this chapter, represent really good investments that can preserve your data as well as your sanity.*

☞ *As cool as DOS 6 is, it's still not perfect. So take a look at the sections on the Norton Utilities 7 and Spinrite later in this chapter for helpful ideas.*

Central Point Backup and Norton Backup

I lump these together because they both do the same thing, and they do it at about the same level. Which one you use is really a matter of personal preference.

Norton Backup is the enhanced version of MSBACKUP (the backup program in DOS 6) and can read and write the same files. The look and feel is the same as MSBACKUP, but Norton Backup allows you to use a tape drive, which you can't with MSBACKUP. Central Point Backup also lets you use a tape drive for your backup and is equally fast and trouble-free.

Tape drives make backups much easier to do, since you don't have to sit there and put a new floppy in every minute or two. Just put the tape in, start the backup, and come back in after lunch and remove the tape.

It doesn't matter what backup software you own, however. It only works if you use it.

SCAN and CLEAN

This pair of shareware utilities from McAfee Associates can handle all your antivirus needs. SCAN is used to check your disks for a virus, and CLEAN is used to remove it once you find one. Both have pretty bare and boring command-line interfaces, but they get the job done. They can be downloaded from a wide variety of bulletin boards, including McAfee's own, or you can order the current version on disk directly. The registration cost is $25 for SCAN and $35 for CLEAN. You can order from

McAfee Associates
3350 Scott Boulevard, Building 14
Santa Clara, CA 95054
Voice: (408) 988-3832
Fax: (408) 970-9727
BBS: (408) 988-4004

Central Point
AntiVirus and Norton AntiVirus

If the bare interfaces of the McAfee pair, SCAN and CLEAN, are just a bit too dull for you, this pair of excellent utilities can handle your antivirus needs. Both are excellent, and both have an easy-to-use look and feel. Both Central Point and Norton have a service that will send you updates periodically so that you don't have to log onto a bulletin board to download them. This is a definite plus if you don't have a modem (or if you do have a modem and find it too spooky to use).

Norton Utilities 7

When I have done something really stupid, which is all too often, and I really need some high-powered help, I call for Peter Norton. He is the originator of this package of utilities, which has been around since the dawn of computer time.

There are other programs and packages that can do similar stuff, but I don't think there is a more comprehensive and powerful tool out there for data recovery. The Norton Utilities include

☞ *Norton Disk Doctor:* This program by itself is worth the price of the package. It can fix problems on hard disks and floppies and do so without requiring you to be a genius or know a lot about the arcane workings of DOS. The faithful Disk Doc can sometimes revive a moribund floppy long enough for you to retrieve the files on it.

☞ *UnErase and UnDelete:* The Norton versions can recover your data when DOS alone will throw up its hands and admit defeat. And if it is your only copy of your doctoral thesis, you don't want anything that admits defeat.

☞ *Calibrate:* This program will exhaustively test your hard disk, marking off any sectors it finds that are bad and moving any data on them to a good area of the disk.

☞ *FileFix:* This will repair damaged Lotus, Quattro Pro, Symphony, WordPerfect, and dBASE files.

The Norton Utilities also include a whole raft of other useful tools that will find files, sort directories, speed up your hard disk, format floppies, and do a whole slew of other little things. If you have Norton Desktop for DOS (or Norton Desktop for Windows), you already have most of what is in the Norton Utilities, so you probably don't need both.

Spinrite

Spinrite is a program that does only one thing, but does it extremely well. If your older hard disk (NOT an IDE drive) has suddenly started to get flaky and you have trouble reading it sometimes, start Spinrite before you go home for the night, and by the time you come back in the morning, it will have gone through and thoroughly inspected and refreshed your hard disk. Any bad sections it finds will be repaired or marked as bad. Data in the bad sections will be moved to good areas of the disk.

COPYIIPC

This is a program that worked so well it destroyed its own market. In the days when all the major software houses except Borland were using copy-protection schemes to prevent users from making copies of their disks, COPYIIPC gave the user a way to make an archival copy. Between COPYIIPC's effectiveness and the complaints from users, the major software companies finally decided that it was just too expensive to keep having to come up with a new copy-protection scheme, only to have COPYIIPC break it in a matter of weeks. But there are still a few programs out there that are copy-protected, and for those that are, COPYIIPC is the way to make a backup copy, just in case.

Chapter 22

A CRIB SHEET FOR RUNNING NINE POPULAR PROGRAMS
(Even If You Don't Know Them)

Marcinko's Maxim: The best way to have a good idea is to have a lot of ideas.

OK, YOU INTERVIEWED for this great job, and you assured your new boss that you know how to run WordPerfect. Of course you've never used WordPerfect in your life, but you didn't let a little thing like that worry you now, did you? So here it is, your first day, and she hands you some scribbled pages and says, "I need this by 10 a.m. Thanks."

Don't panic! Never show fear in front of computers; they can sense it.

Here is just enough information to fake your way through WordPerfect and eight other popular programs you may well run across in the office. If you need more than this, you might actually have to (shudder) read the manual or buy another book, but this should be at least enough to get you started or get the job in the first place.

Fletcher's Rule: The incidence of typographical errors increases in proportion to the number of people who will see the copy.

WordPerfect

WordPerfect is by far the most popular word processing program in the DOS world or in any other. Sooner or later you are likely to have to use it, and then you are in for it! WordPerfect works unlike almost any other program you will run across. None of the keystrokes are even vaguely similar to what you would expect, and very few other programs use similar ones. But not to worry. Once you get some basics down, you can just poke your way around in it to find out how to do other things.

Getting started

The command to start WordPerfect at the DOS prompt is

```
WP
```

You can include a file name after that if you want. For example, if you want to both start WordPerfect and load the file QUARTER3.RPT, type

```
WP QUARTER3.RPT
```

☞ If you get a "Bad command or file name" message from DOS, WordPerfect isn't on your PATH. Try changing to its directory, which will usually be WP51, by typing

```
CD \WP51
```

Then try the WP command again. See "Finding Your True Path" in Chapter 13 for more on paths.

☞ If there isn't a WP51 directory, then see Chapter 15, "Whither Files?" for more on finding files.

Let me out!

The most important thing to learn about any program is how to get out. In WordPerfect you get out by pressing F7, the Exit key. Word-Perfect will ask you whether you want to save the current document. Press Y or N for yes or no. If you answer yes, WordPerfect will prompt you for a file name and will show the current name if it knows it. Press Enter to accept the file name, or type in a new one. If the document already exists, it will ask you to confirm that you want to replace the version that is on your hard disk. Press Y to overwrite the older version, or N to get asked for a name again.

Finally, WordPerfect will ask you the question you have been trying to get at all this time, "Exit WP? No (Yes)," to which you answer with a final Y for yes. You're out! Phew. That was a tough one. WordPerfect seems to think you will never want to leave.

Opening a file

When you first start WordPerfect, you are immediately ready to start typing in your document if it is a new one. If you need to edit an existing document, you will need to open it. The Retrieve key in WordPerfect is Shift-F10. Just press this, and then type in the name of the file you want to edit. If the file is not in your working directory, you will get an error message that the file was not found. Either type in the full path to the file, or press the F5 key to see a list of files.

The F5 key is called the List key in WordPerfect-speak. When you press F5, followed by Enter, you will see a list of files (and directories). You can now use the cursor keys to highlight the file you want to open and press R for Retrieve.

Nine Programs

Saving your work

To save your work in WordPerfect, you press the F10 (Save) key. Word-Perfect will prompt you with what it thinks the file name is. To save the document under this name, press Enter. Press Y to overwrite the older version. To save it under a new file name, type in the new name.

Getting around

To move around in WordPerfect, you use the arrow keys in combination with the Ctrl, Home, and End keys. To move a character or a line at a time, press the arrow key for the direction you want to move. Press Ctrl plus → or ← to move forward or backwards a word at a time, and Ctrl plus ↑ or ↓ to move up or down a paragraph at a time.

The End key takes you to the end of the line, but Home doesn't take you to the start of the line. The Home key plus ← takes you to the left edge of what you see on the screen, and Home,Home,← (press Home twice and press ←) takes you to the start of the line. Home,Home,↑ takes you to the start of the document, and Home,Home,↓ takes you to the end of the document.

Editing 101

Before you can cut, copy, or paste a block of text in WordPerfect, you need to highlight it. Move the cursor to the beginning of the what you want to highlight and press Alt-F4, or F12 on keyboards with 12 function keys. Then move the cursor to the end of what you want to highlight, and press Ctrl-Ins to copy the block or Ctrl-Del to cut the block. Move the cursor to where you want to paste the block in and press Enter.

The Search key in WordPerfect is the F2 key, with Alt-F2 being for Search and Replace. Both are tricky, however, since WordPerfect lets you search for an "Enter" or hard return. Press F2 and type in what you want to search for, and press F7, the Exit key in WordPerfect-speak, to begin the search.

Basic formatting

To create bold text, press F6. Everything you type until you press F6 again will be bold. Underline is F8, same rules. To make existing text boldface, place your cursor at the beginning of it, press F12 to turn on block mode, move your cursor to the end of the text you want to embolden, and press F6. To underline existing text, follow the same steps to highlight the text, but press F8 instead of F6.

To create italic text, you have to press Ctrl-F8, the Font key. Then press A for Appearance and I for Italic. To change back to regular text, press Ctrl-F8 again, followed by N for normal. You can change existing text to italic by highlighting as explained above and going through the whole Ctrl-F8 routine. Ctrl-F8 is also your gateway to changing fonts, sizes, colors, and all sorts of other character-related attributes.

To set different line spacing, page size, and margins; add footers and headers; or change other overall appearance attributes; press the Format key, Shift-F8. This gives you a page of choices. Choose L for line-related things like left and right margins, tab stops, justification, and spacing between lines. Choose P for page-related things like top and bottom margins, page size and orientation, headers and footers, and page numbering.

To center text, press Shift-F6. Everything you type will be centered until you press Enter. Press Alt-F6 to make your text flush right.

To check your spelling

WordPerfect has an excellent spell checker. To use it, press Ctrl-F2 and then D for Document. This will give you a split screen, with your document in the top half and the results of the spell check in the bottom half.

When WordPerfect finds a word it doesn't know, it will highlight the word in the top half, and in the bottom half it will offer you a list of choices to change the highlighted word to. Press the letter to the left of the suggested word you want to substitute for the misspelled word, or choose one of the options from the menu list on the bottom: press 1 to skip this word once, 2 to skip it for the duration of the document, 3 to add it to the words that WordPerfect knows are spelled correctly, 4 to edit the word on the screen, 5 to look up the word using a pattern that you give WordPerfect, or 6 to tell WordPerfect to ignore words with numbers in them.

When WordPerfect has checked the entire document, it will give you a word count on the bottom line. You can exit the spell checker at any time by pressing F1.

Printing it out

To print out your document in WordPerfect, press Shift-F7. From this page of choices, press V for View Document to see what it will look like before you actually print it, F for Full Document to print the entire document, or P to print the current page only.

Canceling a command

In WordPerfect, the Esc key doesn't cancel the current command; instead the F1 key does. Use this key whenever you want to stop a command, cancel one in the middle, or undo the last deletion you didn't really mean to do. Sometimes the F7 key will have a similar effect, but it is actually the Exit key.

Help and how to get it

The Help key in WordPerfect is the F3 key. Press this at any time for help. If you are in the middle of a command, you will either get help on that specific command or a list of choices staring at you. If you are not in the middle of a command, you can then press a letter to get an alphabetical list of help topics that start with that letter. So to get help on the Move command, press F3,M and you will see a list of help topics that start with the letter *M*. Since there are more than will fit on one page, press M again and you will see more help topics that start with M, including a variety of move commands and the keystrokes associated with them. Press the key combination shown for the kind of move you want to do to get a screen of information about that move.

To get an on-screen template to give you a quick reminder of Word-Perfect keystrokes, press F3,F3. This is quite helpful if somehow your keyboard template has sprouted legs and walked away and you just need a quick reminder.

If you need more help than this and are totally intimidated by the manual, open it up to the list of toll-free numbers. This is in the front under "Getting Help." Part of how WordPerfect got to be the number-one word processor was by providing outstanding technical support.

Bechler's Rule: The incidence of missed typographical errors is in direct proportion to the size of the letters in the copy.

Microsoft Word

Microsoft Word is the second most popular word processing program for the DOS world. This section is a quick guide to the use of version 5.5. Earlier versions were quite a bit different, but with version 5.5, Microsoft has moved to a more uniform interface between its DOS product and its Word for Windows product.

One result of this move is that Word 5.5 is much more awkward to use without a mouse than it is with a mouse. If you must use Word, I suggest you get a mouse, no matter how good you are with a keyboard.

All Word documents have the extension .DOC unless you have given them another name. Generally, it is a good idea to stick to a program's preferred extensions. If nothing else, it makes it easy to figure out where the file came from later.

Getting started

To start Microsoft Word, type

    WORD

at the DOS prompt. You can also include a file name to load a document as you are starting up Word.

☞ If you get a "Bad command or file name" message from DOS, Word isn't on your PATH. Try changing to its directory, which will usually be WORD, by typing

    CD \WORD

Then try the WORD command again.

☞ See "Finding Your True Path" in Chapter 13 for more on paths.

☞ If there isn't a WORD directory, try WORD55 or WORD5, or see Chapter 15, "Whither Files?" for more on finding files.

Let me out!

To get out of Microsoft Word, use your mouse to click on File on the menu bar (or press Alt-F) and then select Exit Word. If you haven't saved your document since the last time you changed it, you will be prompted to save before the exit. Select Yes to save the document. If you haven't given it a name yet, you will need to give it one. You can also provide a bunch of optional information about the document in the Summary Information window. Finally, Word will let you out.

☞ *You can have Word bypass the Summary Information window by selecting Utilities from the menu bar, selecting Customize, and toggling the Prompt for Summary Information box off (no X in it).*

Opening a file

Once you get Word started, you need to open a document to get some work done. If you will be working on an existing document, pull down the File menu and select Open from it. Use the dialog box to select the file you want to work with. If you want to create a new file, you are already where you need to be. When you first start up Word, you will get a new, blank document with the temporary name of Document1 (unless you include a file to load on the initial command line). If you want to open another new document, pull down the File menu and select New from it. Word lets you have several documents open at the same time, each in its own window.

Saving your work

To save your work, pull down the File menu and select Save. The shortcut for this is Alt-Shift-F2. To save the current document under a new name, select Save As from the File menu (press Alt-F2).

Getting around

To move around in Word, you use the arrow keys in combination with the Ctrl, Home, and End keys. To move a character or a line at a time, press the arrow key for the direction you want to move. Press Ctrl plus → or ← to move forward or backwards a word at a time, and Ctrl plus ↑ or ↓ to move up or down a paragraph at a time. The End key takes you to the end of the line, and Home takes you to the start of the line. Press Ctrl-Home to move to the beginning of the document and Ctrl-End to move to the end.

Editing 101

To select or highlight a block of text, place the cursor at the beginning of the text you want to highlight and press the Shift key. Hold down the Shift key and use the cursor-movement keys to move the cursor to the end of the block. To cut the block, pull down the Edit menu and select Cut (or press Shift-Del). To copy the block, select Copy from the Edit menu (or press Ctrl-Ins). To paste the block back into the document, place the cursor where you want the block to go and select Paste from the Edit menu (or press Shift-Ins).

To search for something in Word, pull down the Edit menu from the menu bar and select Search. This will open a dialog box where you type in what you want to search for. To do a search and replace, select Replace from the Edit menu, and a similar dialog box opens for the replace operation.

Basic formatting

To create bold text, press Ctrl-B. Everything you type until you press Ctrl-B again will be bold. Press Ctrl-U for underline or Ctrl-I for italic. To change existing text to boldface, underlined, or italic, you must first highlight it. Place your cursor at the beginning of the text you want to highlight, press and hold down the Shift key, and move your cursor to the end of the block. Then press Ctrl-B for bold, Ctrl-U for underline, or Ctrl-I for italic. To change all sorts of other stuff related to how characters look, choose Character from the Format menu.

To set different line spacing, page size, margins; add footers and headers; or change other overall appearance attributes; pull down the Format menu from the menu bar and choose from the various options.

To center text, choose Paragraph from the Format menu. This opens a dialog box that lets you choose from an assortment of paragraph-related formatting options. Select an alignment of Center and press Enter to center your text. Select an alignment of Left to return to a more normal, left-justified look. Select an alignment of Right to set text flush right.

To check your spelling

To use Word's spell checker, press F7. Word will start the spell check from your current cursor position. Word gives you a split screen, with your document in the top half and the results of the spell check in the bottom half.

When Word finds a word it doesn't know, it will highlight the word in the top half, and in the bottom half it will offer you a list of alternative spellings for the word. If the highlighted alternative word is correct, select Change. To select one of the other alternatives, highlight the alternative you want to use and press Enter. If none of the suggested substitutions is the correct word, highlight the one that is closest and then press Alt-S for additional suggestions.

Sometimes the spell checker will highlight a word that is correct but is not in Word's dictionary. To add such word to the dictionary, select Add. To ignore the "error," select Ignore. If you want to edit the highlighted word, type the correction in the Replace With box and select Change. When the spell check reaches the end of the document, it will ask you if it should start over again at the beginning.

☞ *Spell checking is one of the things that Word does very awkwardly with just the keyboard. If you have a mouse, it works much better.*

Printing it out

To print your document in Word, pull down the File menu and select Print or press Shift-F9. This brings up the Print dialog box. Select the appropriate print options, then press Enter or click on OK with the mouse.

Canceling a command

To cancel a command in Word, press the Esc key. You may have to do it more than once, depending on how deep into the menus you are, but don't worry. You can't hurt anything.

Help and how to get it

The Help key in Word is the F1 key. If you press F1 in the middle of a command or where there is a menu of choices available, you will get specific help on that command or menu. Otherwise, you get the main Help index. You can also select Help from the menu bar.

Lance's Lament: The one piece of data you're absolutely sure is correct, isn't.

Quattro Pro

Quattro Pro for DOS is a spreadsheet program that allows you to read and write its own files, which have a .WQ1 extension, files from other spreadsheet programs such as Lotus 1-2-3, and files from database programs such as dBASE and Paradox. If you have an older version of Quattro Pro, it can even mimic the command structure of Lotus 1-2-3. But for this section, we will use its native menus.

Getting started

To start Quattro Pro, just type

Q

and press Enter. If you want, you can have Quattro Pro load a spreadsheet file at the same time by including the file's name on the command line.

☞ If you get a "Bad command or file name" message from DOS, Quattro Pro isn't on your PATH. Try changing to its directory, which will usually be \QPRO, by typing

```
CD \QPRO
```

Then try the Q command again.

☞ See "Finding Your True Path" in Chapter 13 for more on paths.

☞ If there isn't a \QPRO directory, see Chapter 15, "Whither Files?" for more on finding files.

Let me out!

To exit Quattro Pro, press Ctrl-X. Or if you want to do it the hard way, press the / key to activate the menus, then press F for File and X for Exit. Regardless of the method you choose, if you haven't saved your spreadsheet since the last change you made to it, you will be prompted with

```
Lose your changes and Exit?
```

Choose No to cancel the exit, Yes to abandon the changes you have made since the last save, or Save & Exit to save the changes and continue exiting.

If you choose Save & Exit the spreadsheet will be saved first. If there is already a version on your disk, when you go to save it you will be asked to choose between Replace, which will overwrite the version on disk, and Backup, which will save the existing version on your disk by giving it a new name before saving the version you are working on. Get in the habit of selecting Backup. Just in case.

Opening a file

Once you get Quattro Pro started, you need to open a worksheet to get some work done. If you will be working on an existing worksheet, press the / key to activate the menus and select File to pull down the File menu. Select Open from it. Type in the name of the worksheet you want to open or use the dialog box to select the file you want.

If you want to create a new worksheet, you are already there. When you first start up Quattro Pro, you will get a new, blank worksheet to work on called Sheet1 (unless you include a file to load on the initial command line). If you want to open another new worksheet, pull down the File menu and select New. Quattro Pro lets you have multiple open worksheets at the same time.

Saving your work

To save the current spreadsheet in Quattro Pro, press Ctrl-S or use the keystroke sequence /FS (press / to pull down the menus, then press F for File and S for Save). If this is a new worksheet and you haven't saved it before, you will get prompted for a name. If this is a spreadsheet you've already saved to disk, you will be asked if the existing version should be backed up or replaced. Choose backup.

Quattro Pro can have several open spreadsheets at the same time (32 to be exact, but I doubt you will need that many), so to save them all at once in version 4 and later of Quattro Pro, use /FV (press / to pull down the menus, then press F for File, and V for Save All).

Getting around

A Quattro Pro spreadsheet is divided into cells. Each cell is part of a vertical column of cells and a horizontal row of cells. The first column is column A and the last is IV (the letters *I* and *V*, not a Roman numeral 4), for a total of 256 columns. The first row is row 1 and the last is row 8192.

Cells are designated by their column and row, so the first cell in the spreadsheet is A1 and the last possible cell is IV8192. Each cell can contain text, a formula, or a number.

You can move from cell to cell using the arrow keys. To move a screen at a time horizontally, press Tab or Shift-Tab, and to move a screen at a time vertically, press PgUp or PgDn.

Nine Programs

The Home key will always take you to cell A1, and pressing End-Home will take you to the bottom right-hand corner of the used part of the spreadsheet.

Editing 101

In a spreadsheet, you can enter a number, text, a formula, or an address into a cell. If you enter text, it is called a *label*, and a number is called a *value*.

Anything entered into a cell that begins with a letter is assumed to be a label, and anything that begins with a number is assumed to be either a formula or a value.

If you try to enter a label that starts with a number, such as "1st Month Receipts," you will get an error message. Starting the label with a single quotation mark (') will take care of this problem. That initial quotation tells Quattro Pro that you are entering a label.

To enter an address, enclose it in parentheses or begin it with an operator such as + or −. For example, the address of cell A1 would be entered in another cell, such as cell B1, as (A1) or +A1. But what would appear in cell B1 is not "A1" but the *value* of whatever is in cell A1.

To change what is entered in a cell, highlight that cell and press the F2 key. This puts Quattro Pro in Edit mode. The current contents of the cell are shown in the line just below the menus, with the cursor all the way at the end. While in Edit mode, you can use the ← and → keys to move along this line, and you can use the normal typing keys to edit the line. When you press Enter, the changed contents are placed back into the worksheet and you exit Edit mode.

To delete the contents of a cell, move the cursor to the cell and press the Del key. To simply replace the contents, cursor to the cell and start typing in the new contents.

Basic spreadsheet math

To add the contents of cell B1 and cell C1 and place the result in cell D1, move the cursor to cell D1 and type

```
+B1+C1
```

and then press Enter. If cell B1 has 10 in it, and cell C1 has 15 in it, the sum of these two cells, 25, will appear in cell D1. You can still see the formula that created this result on the line just below the menus.

To multiply the same two cells and put the result in cell E1, move your cursor to cell E1 and type

```
+B1*C1
```

The result, 150, will appear in E1 when you press Enter.

Finally, move your cursor to cell F1. There, we will add the values in all the cells from B1 to E1. Type in

```
@SUM(B1..E1)
```

Press Enter and the answer, 200, will appear in cell F1.

☞ *Quattro Pro provides an almost overpowering array of possible formulas and operators. Don't worry. Probably 90 percent or more of all spreadsheet math that is done is a combination of adding, subtracting, multiplying, and dividing. The only real @FUNCTION used for most things is the one we just used, @SUM.*

☞ *For more on @FUNCTIONS and spreadsheet math, you will need to dig out the manuals. Start with the little @Functions and Macros manual. The first half of it contains all the possible functions, arranged in alphabetical order. Just kind of wander through there, looking for a formula that sounds like what you want to do, and then read the examples to see if it looks right.*

Basic formatting

Quattro Pro provides all sorts of tools for advanced spreadsheet publishing. If you need to do much of this, you will need to get some help, either from a manual or someone who is has had a chance to practice with these goodies.

But some things are pretty simple. To draw a line under a column of cells to separate the total from the rest, move your cursor to the cell with the total in it. Press /SL, Enter, then TDQ. This is shorthand for / to activate the menus, S for Style, L for Line Drawing, Enter to indicate we want to draw the line on the current cell, T for Top, D for Double Line, and Q for Quit. You can play around with line drawing to see how it works. One thing to keep in mind. The lines are "attached" to the top and left-hand sides of the cell only. This means that if you have a line under a cell, it is actually a part of the cell below it. Weird, I know, but that is the way it works.

To change the font that is associated with a cell or cells, choose Font from the Style menu, use the cursor keys to highlight the cells to change, and press Enter. A Font dialog box will open, and you can choose typeface, size, color, and attributes of the font.

Changing the look

Quattro Pro can be run in text mode or what is called *WYSIWYG* mode. WYSIWYG is short for "What You See Is What You Get," and it does what you'd think: it lets you see your fonts, lines, and shading fairly close to how they will actually appear when printed. To change to this mode, pull down the Options menu and select Display Mode. The second choice is B:WYSIWYG. Highlight that and press Enter. To make this the way Quattro Pro starts up, select Update from the Options menu.

☞ *WYSIWYG mode is generally slower and uses more memory than straight text mode. If you have a lot of data entry to do, switch to text mode first, even if you normally prefer WYSIWYG. You will be amazed at the difference in speed except on the fastest machines.*

Printing it out

To print your spreadsheet, you will use the Print menu. Click on Print with the mouse, or press the / key to activate the menus and then press P.

The first thing you need to do is decide what you want to print. So choose Block and press Enter. Now, use the cursor keys to go to the upper left corner of the area you want to print. Press the period key. This will anchor that cell as one corner of the block. Now, move your cursor to the lower right corner of what you want to print and press Enter. That defines the print block.

Next, you need to select how and where to print the file. Select Destination. The choices are Printer, File, Binary File, Graphics Printer, and

Screen Preview. You will generally want to choose Screen Preview first to see what your printout will look like.

Now select Spreadsheet Print or Print To Fit. Print to Fit will actually take a print block that is too big and squeeze it down to fit on a single page. Which is great, if it is still readable, but otherwise you may have to spread it across several pages.

When you have it looking like you want in Screen Preview mode, select Graphics Printer from the Destination choices, and then Spreadsheet Print or Print to Fit, whichever you are using.

Canceling a command

To cancel a command or menu in Quattro Pro, press the Esc key. If you are several layers deep into the menu system, each press of Esc will take you back a single layer.

Many menus also have a Quit option, which will take you all the way out of the menu system.

In the few instances where Esc won't work, such as in the middle of a print job, you can use the Ctrl-Break combination.

Help and how to get it

The Help key in Quattro Pro is the F1 key. Press this key at any time and you will get help.

If you are in the middle of a command or menu, you will see help on that command or menu, and if you have an error message on the screen, the help will be about that error message.

If nothing much is happening, you will see the main Help menu. You move around this Help menu by using the cursor keys to highlight the topic you want and pressing Enter or by using the mouse to click on a topic.

Once in the Help system, you can press F3 to get a list of topics to choose from. To exit the Help system, press Esc.

Nine Programs

Rod's Rule: Never put off 'til tomorrow what you can avoid altogether.

Lotus 1-2-3

Lotus 1-2-3 is still the most common spreadsheet you will run into, and it is to Lotus that we owe the debt of using the / key to access the menus. Not one of the world's better decisions, but we're stuck with it now.

Lotus has used various file formats for different versions of 1-2-3 over the years, but the most common format uses the extension .WK1.

Getting started

To start Lotus 1-2-3, just type

    123

and press Enter. If you want, you can have Lotus load a spreadsheet file at the same time by including a −W and the file's name on the command line:

    123 −WSALES

This will start 1-2-3 and load your SALES.WK1 worksheet, if SALES.WK1 is where Lotus expects to find it. Otherwise, you will get an error message and a blank spreadsheet.

☞ If you get a "Bad command or file name" message from DOS, 1-2-3 isn't on your PATH. Try changing to its directory by typing

      CD \123

   Then try the 123 command again.

☞ See "Finding Your True Path" in Chapter 13 for more on paths.

☞ If there isn't a \123 directory, see Chapter 15, "Whither Files?" for more on finding files.

Let me out!

To exit 1-2-3, press the / key to activate the menus, then press Q for Quit. Answer Y for Yes, and you will be out. However, this will not save your current work. To save your work first and then exit, the sequence is

/ F S

Press the Enter key and then immediately type

R / Q Y

This stands for / for the menus, F for Files, S for Save, Enter to accept the file name, R for Replace, which will overwrite the current copy of your worksheet on disk, / to get the menus back, Q for Quit, and Y for Yes, actually quit already.

Opening a file

Once you get 1-2-3 started, you need to open a worksheet to get some work done. If you will be working on an existing worksheet, the key sequence is

/ F R

which is / to activate the menus, F for File, and R for Retrieve. Type in the name of the worksheet you want to retrieve.

If you want to create a new worksheet, you are already where you need to be. When you first start up Lotus 1-2-3, you will get a new, blank worksheet to work on (unless you include a file to load on the initial command line).

Saving your work

To save the current spreadsheet in Lotus 1-2-3, press the / key to get the menus, then press F for File and S for Save. If this is a new worksheet and you haven't saved it before, you will get prompted for a name. If this is a worksheet you've already saved to disk, 1-2-3 will assume the same name is correct. Just hit Enter to accept that name and press R for Replace.

Getting around

A 1-2-3 worksheet is divided into cells. Each cell is part of a vertical column of cells and a horizontal row of cells. The first column is column A and the last is IV (that's the letters *I* and *V*, not the Roman numeral 4) for a total of 256 columns. The first row is row 1 and the last is row 8192.

Cells are designated by their column and row, so the first cell in the spreadsheet is A1 and the last possible cell is IV8192. Each cell can contain text or a formula or a number.

You can move from cell to cell using the arrow keys. To move a screen at a time horizontally, press Tab or Shift-Tab, and to move a screen at a time vertically, use the PgUp and PgDn keys.

The Home key will always take you to cell A1, and pressing End-Home will take you to the lower right corner of the used part of the spreadsheet.

Editing 101

In a spreadsheet, you can enter a number, text, a formula, or an address into a cell. If you enter text, it is called a *label*, and a number is called a *value*.

Characters entered into a cell that start with a letter are assumed to be a label, and anything that begins with a number is assumed to be either a formula or a value.

If you try to enter a label that starts with a number, such as "1st Month Receipts," you will get an error message. Start the label with a single quote to take care of this problem. That initial quote tells 1-2-3 that you are entering a label.

To enter a cell address, enclose it in parentheses or begin with an operator such as + or −. For example, the address of cell A1 would be entered in another cell, such as A2, as (A1) or +A1. But what would appear in cell A2 is not "A1" but the *value* of whatever is in cell A1.

To change what is entered in a cell, highlight that cell and press the F2 key. This puts Lotus 1-2-3 in Edit mode. The current contents of the cell are shown in the line just below the menus, with the cursor all the way at the end. While in Edit mode, you can use the ← and → keys to move along this line, and you can use the normal typing keys to edit the line. When you press Enter, the contents are placed back into the worksheet and you exit Edit mode.

To delete the contents of a cell, move the cursor to that cell and press the Del key. To simply replace the contents, move the cursor to the cell and start typing in the new contents.

Basic spreadsheet math

To add the contents of cell B1 and cell C1 and place the result in cell D1, move the cursor to cell D1 and type

    +B1+C1

and press Enter. If cell B1 has 10 in it, and cell C1 has 15 in it, the sum of these two cells, 25, will appear in cell D1. You can still see the formula that created this result at the top left corner of the screen.

To multiply the same two cells, move your cursor to cell E1 and type

    +B1*C1

Press Enter and the result, 150, will appear in E1.

Finally, move your cursor to cell F1. There, we will add the values in all the cells from B1 to E1. Type in

    @SUM(B1..E1)

Press Enter and the answer, 200, will appear in cell F1.

☞ *@SUM is what is known as an @FUNCTION. Lotus 1-2-3 provides a wide variety of @FUNCTIONS to handle math, logic, date, and string functions.*

☞ *Probably 90 percent of what is done with spreadsheet math is done with nothing more complicated than adding, subtracting, multiplying, and dividing. The only @FUNCTION you have to worry about is the one we just used, @SUM. If you need more, you will have to dig out the manuals or a book on Lotus. Don't panic. Just wade in, looking for only the part you actually need.*

Printing it out

To print your spreadsheet, you will use the Print menu. Press the / key to activate the menus and press P for Print. Next, press P again, this time for Printer.

Now you need to decide what you want to print. Press R for Range and press Enter. Press the Home key to move to the upper left corner of your worksheet. Press the period key. This will anchor that cell as one corner of the block. Now, press End,Home to move your cursor to the lower right corner of what you want to print and press Enter. That defines the print range or block.

Next, press A for Align, then G for Go and finally, when the printing has stopped, press P for Page to force the last page out of the printer. When the printing has finished, select Q for Quit to return to your worksheet.

Canceling a command

To cancel a command or menu in 1-2-3, you use the Esc key. If you are several layers deep into the menu system, each Esc will take you back a single layer. Many menus also have a Quit option, which will take you all the way out of the menu system.

In the few instances where Esc won't work, such as in the middle of a print job, you can use the Ctrl-Break combination.

Help and how to get it

Press F1 to get help in 1-2-3. You can see a list of all the available functions and the syntax for them by selecting @Function Index from the Help menu.

Brian's Observation: Typographical errors will be found only after the letter is mailed.

Paradox

Paradox is one of the most popular database programs for the PC. If you are using Paradox, you may well be completely unaware of it, since the user interface of many Paradox applications is controlled and designed by the programmer. However, if you end up using naked Paradox, don't worry. It is fairly easy to get around in, and with version 4 you can use a mouse for most operations. This quick guide assumes you are using version 4.

Getting started

The command to start Paradox is simple to remember:

    PARADOX

If you are running a custom budget application that someone wrote, called MYBUDGET, you can start it by typing

    PARADOX MYBUDGET

A quick note is in order here. If you are running an application, it may well run directly from the command line and not require that you explicitly load Paradox. With the above example, this would mean that you simply type

    MYBUDGET

If you get a "Bad command or file name" message from DOS, Paradox isn't on your PATH. Try changing to its directory, which will usually be \PDOX40 for version 4, by typing

    CD \PDOX40

Then try the PARADOX command again.

☞ See "Finding Your True Path" in Chapter 13 for more on paths.

☞ If there isn't a \PDOX40 directory, try \PDOX35 or \PDOX. See Chapter 15, "Whither Files?" for more on finding files.

Nine Programs

Let me out!

To exit Paradox, press the F10 key to activate the menus, select Exit, and answer Yes.

It is important that you always follow this procedure when running Paradox and not use Ctrl-Alt-Del to quit. Like most databases, Paradox works with open data files on disk, and simply rebooting the computer can result in a corrupted database.

Saving your work

Since Paradox is a disk-based database, you don't, in the conventional sense of the word, need to save your work. Any changes you make to the database are immediately stored on disk, and simply following the normal exit procedure will result in all your work being saved.

Database Terms for Those Who Care

Databases are organized into *tables*, which are organized into *records* and *fields*. A table is a collection of essentially similar types of data. It is made up of records. Each record has the information on an individual item in that table. The record is divided up into fields. Each field is a particular item of information for that record.

So, for example, an address-book database might have two tables, one for the addresses and one for the phone numbers. Within the address table, there might be records of all your business contacts and their mailing addresses. You might have fields for last name, first name, street address, city, and so on. The phone-book table might contain the same names, but instead of address information it would have home and work phone numbers.

You can view the data in your table in more than one way. *Table view* displays data in tabular format, with columns for the fields and rows for the records. This is the normal Paradox view, but the same data can be viewed in *form view* by pressing F7 once you have the table view open. In this view, you see a page that holds all the fields for a single record.

You can also get a *report view*, in which you print, either to the screen or to a printer, a report of the data in the table. This allows you more control over how the data appears, but you cannot modify the data from this view.

Paradox does have one rule related to saving. Changes you make to the database are not "committed" (made real and final) until you explicitly tell Paradox to "Do-It." The F2 key is the Do-It key.

Getting around

Moving around in Paradox is a bit different from moving around in a conventional word processing or spreadsheet program. The menus allow you to get different views of your data. To access the menus, which are always visible at the top of the screen, press the F10 key and then the first letter of the menu item you want. Or simply click your mouse on the menu item.

To view a database, for example, press F10 and V for View. A dialog box will open. Type in the name of the table you want to open or press Enter to see a list of possible tables to open. If you start typing in the name of the table you want, the cursor will move to it and you can press Enter again to open it.

Once you have a table open on the desktop, you can move around in it using the arrow keys. Pressing Ctrl-Home moves you to the first field in the current record, and Home by itself moves you to the first record of the table. To switch to a form view of the table, press F7. This is a toggle, so you can switch back and forth from form view to table view by pressing F7.

Editing 101

To edit the data in your database, open either a table or form view of the table you want to change. It doesn't matter which one you start with. Then press Alt-F9 to edit the database. (This is called CoEdit mode.) Move your cursor to the record and field you want and make your changes. You can switch between table and form views by pressing F7.

When you move off the current record, any changes will be saved. This process of saving your changes is also called "committing" or "posting" by database geeks. You can undo the last change by pressing F10 and U for Undo.

If you are going to be making a lot of changes to the database and you want to make sure that no one else on the network can work on the database while you are making the changes, press F9 to enter the Edit mode. In this mode, no changes are final until you press F2, the Do-It key.

Printing it out

To print your database you need to make a report. I will not attempt to go into all the details of how to organize a fancy report, but here is what you need to get a simple report of all the data in a table.

Press F10, R for Report, and then O for Output. Press Enter to bring up a list of tables in the current directory. Select the table you want a report of and press Enter again.

Press Enter again to select the standard report, and press Enter a fourth time to send the report to the printer.

Finding something in your database

The reason you stored all your information in your database in the first place, of course, was so that you could find it when you needed it.

One way to find a particular piece of information is to print a report out of the entire table and look for it, and for many simple tasks on small tables this will be perfectly adequate. But if you want to print records that meet a certain criteria, you will need to *query* the database. Paradox uses query by example (QBE), a querying method that is extremely powerful, but fairly easy to understand and use.

Let's look at a simple example: Suppose you want to search your sales contact database to find all the people whose company name has *electrical* in it so you can send them a special offer on switches.

Press F10 to activate the menus and then A for Ask. Choose the table you have your sales contacts in, and you will open up a long skinny window called the Query window. Press the F6 key while your cursor is in the far left-hand side of the window, and little check marks will show up in each field. This will cause the answer to have all the fields in it.

Move your cursor to the company name field and type in **..elect..** This tells Paradox to search the database for any records that contain the text *elect* anywhere within the company name field. Press the F2 key, and when Paradox gets done searching the database it will put up another table view.

This table view is of a special table called the Answer table. In it will be all the records that met your search criteria. The Answer table is a temporary table, and every time you query Paradox, it overwrites the old Answer table with a new one.

This barely touches on the simplest of queries, but it is enough to get started. For more, you will need to go to the manual or third-party books or ask a Paradox guru for help.

Canceling a command

Canceling a command in Paradox is not always done in the same way. First try the Esc key. If that doesn't seem to do anything, try Ctrl-Break. If there is a menu visible that shows a choice for Cancel or Undo, press F10 and choose that.

Help and how to get it

To get help in Paradox, press the F1 key. The Help system is context-sensitive, so if you are in the middle of a menu choice or command, the help you get will be on that command.

To get an index of help topics, simply press the F1 key a second time. To exit the Help system, press the Esc key as many times as it takes to back out.

Stan's Law of Survival: If you want to keep your head while all those about you are losing theirs, be in charge of the guillotine.

---

dBASE

dBASE is the other Borland database, and between it and Paradox, Borland has the vast majority of the database market for PCs. Even more than with Paradox, if you do have to use dBASE, chances are you won't know it. Most people who use dBASE use an application written with it and never actually see the guts of it. But should you fall out of your application and have to deal with raw dBASE, here is what you will need to know to stay afloat.

Getting started

The command to start dBASE is simple to remember:

    DBASE

If you were running a custom budget application that someone wrote called MYBUDGET, you would start it by typing

    DBASE MYBUDGET

A quick note is in order here. If you are running an application, it may well run directly from the command line and not require that you explicitly load dBASE. With the above example, this would mean that you simply type

    MYBUDGET

If you get a "Bad command or file name" message from DOS, dBASE isn't on your PATH. Try changing to its directory, which will usually be \DBASE, by typing

    CD \DBASE

Then try the DBASE command again.

☞ See "Finding Your True Path" in Chapter 13 for more on paths.

☞ If there isn't a \DBASE directory, see Chapter 15, "Whither Files?" for more on finding files.

Let me out!

To exit dBASE, press the F10 key to activate the menus, then select Exit and Quit. Or press Alt-E to go directly to the Exit menu and select Quit.

It is important that you always follow this procedure when running dBASE. Do not use Ctrl-Alt-Delete to quit. Like most databases, dBASE works with open data files on disk, and simply rebooting the computer can result in a corrupted database.

Saving your work

Since dBASE is a disk-based database, you don't, in the conventional sense of the word, need to save your work. Any changes you make to the database are immediately stored on disk, and simply following the normal exit procedure will result in all your work being saved.

Changes you make to an individual record are made permanent when you move the cursor off that record.

Getting around

Moving around in dBASE is pretty straightforward. Press the F10 key to activate the menus, and use the cursor keys to move between records, fields, views, and so forth.

If you should happen to end up with no menus, and nothing but a simple . on the bottom of the screen with a blinking cursor, you have accidentally found your way to dBASE's friendly "dot prompt." To return to the more friendly Command Center, type

    ASSIST

If you were running an application, such as MYBUDGET, type

    DO MYBUDGET

and you will be back in your application.

☞ *If you regularly use several different applications, make a list of the different application names and what application they actually run. That way if you end up at the dot prompt you know what to run.*

☞ *To exit dBASE from the dot prompt, type*

    QUIT

Canceling a command

The general cancel command is the Esc key. This will back you out of a menu or command, one step at a time.

If you back out too far, you will end up at the dot prompt. Don't panic! Just type

    ASSIST

to get back to the menus.

Help and how to get it

To get help in dBASE, press F1. Once you are in the help system, you can get a list of help topics by selecting CONTENTS at the bottom of the Help screen. Press the F3 key to see the previous screen of help and the F4 key to see the next. Pressing Esc will get you out of the Help system and back to dBASE.

Traffis's Truism: The attention span of a computer is only as long as its electrical cord.

Harvard Graphics

Harvard Graphics is easily the most popular DOS-based application for doing those important corporate dog-and-pony shows. You can use Harvard Graphics to create slide shows you run from your computer, make flimsies, create 35mm slides, or print out reports.

Harvard Graphics makes it easy to create charts, graphs, organization charts, and text charts. And it's a breeze to print them out in whatever form you need for that all-important presentation.

Getting started

To start Harvard Graphics, type

    HG

from the DOS command line. If you get a "Bad command or file name" message from DOS, try

    HG3

which is the command for version 3 of Harvard Graphics. If you still get a "Bad command or file name" message, then Harvard Graphics isn't on your PATH. Try changing to its directory, which will usually be HG or HG3, by typing

    CD \HG

Then try the HG or HG3 command again.

☞ See "Finding Your True Path" in Chapter 13 for more on paths.

☞ If there isn't a HG directory, try HG3. If you still can't find the Harvard Graphics files, see Chapter 15, "Whither Files?" for more on finding files.

Let me out!

To exit Harvard Graphics, press the Esc as many times as it takes to get back to the main menu. Then press E for Exit.

Saving your work

To save a chart, press Ctrl-S. You will be prompted for a name if Harvard Graphics doesn't already have a name for the chart.

Getting around

Getting around in Harvard Graphics is pretty easy. You can use your mouse to click on the menu choices or press the function keys that are shown at the bottom or top of the screen.

Pressing F2 displays the current chart, F3 is the Save key, and F10 is the key you use to tell Harvard Graphics that you are satisfied with the current task and want to go to the next. Other function keys have different uses, depending on where in the menu system you are and what you are doing.

Creating a basic pie chart

Pie charts are among the most common and useful charts used in business presentations today. They are perfect for showing how different items contribute to a whole—for seeing that the biggest chunk out of your paycheck goes to taxes, for example.

To create a simple pie chart, select Create New Chart from the main menu. This will bring up a menu called the Create New Chart menu. Original, isn't it? Select the type of chart you want to make, in this case Pie, from that menu. Now you will see a data-entry screen that lets you enter the data for the chart, as well as its title, subtitle, and so forth. Type in labels for each slice of the pie, along with the value for each slice.

To see what your chart looks like, press the F2 key. When you have everything where you want it, press F3 or Ctrl-S to save the current chart.

Making other kinds of charts is essentially the same as making a pie chart. Experiment! After all, the whole idea is to wow them with this presentation.

Ross's Rule of Presentations: The weaker the math, the more elaborate the graphics need to be.

Basic chart types

There are a number of basic chart types supported by Harvard Graphics, depending on the version you have, though the variations within each type make the actual number a whole lot higher. Some of the most important types are

- ☞ *Text charts,* which let you create bulleted lists, title pages, and multiple column charts.

- ☞ *Pie charts*, which are useful for showing how individual components contribute to the whole.

- ☞ *Bar & Line charts*, and the variations on these, such as stacked bar, which are best for showing trends over time. Choose bar charts for simple comparisons and presentations, and one of the line types when you want to focus on the change from one point to another.

- ☞ *Area charts* are good for showing volume changes, especially for emphasizing the effect that one component is having over time. They are more dramatic than line charts.

- ☞ *High/Low/Close charts* are special charts that are useful for showing distribution within a group, such as income within a job title.

- ☞ *Organization charts* let you show the structure of your department, company or group.

To check your spelling

To check the spelling of your chart, press F4 from the main menu. Harvard Graphics will check the spelling and look for doubled words and numbers with improper punctuation.

Printing it out

To print out your chart, select Produce Output from the main menu, or press Ctrl-P for print. Then select what kind of output device you want. This can be a printer, a plotter, a film recorder for 35mm slides, or various slide-show options.

Canceling a command

In Harvard Graphics, press the Esc key to back out of whatever you are in the middle of, one step at a time.

Help and how to get it

Press F1 at any time to get into the Help system. This will bring up help on the operation or menu you are in the middle of.

To get an index of help topics, press Shift-F1 while you are in the Help system.

To exit the Help system, press Esc one or more times.

Muranaka's Maxim: Adding staff to a late project makes it later.

Procomm Plus

Procomm Plus is a very popular communications program for the PC. If you have a modem attached to your computer, you will need some sort of communications software such as Procomm to be able to use that modem. And probably a fair amount of help.

There is nothing simple about using modems. Modem commands use a truly inspired language whose structure and syntax appear to have had their origins on Arcturis IV. Don't even think about trying to figure them out yourself. Get help.

If it's that hard, why would you want to do it at all? Probably the best reason is that it brings the outside world to your computer, and you to the outside world. Your modem connects your computer to a telephone line, and that telephone line is your gateway to a world of information, services, and people. You can use your modem to write and collect mail, research a term paper, order airline tickets, have flowers sent to your mother in Boise, or just to chat with friends you only know through the computer.

While this section focuses on Procomm Plus, the commercial version of the program, there is also a shareware version for which most of this will apply as well.

Getting started

To start Procomm Plus, type

    PCPLUS

If you get DOS's favorite "Bad command or file name" response, it means that Procomm isn't on your PATH. You need to change to the Procomm Plus subdirectory, which will usually be PCPLUS. Type

    CD \PCPLUS

and try the PCPLUS command again.

☞ See "Finding Your True Path" in Chapter 13 for more on paths.

☞ If there isn't a \PCPLUS directory, see Chapter 15, "Whither Files?" for more on finding files.

Let me out!

To exit Procomm, press Alt-X. Like most of Procomm's commands, this is the Alt key in combination with a letter that is a mnemonic (e**X**it) for the action you want.

Dialing a phone number

Here, as elsewhere, I am assuming that someone has already set up your copy of Procomm Plus. If they haven't, get some help to get everything set up before you start.

To get a list of phone numbers to dial, press Alt-D for Dialing Directory. A dialing directory contains a list of places you can call, and all the settings for your modem to use when calling that place. If someone has done a really good job of setting it up, it will even have an automatic script that logs you on to the bulletin board or service without your having to remember your password or any special commands that the service needs. To dial a number, just highlight the line and press Enter.

Your modem will usually make some weird modem and dialing noises, followed by a high-pitched computer warbling noise when it connects. Procomm will usually beep at you at this point and return to its main screen. If you have an automatic logon script for this number, it will now run.

If there is no automatic script to log you onto the computer you are calling, you will have to follow the prompts on the screen. This is the other computer telling you what information it wants before it lets you log on.

If you call a particular computer or service regularly and you don't have a logon script that handles everything automatically, you might want to ask for help creating one so you don't have to remember everything.

Logging on

The commands to log on (connect) to another computer, bulletin board, or online service will vary greatly depending on the software being used on the other end and what kind of service it is. Usually you will see some sort of introductory greeting asking you to enter your UserID (short for User Identification). If you have an automatic logon script already, then it should take over, logging you onto the other computer. If you don't, you will have to follow the prompts and answer the questions about who you are and what your password is to actually get logged onto the service.

If all you see on the screen is a bunch of weird characters, try pressing Alt-B to send a break signal to the other computer. Sometimes this will help. If that doesn't work, try pressing Enter. If that doesn't do it, press Alt-H to hang up, and get some help setting up the options on your modem to match the service you are connecting to.

Capturing what is on the screen

Frequently, what you want to do is simply "capture" everything that is happening on the screen so you can look at it later when you aren't running up your phone bill or CompuServe bill. To do this, press Alt-F1 and type in a name for the log file. Any old DOS name will do. Now, everything that happens will get saved into this file, and you can look at it later with your word processor or DOS EDIT. To turn the capture file off again, press Alt-F1.

Uploading/downloading

Frequently, the reason you connect to another computer with a modem is to upload or download a file. This could be a new mouse driver from your mouse company's bulletin board or the chapter for your new book that you are uploading to your publisher.

In order to send or receive a file, the two computers have to agree on a method to make sure that the file gets through without errors and that errors that are there get fixed. This method is called a *protocol*, and there are several different ones available. Procomm Plus knows most of them, so it is merely a matter of choosing one that the computer on the other end likes.

Common protocol names include XMODEM, YMODEM, KERMIT, and CompuServe QuickB. XMODEM is usually a safe bet, since almost everyone has it available.

In order to download a file from the other computer to your computer, you first need to select it from the other computer. The methods will vary, depending on the software the other computer is using. But once you have selected it, you will also have to tell the other computer what protocol to use. Once everything is done though, you will see a message on the screen that says something like "Starting Transfer." At that point, press the PgDn key. Procomm will ask you to select a protocol. Pick whichever one you selected for the other computer, then tell Procomm what name to give the file and press Enter. The file transfer will begin. Procomm Plus puts an informational window on the screen that tells you how the download is proceeding. When the transfer is complete, it beeps at you.

For uploading a file, the steps are pretty similar, except that you press the PgUp key when you are ready to have Procomm start the upload.

Disconnecting

To disconnect from the other computer, you should first *log off* from it. This means you need to tell it that you are going to disconnect. If you just hang up the modem and don't politely log out first, the other computer will eventually figure out that you aren't logged on anymore, but it will be in no hurry about the process. The exact command to log off will depend on the software on the other end, but will usually be something like Exit, Bye, or G for good-bye.

Most bulletin boards and commercial service software have a built-in help system for you. Try pressing the ? key and see what it says. Usually this will give you a list of commands, one of which should be how to say good-bye.

Once you have figured out how to tell the other computer you want to log off and done so, press Alt-H to hang up the modem. And if you can't figure out how to politely log off, Alt-H by itself will get you off the rude way.

Canceling a command

To cancel a command in Procomm, press the Esc key. This will stop Procomm from completing the dialing it has started, but it will not tell it to disconnect from another computer once you have actually connected.

Help and how to get it

Press Alt-Z at any time to get help on the current operation and a list of possible commands you can issue. You can then directly issue the commands without leaving the Help system, or you can exit Help by pressing the Esc key one or more times.

Windows

By itself, Windows is cute, but useless. However, it provides an operating environment that is becoming more common every day. If your computer has the hardware to support it (and it *is* a hardware hog), Windows provides a useful and easy-to-use environment to work in. Plus, you get access to the whole range of new programs that require Windows while still having all your old DOS favorites available.

One word of warning. While you can, technically, run Windows without a mouse, in fact it just isn't real. So if you don't have a mouse, pass on Windows until you can get one.

For a complete guide to surviving in Windows, go back to the bookstore and buy a copy of *Murphy's Laws of Windows* (SYBEX, 1993). But for a quick crib, read this.

Getting started

To start Windows, just type

```
WIN
```

at the DOS prompt. If you get a "Bad command or file name" response, it means that Windows isn't installed, or for some reason it isn't on your PATH. Since Windows gets pretty fussy about wanting to be on your PATH, refer to "The PATH Command" in Chapter 13 for help on adding the Windows directory to your PATH. Then try again after you have rebooted your computer.

To start a program from within Windows, double-click on its *icon*. The icon is the little graphic square that is supposed to tell you which program it is for. Some of them even do.

Many computers that have large hard drives and lots of programs on them get so cluttered with possible icons that it gets hard to find the one you want. Get some help from someone who uses Windows all the time to set your Windows environment up so that you can easily find the programs you actually use without having to hunt around for them.

Let me out!

To exit from Windows, or any Windows-only program, select File from the main menu bar and then select Exit, or simply press Alt-F4, the universal Windows command to tell a program enough already. Windows will usually ask you to confirm that you really want to leave if you are leaving Windows completely. If you are leaving a Windows program and you haven't saved your work since the last change, you will be offered an opportunity to do so before the program terminates.

Nine Programs

Always make sure you exit all the way out of Windows before you turn off your computer. It is easy to think you are back at the DOS prompt, even when you're still in Windows. If you are at the DOS prompt and ready to turn off your computer, type

    EXIT

first to make sure. If you are still in Windows or any other program, this will send you back to that program. From there, you can exit properly to the DOS prompt before turning off your computer.

Opening a file

Once you get a Windows program started, you need to open a document or worksheet to get some work done. If you will be working on an existing document or worksheet, pull down the File menu and select Open from it. Use the dialog box to select the file you want to work with and open it up.

If you want to create a new file, you are probably already where you need to be. When you first start up a Windows program, you will get a new, blank document or worksheet to work on, unless you include a file to load on the initial command line. If you want to open another new document or worksheet, pull down the File menu and select New from it. Many Windows programs allow you to have multiple documents or worksheets open at the same time.

Saving your work

Windows programs are pretty consistent. To save your work in any Windows program (as opposed to a regular DOS program that you just happen to be running under Windows), select Save from the File menu.

Getting around

Windows programs can be run full-screen, so that they take up the entire screen on your computer, or they can be run in a smaller window so that you can see more than one program at a time. You can even shrink them down to little tiny icons that line up along the bottom of the screen.

To switch between open windows, just click the mouse anywhere in the window you want.

If the program you want is *iconized* (turned into one of those little graphic things on the bottom of the screen), you will need to double-click on the icon to open it.

If you have a program running full-screen and can't see anything else, press Shift-Tab repeatedly to cycle through the list of available programs, or press Ctrl-Esc to pop up a Task List of all the open programs. Double-click on the one you want to run.

Editing 101

Most Windows programs follow one of two conventions for the basic editing commands. Programs written for Windows 3.0 use Ctrl-Del to cut a block to the Clipboard, Ctrl-Ins to copy a block to the Clipboard, and Shift-Ins to paste the block back into the document.

Programs written to the newer Windows 3.1 standard use Ctrl-X to cut a block, Ctrl-C to copy a block, and Ctrl-V to paste it back in. Many Windows programs will accept both the old and new commands.

Printing it out

To print from most Windows programs, you simply select Print from the File menu. This menu will also allow you to choose which printer to print to by selecting Printer Setup.

Canceling a command

To cancel a command or exit a menu in Windows or a Windows program, press the Esc key one or more times.

If you make a mistake in a Windows program and want to undo your last command, press Alt-Backspace. This will usually undo the last command or edit. In Windows 3.1, this is being replaced by Ctrl-Z, though most programs will still accept Alt-Backspace.

Nine Programs

Help and how to get it

The majority of Windows programs have excellent help systems. To get help on any part of a program, just press the F1 key or pull down the Help menu from the main menu bar. This will always be the last menu choice on the far right-hand side of the menu bar across the top of the program or across the top of the Windows Program Manager.

Murphy's Last Rule: If something doesn't go wrong, in the end it will be shown that it would have been ultimately beneficial for it to have gone wrong.

Chapter 23

DOS COMMANDS YOU WILL ACTUALLY USE

Murphy's Sixth Law: There are no real secrets—only obfuscations.

DOS COMMANDS RANGE from the everyday-useful to the hopelessly abstruse. In this chapter you'll find the dozen and a half commands that pop up pretty frequently. See Chapter 24 for commands that you'll use infrequently or not at all. Chapter 25 covers the commands that you should definitely leave alone.

The only switches and parameters shown here are the ones you're likely to be using. You can find every single possible switch and parameter by typing in the name of the command you want followed by /?. Elements that appear in regular type must be entered exactly as shown. Elements in italic are placeholders for information you have to supply. For assistance interpreting the syntax, you may want to look at "Command Line Syntax" in Chapter 2.

BACKUP

This is something you'll use only if you have DOS 5 or earlier. You should be backing up often to safeguard your files, but get someone else to set up this command for you.

CD

By itself, this command will display the name of the **C**urrent **D**irectory. With additional parameters, you can use it to **C**hange **D**irectories.

Syntax

```
CD [drive:] [path]
```

Drive specifies the drive you want CD to operate on. Not necessary if you want to stay on the current drive. *Path* specifies where you want to change to. For more on using this command, see "Moving around in Directories" in Chapter 13.

CHDIR

Same as CD.

CHKDSK

Checks out your disk and reports on what it finds.

Syntax

```
CHKDSK [drive:] [/F]
```

If you don't specify a drive, CHKDSK will report on the current drive. The /F switch tells CHKDSK to repair file errors it finds. For more on CHKDSK, see "How Much Room? The CHKDSK Command" in Chapter 13.

CLS

CLears the **S**creen. Just type in

```
CLS
```

at the DOS prompt and you can clear the screen of everything except the prompt. Useful for clearing off embarrassing error messages before you call in the DOS guru.

COPY

Copies one or more files from one location to another.

Syntax

```
COPY fromwhere towhere
```

OK, so those aren't official DOS parameters, but you know what I mean. The drive, path, and file names are part of *fromwhere* and *towhere*. See Chapter 3, "Files and the Things You Do with Them," for the scoop on copying.

DEFRAG

A command you should run every week or so. Reorganizes the files on your hard disk. Just type in

```
DEFRAG
```

at the DOS prompt and follow the instructions. For more on why you need to run DEFRAG, see "DEFRAG This, Jack!" in Chapter 13.

Useful Commands

DEL

Deletes the files you tell it to.

Syntax

```
DEL [drive:] [path] filename
```

The drive and path only have to be included if the file is not in the same directory as you are. Before you start deleting files see the precautions in "Deleting Multiple Files" in Chapter 3.

DIR

Displays a iist of files and directories in the directory you specify.

Syntax

```
DIR [drive:] [path] [/P] [/W] [/B]
```

Drive and *path* only have to be included if you want a listing in a directory other than your current one. The switches are

/P   Displays a **P**age-at-a-time

/W   Displays five columns **W**ide

/B   Displays just the **B**are names

See "The DIR Command" in Chapter 15 for more on the DIR command.

DISKCOPY

Copies everything on one floppy disk to another floppy of the same size and type, including the volume name and any hidden files.

Syntax

```
DISKCOPY [drive1:] [drive2:] [/V]
```

To make a copy of your disk in drive A, just type in

```
DISKCOPY A: A:
```

You'll be prompted to put in the source disk (the original) and the target disk (the copy). Add the /V switch if you want DOS to **V**erify that the copy is identical to the original. This slows the process a lot but is comforting when you want to be absolutely sure that the copy is good.

☞ See "Copying a Floppy onto Another Floppy of the Same Type" in Chapter 9 for more on DISKCOPY.

ERASE

Same as DEL.

FASTHELP

In DOS 6, just type

```
FASTHELP
```

at the prompt to get a one-line summary of each DOS command. To get the same in DOS 5, type

```
HELP
```

at the prompt.

FORMAT

All floppies must be formatted before they can be used by DOS.

Syntax

```
FORMAT drive: [/F:size] [/S]
```

You only need to use the /F switch if you are formatting a low-density disk in a high-density drive. If the disk is a 5¼-inch low-density disk, the switch will be /F:360. If it's a 3½-inch low-density disk, the switch is /F:720. See "How to Format a Floppy" in Chapter 9 for information on how to use FORMAT. Remember, you never want to format a disk other than a floppy.

The /S switch copies the system files to the floppy and makes it bootable. See "How to Make a Boot Floppy and What to Do with It" in Chapter 16 for information on bootable disks.

☞ *If you have a version of DOS before 5.0, the process of formatting a disk of a density different from your drive's is much messier. Get a DOS expert to show you how and then write down the instructions, because you'll never remember them the next time.*

HELP

To get help on a specific command, type in **HELP** followed by the name of the command (DOS 5 and DOS 6 only). In DOS 6, type **HELP** alone to get a whole list of commands to choose from. Use your mouse to highlight the command you want help on. Double-click on it to get *pages* of information.

MD

Makes a **D**irectory.

Syntax

    MD [*drive:*] *path*

See "Making a New Directory" in Chapter 13 for a good example of how to use this command.

MKDIR

Same as MD.

MOVE

Moves one or more files to the location you specify. This command is in DOS 6 only.

Syntax

```
MOVE fromwhere towhere
```

More unofficial commands! Basically remember that *fromwhere* means the identification of the file you want to move (its name and path) and *towhere* is the path to the destination. So, if you want to move ALFIE.TXT to the LETTERS directory on drive C, the command is

```
MOVE ALFIE.TXT C:\LETTERS
```

If you want to rename the file at the same time, it's

```
MOVE ALFIE.TXT C:\LETTERS\ALFREDO.TXT
```

You can even rename the directory from LETTERS to MEMOS by typing in

```
MOVE C:\LETTERS C:\MEMOS
```

See "Moving Files—A Reason to Get DOS 6" in Chapter 3 for help in using this command. If you don't have DOS 6, see "Moving Files If You Don't Have DOS 6" in the same chapter.

MSAV

This is the program in DOS 6 that scans your computer looking for viruses. If you don't have it in your AUTOEXEC.BAT file, you'll want to run it often.

At the DOS prompt, type in

```
MSAV
```

Select Detect to scan your drive for viruses; select Detect & Clean to scan for viruses and remove any that are found.

Useful Commands

☞ For more on viruses and how to avoid them, see Chapter 14, "An Ounce of Prevention."

REN

REName changes the name of a file.

Syntax

    REN filename1 filename2

Include the path to *filename1* if the file is not in your current directory. You can't use REN to rename files across drives, to rename subdirectories, or to move files. Use the MOVE command, above, to do that.

☞ See "Renaming Files" in Chapter 3 for more information on RENAME.

RESTORE

This is the reverse of BACKUP, the backup command used in DOS 5 and earlier. Have someone else set up BACKUP and RESTORE for you.

UNDELETE

Restores files deleted using the DEL command (DOS 5 and DOS 6 only).

Syntax

    UNDELETE filename

or

    UNDELETE /LIST

The /LIST switch gives a listing of all the files that DOS deems to be recoverable.

☞ "Undeleting a File" in Chapter 3 has lots more on the UNDELETE command.

Chapter 24

DOS COMMANDS YOU WILL USE ONLY ONCE...
(Or Only Once in a While)

Tauber's Truism: When all else fails, read the instructions.

THE COMMANDS IN this chapter are those that may cross your path in a very limited way. Some, like DBLSPACE or MEMMAKER, are one-time-only commands. You run them once to set up your hard disk and your memory and then forget about them. Others are commands that you might have occasion to use only rarely. If you live a good clean life you may never have to use them at all.

ATTRIB

With this command you can add or remove the read-only, hidden, archive, or system **ATTRIB**utes of certain files or directories. It is not a good idea to fool with attributes unless you are sure you know what you're doing. Some information about ATTRIB is in "Bad Guests—Files That Refuse to Leave" in Chapter 3.

COMP

COMPares the contents of two files to see if they're identical (DOS 5 and earlier).

Syntax

```
COMP firstfile secondfile
```

You need to include paths for files that are not in your current directory.

DATE

To change the date in your computer, type in

```
DATE
```

at the prompt. You'll get a display of the current date and the chance to enter a new date.

DBLSPACE

This command to increases the capacity of your hard disk. You'll probably only use it once. See "Double Your Hard Disk, Double Your Fun" in Chapter 13 for more on DBLSPACE.

DISKCOMP

Compares two disks to see if they're identical. It works only with floppy disks and is not very useful. But if you *insist*, you can compare two floppy disks of the size that fit in your drive A by typing

```
DISKCOMP A: A:
```

You'll get prompts telling you how to proceed.

ECHO

You're unlikely to use this command unless you start messing around with batch files. However, you are likely to see it in your AUTOEXEC.BAT. The instruction ECHO ON means that the contents of the batch file are displayed on the screen while the batch file is running. If the command is changed to ECHO OFF, the file still runs but the text is hidden.

FC

This command, which stands for **F**ile **C**ompare, compares two files and displays any differences between them. See "It Worked Yesterday" in Chapter 16 for a demonstration of how to use FC.

FIND

Looks for text that you specify.

Syntax

```
FIND /I "string" [drive:] [path] filename
```

The switch /I tells the command not to be case-sensitive. "*String*" stands for the text you want to find; make sure you enclose it in quotes. Specify a drive and path if you want to direct the search to a particular area. For example, if you want to find all files in the directory LETTERS that contain the words "my lawyer will be in touch," type in

```
FIND /I "my lawyer will be in touch" C:\LETTERS
```

Sometime Commands

LABEL

Use LABEL to add a volume label to a disk. See "Copying a Floppy onto Another Floppy of a Different Type" in Chapter 9 for an example of how to use LABEL.

MEM

Displays all sorts of confusing information on used and available memory on your computer. For all you could possibly want to know about memory and more, see Chapter 6, "Memory (What You Need and What You Don't)."

MEMMAKER

A program you'll probably run only once. See "Getting More Conventional Memory Using DOS 6" in Chapter 6 for instructions.

MORE

If you are in the habit of viewing long files at the DOS prompt, you will need this command. It lets you view such a file, one page at a time.

Syntax

```
MORE < filename
```

You'll get the first page of the file with the prompt "-More-" at the bottom of the screen. Press any key to see the next screen.

PATH

The PATH command, which can be found in your AUTOEXEC.BAT, designates which directories DOS should search for files. (See "The PATH Command" in Chapter 13 for information on how to change your PATH statement). To get a display of what the current search path is, just type in

    PATH

at the DOS prompt.

PRINT

Prints a text file while you are doing something else. See "Putting it on Paper" in Chapter 3 for more on this command.

PROMPT

Use PROMPT to customize the look of your DOS prompt.

Syntax

    PROMPT [*text*]

The text is whatever you want to see. "Playing with Prompts" in Chapter 11 tells you how to get both normal and weird variations on the prompt.

RD

Removes a directory, but only after you have removed all the files in the directory.

Syntax

    RD [*drive:*] *path*

The parameter [*drive:*] *path* specifies the location and name of the directory you want to delete.

REM

This is short for **REM**ark. You may see this in your AUTOEXEC.BAT or CONFIG.SYS file. It means that the words that follow it are comments or a disabled command. DOS will not act on an instruction preceded by REM.

REPLACE

Replaces files in a destination directory with files in a source directory that have the same name.

Syntax

```
REPLACE fromwhere towhere [/P] [/U]
```

Fromwhere is the location, including the path, of the source files. *Towhere* is the destination, including the path. If you add the /P switch, you'll get a prompt before a file is replaced.

Add the /U switch and the command will only replace the files on the destination directory that are older than those in the source directory. This is really useful if you're working on two computers and ferrying files back and forth. With REPLACE you can always have the newest version of each file on your hard disk.

RMDIR

Same as RD.

SYS

Creates a bootable disk by copying the system files to the disk.

Syntax

```
SYS drive:
```

Drive: specifies where you want the files copied *to*. The disk needs to be formatted first. If it isn't, you can save a step by using the command

    FORMAT *drive:* /S

See "How to Make a Boot Floppy and What to Do with It" in Chapter 16 for more on bootable disks.

TIME

To see what time your computer thinks it is, type in

    TIME

at the DOS prompt. You can type in a new time or press Enter to accept the time displayed. See "Pardon Me, Do You Have the Time?" in Chapter 11 for more on the TIME command.

TREE

TREE will give you a graphical representation of a directory's structure.

Syntax

    TREE [*drive:*] [*path*] [/F]

If you don't include a path, you'll get a display of *all* the directories on the drive. Include the /F switch if you want all the files in the tree shown too. If the display goes scrolling by too fast, use the same command as before but add a space and then

    ¦ MORE

That's the pipe character, another space, and the command MORE. That will give you one screen's worth at a time.

☞ If you have DOS 5 or DOS 6 you can get the same effect using DOS Shell. See Chapter 4 for information on using DOS Shell.

TYPE

This command will display on screen the contents of a text file.

Syntax

```
TYPE [drive:] [path] filename
```

If the file is longer than a screen's worth, use the same command, add a space, and type in

```
¦ MORE
```

That's the pipe character, another space, and the command MORE. That will give you one screen's worth at a time.

UNFORMAT

Recovers a disk that was erased by using the FORMAT command.

Syntax

```
UNFORMAT drive:
```

See the section called "Format C:—How to Unformat" in Chapter 16 for information on the UNFORMAT command.

VER

Type in this command at the DOS prompt to see what version of DOS is installed.

VOL

If the disk has a volume label and serial number, this command will display what they are.

Syntax

```
VOL drive:
```

VSAFE

VSAFE is a command in DOS 6 that, when loaded, continuously monitors your system to guard against viruses. For information on when and how to run VSAFE, see "The Ultimate Security against Viruses" in Chapter 14.

XCOPY

This command copies directories, their subdirectories, and files, unlike the COPY command, which only does files.

Syntax

```
XCOPY fromwhere towhere [/S]
```

Fromwhere includes the location of the files you want to copy. *Towhere* specifies the destination of the files you want to copy. Include the /S switch and all subdirectories will be included unless they are empty. More information is in "Including Subdirectories (The XCOPY Command)" in Chapter 3.

Chapter 25

DOS COMMANDS YOU SHOULD LEAVE ALONE

McEtchin's Postulate: Facts are not all equal. There are good facts and bad facts. Science consists of using good facts.

THE FOLLOWING COMMANDS are either useless to you or positively dangerous. Feel free to look them up in the Help system, but be sure you know what you're doing before you start fooling around with them—especially those with the Warning sign.

This book tries to avoid the DOS commands that are too silly to talk about. However, the ones that have crept in are in this chapter.

APPEND
Allows DOS to look in directories other than the current one to find data files. Not nearly as useful as it sounds and not worth the trouble.

ASSIGN
Assigns a different drive letter to an existing drive. You don't want or need to do this (DOS 5 and earlier).

BREAK
Controls how often DOS checks for Ctrl-C (or Ctrl-Break) while running programs. The default setting is OFF, which is what it should be.

CHCP
CHanges the **C**ode **P**age that devices use to generate characters. Not something you could do easily, even if you wanted to.

COMMAND
This is actually the file COMMAND.COM and it's what runs the command interpreter of DOS. Don't delete it.

CTTY
This command can disconnect your keyboard and monitor so that you have to use the reset button to get your computer back. It's not usable for anything you have to do.

DEBUG
This sounds like something you might want to do. It isn't. It's a nerdish tool that not even nerds use any more.

DELTREE
New in DOS 6, this command allows you to delete an entire directory and all its files and all its sub-directories and all *their* files—all at once. This is very powerful and very dangerous. Even UNDELETE won't save you if you use this command in error. (But UnErase in the Norton Utilities can save the day if you act *immediately*. See Chapter 21, "Seven Programs That Can Save Your Cookies.")

EXPAND
If you mess up one or more of your necessary DOS files, a DOS expert can use this command to get them back from your original installation disks.

FASTOPEN	This is supposed to speed up the process of opening frequently used files and directories. It doesn't work very well and causes mysterious problems.

FDISK	You should never have to run this program. It prepares your hard disk for formatting when it is new. This was done when the disk was new and doing it again can cost you the contents of your hard disk. This one is strictly for experts.

GRAPHICS	A specialized command that loads a memory-resident program to let you use the Shift-PrintScreen keys to send a graphic screen to a Hewlett-Packard or IBM printer. If you need this, and you probably don't, have an experienced DOS user set it up for you.

JOIN	An old-time DOS command that makes a whole drive look to be a subdirectory on another drive. This command was dropped in DOS 6 and was archaic even in DOS 5. Both useless and dangerous.

KEYB	This command lets you install a foreign-language keyboard driver. If you need this, get a guru to set it up for you.

MODE	A gut-level command that configures hardware attached to your computer. Most of this is done automatically by software these days. If you need to use it, you'll likely need help.

RECOVER	This is a really nasty command that purports to recover data from a defective hard disk. Its reputation is so lousy that it's not even included with DOS 6. You do not want to use this command under any circumstances. If you are having difficulties with your hard disk, get some help either from a DOS expert or a program like the Norton Disk Doctor. (See Chapter 21 for "Seven Programs That Can Save Your Cookies." Information on hard disk problems is in Chapters 16 and 17.)

Commands to Forget

SET

This command controls what are called environment variables. You don't care what they are. If you insist, type **SET** at the DOS prompt and press Enter. Didn't I tell you?

SETVER

This has to do with the DOS version table. Don't tamper with this and you'll stay happy.

SHARE

Your mother always said it was nice to SHARE. But you don't have to unless you're on a network—and then it's the administrator's problem. If a program, such as a database, needs to have SHARE running even when you aren't on a network, it will tell you. Otherwise, you don't need it.

SUBST

This is a command that tricks DOS into thinking that a directory is actually a drive. Tricky business that should be left to experts.

VERIFY

This is an older fail-safe command designed to double-check that files are being written correctly to a disk. This falls in the category of wearing a belt, suspenders, *and* colorful underwear in case both fail. It slows your computer down dramatically and doesn't work very well. Normally it's OFF.

Glossary

FORTY-SIX TERMS THAT WILL IMPRESS YOUR FRIENDS
(And Confound Your Enemies)

Address The location of a given bit of memory. The numbers are expressed in the numbering system called hexadecimal (base 16), which is just as bad as it sounds.

ANSI Stands for **A**merican **N**ational **S**tandards **I**nstitute (pronounced *AN-see*). This is a numerical code for characters that is becoming more common since it is used by Windows and Windows programs.

Application An application is a collection of files that may include several programs. Lotus 1-2-3 is an application consisting of a number of files that together constitute a single package. Applications are also grouped by type, such as word processing applications, database applications, and so forth.

ASCII Stands for the **A**merican **S**tandard **C**ode for **I**nformation **I**nterchange (pronounced *AS-key*). Developed back in the sixties as a standard numerical code for characters used on all computers. Today, the usual use is to mean a normal text as opposed to one in code unreadable by humans.

Attribute A bit of code in a file that gives DOS specific information about the file's status. Two attributes are handled by DOS (the directory attribute and the volume label attribute). The other four are read-only, hidden, archive, and system. A file can have none or any number of the attributes. You can modify these but you shouldn't.

Baud The speed at which data is transmitted over a communications line or cable. This is not the same as BPS (bits per second), but it matters not.

Bit Short for **b**inary dig**it**. Represents a single switch inside a computer set to 0 or 1. There are millions of them in every computer. Eight bits make up a byte, the basic unit of data storage.

Boot A simple name for the complicated process your computer goes through when starting up. Restarting by pressing Ctrl-Alt-Delete is a "warm boot." Starting up from a power-off is a "cold boot."

Bootable disk When your system starts up, it looks for a disk first in drive A. If none is there it goes to drive C. When a disk is found, the computer examines the disk to see if it contains the *system* files. When a disk with system files is found, the computer uses that disk's information to start the system running. If a disk with system files is in drive A, that disk will be used to tell the computer about itself. Computers can normally be booted only from drive A or drive C.

BPS **B**its **p**er **s**econd. A unit of measurement for the communication speed of modems and fax modems.

Buffer An area of memory set up to speed the transfer of data, allowing blocks of information to be moved at once.

Byte A basic measurement of capacity. A byte is eight bits. For all intents and purposes, a byte equals a single character.

Clone A copy of the original IBM PC and PC/AT. All PCs that aren't made by IBM are technically clones.

CMOS Stands for **C**omplementary **M**etal-**O**xide **S**emiconductor. It's the area in your computer that stores the most basic configuration information about what hardware is in your machine.

Default Means the setting that the device or program will have without any intervention from you. Usually you can change the default settings, but you shouldn't unless you have a good reason.

DIP switches Stands for **D**ual **I**nline **P**ackage. These are tiny little switches mounted directly on a printed circuit board (on a printer you can see the switches but not the circuit board). Usually used for changing the default settings for a device. Don't use a pencil to change a DIP switch, since the lead can break off and cause problems. Always change DIP switch settings when the power is off.

Download To download a file is to get it from somewhere else to you. In the case of a printer, downloading can mean sending a soft font to the printer to be stored in the printer's memory.

Driver A program made up of instructions to operate things that are added on to your computer, such as printers, a mouse, expanded memory, and so forth.

Expanded memory A kind of "paged" memory that is used to get around the limitations of DOS, which will only use a maximum of 640K of memory.

Extended memory Memory whose address is greater than 1 megabyte. Not available on older XT-compatible computers, and still not used by most DOS programs. But Windows loves this kind of memory.

IDE Stands for **I**ntegrated **D**rive **E**lectronics. Used to describe the most common type of hard drive in PCs these days. IDE drives are like BIC pens. They work really well and are really cheap, but when they break down you can't fix 'em. You gotta get a new one.

Initialize To prepare for use. With disks, this means to format the disk so that DOS can read it. Programmers use this term to mean to get everything in the program to a known, beginning state.

Kilobyte One thousand bytes (actually 1024). Abbreviated as K and KB.

Macro Essentially a little program that you write yourself to automate a frequently performed task. Most word processing and spreadsheet applications have ways for you to write macros. DOSKEY is the program for writing macros in DOS.

Megabyte One million bytes (or 1,048,576 bytes). Abbreviated as M or MB.

Memory-resident A program that starts when your computer starts but then retreats into the background and waits for you to activate it. Also called a TSR (for **T**erminate and **S**tay **R**esident). All memory-resident programs use up chunks of your conventional memory, so there's a real limit to how many can be running at a time.

Mode The state a program or device is in. When used with video equipment, this could be "graphics mode" or "text mode." Also, a DOS command to control how DOS will communicate with various peripheral devices.

Modem A contraction for **mo**dulator-**dem**odulator. A device that hooks up to phone lines so your computer can communicate with other computers.

On-line To be in a state of readiness. A printer is said to be on-line when it's ready to print. On-line is also used to mean being connected to another computer via modem.

Optimize Computer jargon for "improve the performance of."

Parallel A port on your computer usually used to connect to a printer. Can also be used to connect other devices, such as external drives or network cards, to your computer.

Parameter An optional instruction that alters the default setting of a DOS command when added. Some parameters are switches, but others are values or codes of some kind. The Help screen for each command shows the possible parameters.

Peripheral A device attached to the outside of your computer. Some common peripherals are the monitor, keyboard, mouse, and printer.

Port A connector on your computer for plugging in external devices. At a minimum, computers will have one serial port and one parallel (printer) port.

PostScript A page description language. Used on many printers to provide high-quality text and graphics output, but can also be used to control video displays.

Protocol A set of rules that determine the flow of data and how it's used. The modems at either end of a communication line have to be using the same protocol to talk to each other.

Scalable font A font that can be "scaled" up or down. These are the kind to have since they don't take up a lot of storage space on your hard drive.

Scanner A truly cool device that lets you "read" a letter or a picture or a drawing so that it becomes a file on your computer. With appropriate software you can then manipulate the file or even send it off to someone via fax.

SCSI Stands for **S**mall **C**omputer **S**ystems **I**nterface. This is an almost(!) standard way to connect a wide variety of peripheral devices to your computer. But still mostly for nerds.

Serial A particular type of port. Mostly used by modems but also occasionally by a mouse, a scanner, or a weird printer. Communicates one bit at a time.

Shareware A special type of software developed by guys in a garage as well as by real companies, shareware is try-before-you-buy. Use it and if you like it, pay the (usually) modest fee to register it. Shareware is available through bulletin boards, some retail outlets, catalogs, and (most often) from a friend.

Soft font This is a font that is not normally present in your printer, but that you can download to it. Normally stored on your hard disk.

String Computer talk for any group of characters that a DOS command handles as a single unit. When supplying a string for a DOS command you can use any characters on the keyboard, including blank spaces.

Switch   A parameter in a DOS command preceded by a slash (/). Like other parameters, switches change the default setting of the command.

Syntax   The grammar of DOS. In other words, the form and order in which instructions must be entered.

System Files   A bootable has on it COMMAND.COM (the DOS command processor) and DOS's two system files, IO.SYS and MSDOS.SYS (in PC-DOS, it's IBMBIO.COM and IBMDOS.COM). The system files are hidden, so you'll need a file viewer like Norton Commander or LIST to see them. You don't need to though, there's certainly nothing special to look at.

Upload   Send a file to another computer, using a modem and communications software.

Mega-Index

Are you ornery enough to take on The Murphy's Mega-Index?

There is a **MURPHY'S LAW OF INDEXES** too. It says that even if you list something in an index ten different ways, someone will always come along ornery enough to look for it an *eleventh* way!

If you look for some information in our index, and you do not find it listed the *first way you look it up*, let us know. We'll add your eleventh way of looking it up to future indexes AND you will earn yourself a place in Indexer's Heaven!

Symbols

This index contains certain typographical conventions to assist you in finding information. **Boldface** page numbers are references to primary topics and explanations that are emphasized in the text. *Italics* indicate page numbers that reference figures.

This index contains certain typographical conventions to assist you in finding information. **Boldface** page numbers are references to primary topics and explanations that are emphasized in the text. *Italics* indicate page numbers that reference figures.

This index contains certain typographical conventions to assist you in finding information. **Boldface** page numbers are references to primary topics and explanations that are emphasized in the text. *Italics* indicate page numbers that reference figures.

This index contains certain typographical conventions to assist you in finding information. **Boldface** page numbers are references to primary topics and explanations that are emphasized in the text. *Italics* indicate page numbers that reference figures.

This index contains certain typographical conventions to assist you in finding information. **Boldface** page numbers are references to primary topics and explanations that are emphasized in the text. *Italics* indicate page numbers that reference figures.

This index contains certain typographical conventions to assist you in finding information. **Boldface** page numbers are references to primary topics and explanations that are emphasized in the text. *Italics* indicate page numbers that reference figures.

I

This index contains certain typographical conventions to assist you in finding information. **Boldface** page numbers are references to primary topics and explanations that are emphasized in the text. *Italics* indicate page numbers that reference figures.

This index contains certain typographical conventions to assist you in finding information. **Boldface** page numbers are references to primary topics and explanations that are emphasized in the text. *Italics* indicate page numbers that reference figures.

This index contains certain typographical conventions to assist you in finding information. **Boldface** page numbers are references to primary topics and explanations that are emphasized in the text. *Italics* indicate page numbers that reference figures.

This index contains certain typographical conventions to assist you in finding information. **Boldface** page numbers are references to primary topics and explanations that are emphasized in the text. *Italics* indicate page numbers that reference figures.

file allocation tables, **174**
floppy disks, **109–110**, *110*
from viruses, **181–186**
protocols, 66
definition of, 325
for file transfers, 293
punctuation in commands, 24. *See also*
specific punctuation symbols
purchasing
floppy disks, **106–107**
software, **149–152**

Q

$Q parameter for PROMPT, 145–146
QBE (query by example), 282
QD (quad-density) floppy disks, 106
QEMM memory manager, 80–81, **249**
Quattro Pro application, **267**
appearance of, **272**
executable file for, 15–16
formatting in, **271–272**
help for, **273**
math in, **270–271**
moving around and editing in,
269–270
opening files in, **268–269**
printing in, **272–273**
saving files in, 269
starting and exiting, **267–268**
querying Paradox records, **282–283**
question marks (?)
for command help, 12–13
in deleted files, 209
as wildcard character, 197
questioning experts, 225
Quicken application, executable file
for, 16
quitting programs. *See* exiting
quotation marks (')
in Lotus 1-2-3, 276
in Quattro Pro, 270
QWERTY keyboard layout, 85

R

R file attribute, 41–42
RAM (random access memory). *See*
memory
raster fonts, 119
RD command, 311
read errors, 223, 230
README files, 152, 154–155
read-only attribute, 41–42
read-only files, 308
deleting, **41**
error message for, 228
reading file contents, **11–12**, **246–247**,
314
rebooting, **17–18**
quitting applications by, **243**
for system file changes activation, **138**,
210
receiving files with Procomm Plus, **293**
records, database, 280–283
RECOVER command, 243, 319
recovering
files, 319. *See also* undeleting files
from formatting, **213**
Reference Manuals, 158
reformatting floppy disks, 109
refresh rate for monitors, 100
refreshing hard drives, **254**
registering shareware, **159–160**
registration cards, 155
reinforcing hub rings, 106
reinitializing printers, 125
REM command, 312
remarks in system files, 312
removing (deleting). *See* deleting
removing (withdrawing) floppy disks,
10–11, 240
REN (RENAME) command (DOS), **44–45**,
229–230, **306**
Rename command (DOS Shell), 53

This index contains certain typographical conventions to assist you in finding information. **Boldface** page numbers are references to primary topics and explanations that are emphasized in the text. *Italics* indicate page numbers that reference figures.

This index contains certain typographical conventions to assist you in finding information. **Boldface** page numbers are references to primary topics and explanations that are emphasized in the text. *Italics* indicate page numbers that reference figures.

This index contains certain typographical conventions to assist you in finding information. **Boldface** page numbers are references to primary topics and explanations that are emphasized in the text. *Italics* indicate page numbers that reference figures.

This index contains certain typographical conventions to assist you in finding information. **Boldface** page numbers are references to primary topics and explanations that are emphasized in the text. *Italics* indicate page numbers that reference figures.

W

X

Y

Z